Practical Planning for Network Growth

Hewlett-Packard Professional Books

Blinn	Portable Shell Programming: An Extensive Collection of Bourne Shell Examples
Blommers	Practical Planning for Network Growth
Cook	Building Enterprise Information Architectures: Reengineering Information Systems
Costa	Planning and Designing High Speed Networks Using 100VG-AnyLAN, Second Edition
Crane	A Simplified Approach to Image Processing: Classical and Modern Techniques in C
Fernandez	Configuring CDE: The Common Desktop Environment
Fristrup	USENET: Netnews for Everyone
Fristrup	The Essential Web Surfer Survival Guide
Grady	Practical Software Metrics for Project Management and Process Improvement
Grosvenor, Ichiro, O'Brien	Mainframe Downsizing to Upsize Your Business: IT-Preneuring
Gunn	A Guide to NetWare® for UNIX®
Helsel	Graphical Programming: A Tutorial for HP VEE
Helsel	Visual Programming with HP VEE
Kane	PA-RISC 2.0 Architecture
Knouse	Practical DCE Programming
Lewis	The Art & Science of Smalltalk
Lund	Integrating UNIX and PC Network Operating Systems
Malan, Letsinger, Coleman	Object-Oriented Development at Work: Fusion In the Real World
Madell, Parsons, Abegg	Developing and Localizing International Software
McFarland	X Windows on the World: Developing Internationalized Software with X, Motif®, and CDE
McMinds, Whitty	Writing Your Own OSF/Motif® Widgets
Phaal	LAN Traffic Management
Poniatowski	The HP-UX System Administrator's "How To" Book
Poniatowski	HP-UX 10.x System Administration "How To" Book
Thomas	Cable Television Proof-of-Performance: A Practical Guide to Cable TV Compliance Measurements Using a Spectrum Analyzer
Witte	Electronic Test Instruments

Practical Planning for Network Growth

John Blommers

Network Performance Specialist
Hewlett-Packard, Bellevue, WA

HEWLETT
PACKARD

Prentice Hall PTR
Upper Saddle River, New Jersey 07458

Editorial/production supervision: *Camille Trentacoste*
Cover design: *Talar Agasayan*
Cover design director: *Jerry Votta*
Composition: *Omegatype*
Manufacturing manager: *Alexis R. Heydt*
Manager, Hewlett-Packard Press: *Patricia Pekary*
Acquisitions editor: *Karen Gettman*
Editorial Assistant: *Barbara Alfieri*

© 1996 by Hewlett-Packard

Published by Prentice Hall PTR
Prentice-Hall, Inc.
A Simon & Schuster Company
Upper Saddle River, New Jersey 07458

The publisher offers discounts on this book when ordered in bulk quantities.
For more information, contact:
    Corporate Sales Department
    Prentice Hall PTR
    One Lake Street
    Upper Saddle River, NJ 07458
    Phone: 800-382-3419 Fax: 201-236-7141
    E-mail: corpsales@prenhall.com

All rights reserved. No part of this book may be reproduced, in any form or by any means, without permission in writing from the publisher.

All product names mentioned herein are the trademarks of their respective owners.

Printed in the United States of America
10 9 8 7 6 5 4 3 2 1

ISBN 0-13-206111-2

Prentice-Hall International (UK) Limited, *London*
Prentice-Hall of Australia Pty. Limited, *Sydney*
Prentice-Hall Canada Inc., *Toronto*
Prentice-Hall Hispanoamericana, S. A., *Mexico*
Prentice-Hall of India Private Limited, *New Delhi*
Prentice-Hall of Japan, Inc., *Tokyo*
Simon & Schuster Asia Pte. Ltd., *Singapore*
Editora Prentice-Hall do Brasil, Ltda., *Rio de Janeiro*

This book is dedicated in loving memory and thanks to a very special cat named "hp" . . . for the hours and hours of dedicated lap time he contributed to support my sanity while writing this book, and for a love we shared that will always be remembered.

Contents

1 ANSWERING SOME REAL WORLD NETWORK PERFORMANCE QUESTIONS *1*

    1.0   Introduction   1

    1.1   Why do we try to predict network performance?   1

    1.2   How much does a poorly performing network cost the business?   3

    1.3   How can investing in performance studies reduce risk?   4

    1.4   How does user response time increase with number of users?   5

    1.5   What speed should a remote network link be?   7

    1.6   Should a server be upgraded or should a second server be installed?   8

    1.7   How many X-stations can be supported on this Ethernet LAN?   8

    1.8   Can we add a new application to the enterprise network?   9

    1.9   How suitable is frame relay for interactive applications?   10

    1.10   Will an FDDI backbone for the file servers support future needs?   11

2 COLLECTING NETWORK PERFORMANCE DATA *13*

    2.0   Introduction   13

    2.1   The need for benchmark performance data   13

    2.2   SNMP historical data collection   14

    2.3   LAN analyzer tracing and statistics monitoring   18

	2.4	Segment monitors, RMON, and HP EASE 20
	2.5	UNIX tracing functions 32
	2.6	The ubiquitous *ping* command 32
	2.7	Using performance information from the UNIX BSD *netstat* command 35
	2.8	Processing packet traces using UNIX's *awk* 36
	2.9	Sampling frequency of performance data 40
	2.10	Traffic characteristics: Packet size distribution and arrival rate 41
	2.11	Synthesis and estimation of traffic 42

3 QUALITY OF NETWORK PERFORMANCE DATA 45

- 3.0 Introduction 45
- 3.1 Dealing with contamination of the data during measurement 45
- 3.2 Number of light, medium, and heavy users during testing 47
- 3.3 Understanding the business cycle impact on network traffic 48
- 3.4 Mixtures of different user workloads 50

4 THE PERFORMANCE PROPERTIES OF NETWORK DEVICES AND TOPOLOGIES 51

- 4.0 Introduction 51
- 4.1 Hub, bridge, router, and switch performance characteristics 52
- 4.2 Tunable parameters on routers: Priority queues and compression 58
- 4.3 Client location impact on performance 60
- 4.4 How server performance can impact the network 62
- 4.5 A generic model for a file server 63
- 4.6 Reality check—NFS server performance and tuning parameters 64
- 4.7 Locating servers for best performance 69
- 4.8 Ethernet, Token Ring, and FDDI simulation design curves 71
- 4.9 Performance myths about Ethernet and Token Ring 75
- 4.10 T-1, Frame Relay, and X.25 as design bottlenecks 77
- 4.11 Specmanship by equipment vendors 86
- 4.12 Using Decision Analysis to select among alternative solutions 89

5 INDICATORS OF NETWORK PERFORMANCE 92

- 5.0 Introduction 92
- 5.1 Psychology of response time 93
- 5.2 Average response time and percentiles 93

5.3	Transaction rate 95
5.4	Utilization percentage 96
5.5	Collision rate 98
5.6	Protocol overhead and efficiency 100
5.7	Maximum number of concurrent users 101
5.8	Time to perform a large file transfer 102
5.9	Time taken to display a color image 103
5.10	Correcting the direction of finger pointing 104
5.11	Dropped packet rate and transport retransmissions 106

6 NETWORK STATISTICS 101: THE ESSENTIALS 107

6.0	Introduction 107
6.1	Basic measurements: Average and variation 107
6.2	Useful statistics distributions: Normal, exponential, Poisson, uniform, and fixed 109
6.3	Examples of statistics distribution in networking 115
6.4	Combining statistical values 115
6.5	Specifying that 99% of response times are less than 5 seconds 117
6.6	Using *ping* output statistics to characterize network performance 120
6.7	Trend analysis: Predicting future performance from past measurements 123

7 PREDICTING AVERAGE VALUES FOR RESPONSE TIME AND THROUGHPUT 129

7.0	Introduction 129
7.1	Document retrieval over a frame relay network 129
7.2	Response time for telnet users on a 56 kbps WAN 132
7.3	The effect of multiple WAN hops on response time 133
7.4	Response time vs. throughput issues: The network round-trip time 133

8 WORST-CASE ANALYSIS 135

8.0	Introduction 135
8.1	Analyzing the busy hour 135
8.2	Network behavior on the last day of the business financial quarter 138
8.3	Behavior of fully utilized resources 139
8.4	Maximum number of concurrent users 141
8.5	When everybody hits the ENTER key at once: Multiple concurrent requests 144

	8.6	Comparing the worst case with the best case 144
	8.7	Pricing a network designed for the worst-case traffic 147

9 APPLIED QUEUING THEORY   151

- 9.0   Introduction   151
- 9.1   Transactions and service   152
- 9.2   Exponential service time and interarrival time   153
- 9.3   Other statistical distributions   154
- 9.4   Calculating the average length of the queue   155
- 9.5   Average wait time in the system   156
- 9.6   When queuing theory gives good results   158
- 9.7   Validating queuing theory results   159
- 9.8   Single-server queues and multi-server queues   160
- 9.9   Helpful tables in queuing theory analysis   169
- 9.10 Transactions moving serially through multiple servers   172
- 9.11 Queuing theory applied to a spooled network printer   173
- 9.12 Deciding whether to upgrade or replicate   175
- 9.13 Predicting buffer overflow and packet loss in bridges and routers   176

10 SIMULATING DISCRETE TIME EVENTS   180

- 10.0 Introduction   180
- 10.1 Simulating discrete time events   180
- 10.2 Statistical methods of simulation   190
- 10.3 Using C-language modeling libraries   193

11 USING SPREADSHEETS FOR CAPACITY PLANNING   195

- 11.0 Introduction   195
- 11.1 Functions available in spreadsheets   196
- 11.2 Converting performance formulas to columns and rows of values   201
- 11.3 Producing charts and graphs from rows and columns   202
- 11.4 A queuing example with discrete event simulation   205
- 11.5 Visualizing the worst-case performance example   208
- 11.6 Graphical solutions with spreadsheets   209
- 11.7 Iterative methods using spreadsheets   212
- 11.8 Producing documentation from a spreadsheet   216
- 11.9 Available commercial spreadsheets   218

12 MATHEMATICS SCRATCH PADS 219

- 12.0 Introduction 219
- 12.1 What is Mathcad? 219
- 12.2 A sample Mathcad document (Figure 12-1) 221
- 12.3 Using Mathcad to handle messy formulas easily 222
- 12.4 Graphing and displaying results in Mathcad 223
- 12.5 Producing documentation with Mathcad 225
- 12.6 Commercially available math scratchpads 226

13 USING THE SYSTEMS & NETWORKS PLANNET SIMULATION TOOL 227

- 13.0 Introduction 227
- 13.1 Components of the PlanNet simulator 228
- 13.2 PlanNet's library of standard network components 229
- 13.3 Creating custom network components with BONeS Designer 230
- 13.4 Creating the network topology and running the PlanNet simulator 231
- 13.5 Standard and user-written traffic generator modules 232
- 13.6 PlanNet report generation 235
- 13.7 Content of a professional modeling and simulation report 236
- 13.8 Validating simulation results 237
- 13.9 What-if scenarios, or modeling alternative topologies 238
- 13.10 A sample PlanNet simulation explained 239
- 13.11 Choosing a client-server protocol—FTP, NFS, or X Windows 246
- 13.12 Expanding a centralized application to remote locations 249
- 13.13 Validating a network design for Email and telnet users 251
- 13.14 Commercially available simulation tools 255
- 13.15 Searching for simulation information on the World Wide Web 256

14 COMPARING AVERAGE, WORST CASE, QUEUING, AND SIMULATION METHODS 257

- 14.0 Introduction 257
- 14.1 Suitability for large network models 257
- 14.2 Accuracy comparison of the four methods 258
- 14.3 Ease of use and reusability 258
- 14.4 Work time requirements 259
- 14.5 Training and experience needed to use the methods 260
- 14.6 Quality of documentation produced by the tools/methods 260
- 14.7 Using one method to validate another 261

15 DIFFICULTIES IN PREDICTING NETWORK PERFORMANCE   263

15.0   Introduction   263
15.1   Broadcast activity and its effect on system and network performance   263
15.2   Media error recovery, interruptions to service, CRC errors, and restarts   264
15.3   Protocol bugs and features   265
15.4   Operating system implementation effects on the network   266
15.5   Impact of system and network component upgrades   266
15.6   Configuration errors in network electronics   267
15.7   Mixing protocols such as IP, IPX, DECNet, and AppleTalk   268
15.8   Router overhead: RIP, OSPF, SNMP, ICMP, accounting, and compression   269
15.9   Special transport-layer features: Van Jacobson TCP and Netware burst mode   270

16 HOW TO FIND BOOKS AND PAPERS FOR REFERENCE AND FURTHER STUDY   271

16.0   Introduction   271
16.1   Using the World Wide Web to find network performance information   271

BIBLIOGRAPHY   275

INDEX   276

Preface

To solve network performance problems such as poor response time or high congestion, you need to use straightforward methods to collect the necessary data and process it to get results you have confidence in. You will also have to convince management that your analysis is accurate and that the time and money you're asking them to invest will pay off. To help you prepare your presentation, we've even included some sample reports in the book.

This book will give you the fundamentals of network performance analysis, explain the parameters found in media such as Ethernet, Token Ring, and FDDI; interconnect devices such as hubs, bridges, routers, and Ethernet switches; and wide area technologies such as T-1, frame relay, and X.25. Server architecture is also covered. In each chapter, we guide you through techniques such as queuing theory, worst-case analysis, and even simulation and explain how to use tools such as spreadsheets, math scratchpads, and discrete event simulators. As a bonus, the included floppy disk in MS-DOS format contains all the examples from the text to help you practice and apply all these techniques in your next assignment.

Extensive illustrations make this book a pleasure to use. Many graphs are provided for design purposes and tables are also provided where appropriate. It is possible to skim this book by looking at each illustration and reading only the captions.

While prowling the bookstores for texts about network performance prediction, it became frustratingly plain to me that a practical, well-rounded, vendor-independent, and technology-independent work was missing from the shelves. Many texts discussed TCP/IP, LANs, SNA, and other existing technologies. Many focused attention on mathematical analysis of theoretical networks. Yet others presented methods in queuing theory, linear programming, and statistical analysis. Even volumes about spreadsheets, mathematics scratchpads, and simulation languages abounded

During this book's development, I drew heavily upon my experiences in analyzing the performance of new customer network designs. Memories of solving performance problems on existing customer networks resurfaced. Enthused, I went into my filing cabinet, reviewed disk files on my HP 9000 workstation, reacquainted myself with texts on my bookshelf, and collected performance reports I'd written. So armed, I started to write, did more analysis, and fleshed out this book.

Consequently, this book is about practical ready-to-use methods that let the network manager and designer estimate network utilization and user response time with reasonable accuracy and confidence. Practical tools like Lotus 1-2-3 or similar spreadsheets are used to present analysis of realistic situations. The Mathcad tool is also used for situations where unpleasant math formulas are needed to solve problems in performance. Instead of writing throw-away programs in BASIC, FORTRAN, or C, Mathcad is used to directly solve summation formulas in the native notation. This will encourage the network manager to proceed with the analysis rather than be intimidated with a messy numerical programming task. The author has used all these tools in his work and shares his experiences with the reader.

Real-world examples are clearly described, developed, and analyzed. Useful tables are included to allow the methods to be applied to a wide range of problems. The included MS-DOS diskette contains all the examples in the text so the techniques can be applied directly. This helps build up confidence.

The performance aspects of LAN technologies such as Ethernet, Token Ring, FDDI, and ATM are presented to build a foundation for the reader. WAN technologies such as T-1, frame relay, and X.25 are also discussed at the building block level. Because the author builds up the reader's ability to analyze performance aspects of these technologies, new technologies can be analyzed with confidence. The methods given are not dated and can be used in the coming years. Also, analysis methods are not dependent on a particular protocol—TCP/IP, Netware, SNA, or AppleTalk can be handled.

Several analysis methods are covered. Worst-case analysis is useful in designing robust networks that may be overprovisioned to meet business needs. Queuing theory is another method that can by very easy to use in many practical situations—especially if the design tables are used or if Mathcad is available to handle the math involved. When queuing theory doesn't fit the problem, the reader is invited to the world of graphical simulation tools. Actual simulations are presented and reproduced to show the power of the method. The relative accuracy of these methods is compared to help the reader choose among them.

About the Author

John Blommers is a Network Performance Specialist who works for Hewlett-Packard's Professional Services Organization. Much of his time is spent troubleshooting performance problems for customers and preparing network capacity plans for new network designs. He has also conducted capacity studies for several large customers who have implemented the SAP business software across their enterprise. This book is based on his experiences working at HP, and it is written to share the many secrets of network performance analysis that he has developed and applied successfully to real-world customer situations.

John also teaches classes at the University of Washington Extension, in the areas of LAN Troubleshooting and Diagnosis, UNIX TCP/IP and Network Administration, and LAN/WAN network design. He holds a Masters degree in Applied Mathematics and Bachelors degree in Electrical Engineering.

His hobbies include dabbling at woodworking and collecting antique radios and test equipment.

1

Answering Some Real-World Network Performance Questions

1.0 INTRODUCTION

In our first chapter we cover real-world questions that network designers grapple with and introduce methods for answering them. Detailed tools and methods are covered in later chapters. Performance analysis methods include rules of thumb, linear extrapolation, queuing methods, and simulation. Benchmarking techniques are reviewed in the context of providing data for these methods.

We go into the reasons for predicting network performance, review the business costs of a badly performing network, and discuss how network capacity plans reduce risk. Next we review what impacts user response time, consider how to size WAN links, and worry over server sizing. We touch on issues regarding X-terminal traffic and new enterprise applications. Finally we study an approach to figuring out the suitability of frame relay and FDDI rings.

1.1 WHY DO WE TRY TO PREDICT NETWORK PERFORMANCE?

Networks are built to support business functions such as word processing, computer-aided drawing, electronic mail, and imaging. One very critical success factor is that each business function be performed in real time. The definition of real time depends on the application and can vary from milliseconds to hours.

A word processing user loads a document, makes changes to it, and writes it back to the file server. The read and write operations should be very quick—a few seconds at most. Computer-aided drawing activities are very iterative and users expect subsecond response time when loading a library symbol or deleting a component from the drawing. Electronic mail sent between parties may take minutes or hours without users invoking their wrath upon the network. Imaging users prefer that complete images be available within a few seconds and then spend minutes to hours studying or modifying them.

User productivity declines rapidly if the applications they use don't respond quickly enough. Frustration sets in, attitudes deteriorate, real work output slows down, and confidence in "the network" reaches new lows. The business starts to become paralyzed as operations slow to a crawl or stop altogether. Customers cannot be serviced in a timely manner, errors are made, business is lost, and any competitive advantage the network once promised is lost.

We try to predict the performance of a network to make sure it can provide the responsiveness that all the users require. This performance must be available at all times of the day and night. Response time must be provided when needed most—at the end of the fiscal quarter, on Monday morning, and at month's end. That response time has to be available when additional users are added to the network, when a new department moves onto the network, when a new application is deployed enterprise-wide, and when additional networked printers are installed. When remote sites are connected to the network, those users expect good response time as well.

There are two common metrics for network performance. User response time is the most important of these. It is determined by adding up all the little delays that application packets have to endure before a response is returned to the user. These delays include the client-side think time, the network delays in forwarding packets, and server-side delays in processing these packets. The user is equally likely to blame the network or the server system for response time problems. To correct the direction of finger pointing, the ability to calculate response time is critical.

Network utilization is the other common performance metric. It is the favorite of network managers because they need to provide available bandwidth to support the users. Utilization is directly measurable with LAN/WAN analyzers, segment monitors, and with SNMP-compliant network electronics such hubs, bridges, routers, and switches. Using historical performance data, network managers can make predictions about network utilization when additional traffic is anticipated and can provision accordingly.

When facing the prospect of adding users to the network, we need to anticipate the performance impact in advance. If the additional user traffic can safely be carried, then implementation can proceed at once. If analysis indicates that additional user traffic will

---

Reasons for Predicting Network Performance
Keep user response time low.
Increase user productivity.
Supply adequate network bandwidth.
Provide for future growth.
Ensure successful deployment of new applications.
Validate response time goals of new network designs.
Troubleshoot for bottlenecks.
Choose among several competing network applications.
Choose the best alternative network topology.

degrade response time to unacceptably high levels, then the deployment should be rescheduled to coincide with the selection and implementation of appropriate network upgrades. It's unacceptable to add users to a network with one's fingers crossed.

Likewise, if the company plans to add an enterprise-wide application, the impact must be assessed in advance and appropriate network upgrades and redesigns must be implemented. Application traffic information may be available from the vendor. It can be measured with a LAN analyzer during a benchmark test, with users and server systems on an isolated LAN. If a limited pilot project is conducted to evaluate the application before committing to it, then we have another opportunity to measure the impact of the new application. The location and number of servers and users can be projected onto the existing network traffic and any upgrades can be made in advance to ensure adequate response time at full deployment.

Developers of client-server applications are very interested in understanding the traffic levels created by their code. Even in the design stage, they want to estimate the network bandwidth needed to support typical user counts and workloads. Bad news here allows the developers to adjust their designs early in the development cycle, when it's relatively inexpensive to do so. At each project checkpoint, the LAN traffic is measured and the full-scale performance analysis is redone to ensure that the design goals are met.

In problem-solving situations, it can pay to look at things from a performance perspective. Perhaps work habits are changing and network traffic or server utilization is increasing. A performance analysis will offer an appropriate range of solutions that can be proven to solve the existing problem. It would be unfortunate to upgrade a file server only to find that the bottleneck is caused by electronic mail traversing the LAN.

We try to predict the performance of an existing network because that exercise locates the bottlenecks that affect response time the most and provides alternative solutions in advance. One of these alternatives can usually be selected based on criteria such as low cost, ease of expansion, or low risk. We know it is folly to simply allow the network to grow unchecked. Networks never shrink, because the advantages of the connectivity brings converts in droves. The cost of ignoring the infrastructure until it's too late is much greater than the cost of maintaining and expanding the network along computed lines. The network administrator will be answerable for unacceptable network performance management practices.

A brand new network design usually consists of a logical and a physical design. A good design is always supported by a performance study. These studies take into consideration all available estimates and measurements of the anticipated traffic, where it originates, where it goes, and how often it flows. Traffic information is used to set network link speeds and choose LAN/WAN technologies. It also helps the designer choose among alternative topologies. Once the new network is installed and all users and systems have migrated onto it, everybody expects superior performance. If the new network won't deliver the necessary performance, the designers will answer for it.

1.2 HOW MUCH DOES A POORLY PERFORMING NETWORK COST THE BUSINESS?

Putting a dollar figure on network downtime is an exercise in estimation. A poorly performing network is considered to be down when users can no longer work. A salesperson writing up a quotation for a customer risks losing business if the quotation can't be

> **Costs of a Poorly Performing Network**
> Lost sales opportunities   Low customer and user satisfaction
> Slipped schedules   Low morale

delivered on time. A customer care agent for a communications service provider cannot satisfy customer requests. A consultant working on a report cannot meet a delivery deadline. A point-of-sale clerk who cannot authorize a customer's credit card will lose a sale and possibly a customer. Electronic mail between a contractor and a supplier is delayed and a critical order date is missed. Write in your worst nightmare here.

Consider a Fortune 500 company with offices across the United States and Canada. It typically has a central corporate office and numerous field offices and manufacturing sites interconnected with a wide area network. The field offices provide sales and support services to customers and transmit sales orders to the corporate office. The corporate office communicates with the appropriate manufacturing sites to schedule coordinated product shipments to customers. The field offices also communicate with the manufacturing sites for product support purposes. The enterprise network is mission critical to such companies. Performance problems can purportedly cost millions of dollars in lost sales.

Productivity losses due to network performance problems can be estimated more easily. For example, suppose the loaded cost of a full-time administrative assistant is $60 per hour, and 10% of that person's time is unproductive because the access to the file server is slow in the afternoons. Assuming 265 eight-hour working days per year, $12,720 is wasted per assistant. With 100 administrative assistants the waste is $1,272,000 dollars annually or $106,000 monthly. The cost of a performance analysis to validate a network design may be around $30,000 up front, depending on the scope of work.

Consider a software company with an impending product release. Forty developers and testers at three sites access seven development systems, each acting as a repository for source code and each equipped with software development tools. Periodically, a "build" is done. All source code and data files are compiled and linked to produce the final product. For the company to remain competitive, the turnaround time of these builds should be less then 12 hours so that testing can resume in the morning. If the builds start to take longer and longer, the next release will slip because developers can't test until late the next morning. Assume that this release will generate $1 million in revenue over the next six months. A slip of just one month represents a direct loss of almost $167,000.

The cost of poor network performance is not always easily expressed in dollars and cents. The cost of a late delivery, a missed deadline, or an inoperative application is just as real.

1.3 HOW CAN INVESTING IN PERFORMANCE STUDIES REDUCE RISK?

The telephone industry pioneered the study of voice traffic patterns in order to design and provision a profitable switching network. Traffic engineers understand how to design a nonblocking switching system that guarantees all users can get a dial tone anytime. The cost of building and servicing such a system is prohibitive so the user fees will be high and the customer base will remain small along with profits. Conversely, if the network is underdesigned, too many users will be denied service and again profits will remain small. To find a happy medium, traffic studies are used to design a network that will provide service most of the time. In this way the telephone industry reduces its risks and maximizes its profitability (see Figure 1-1).

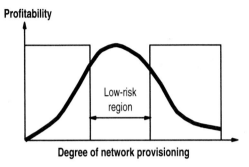

Figure 1-1 The best reason for doing performance analysis on a network is to locate the point where the provisioning levels maximize profit. Building the fastest network will not deliver a return on investment beyond the profitability peak. The region of the peak is also a low-risk area.

When a data network is designed, there are also two types of risk. The risk of overprovisioning is that money is spent needlessly on hardware and services that remain underutilized. The risk of underprovisioning is that users immediately suffer a fixed period of lost productivity while additional time and money is spent to upgrade the network. If the upgrade is done without the benefit of a proper performance analysis, there is the risk that the upgrade may still not provide the necessary response time to the users.

Performance studies deliver a documented reproducible methodology that locates the optimum between the high cost of overdesigning and the high cost of underdesigning.

An existing network's performance should be measured operationally. This data is plowed back into a performance analysis on a periodic basis with an eye towards forecasting peak traffic trends. This reduces the risk that the network will fail to provide the necessary performance at some future time by providing accurate information about how the upgrades may be done most effectively.

1.4 HOW DOES USER RESPONSE TIME INCREASE WITH THE NUMBER OF USERS?

Experience tells us that response time increases in some manner with the number of active users and the amount of resources they consume. When most employees read their Email first thing every morning, the mail system becomes sluggish. Later in the day it's responsive. Users who move four-megabyte images between the file server and their display screens wait longer than word processing users editing one-page memos.

Department managers may have to generate month-end reports. Their administrative assistants generate more printouts during these last few days and find themselves waiting impatiently for their printouts. Even the 17 PPM laser printers can't keep up with the work flow and the administrative assistants discover another way to measure response time—their position in the print queue. They also learn that adding just one or two more printers to the pool reduces their wait time drastically.

> **How Does Response Time Vary?**
>
> Increases with the number of *active* users.
> Increases with user workload intensity.
> Increases with the volume of data moved.
> Increases with the queue depth.
> Increases with the network utilization.

Generally, response time remains independent of the number of users so long as the resource utilization remains low. Users don't have to wait when only a few images are accessed each hour. Email systems respond quickly when there is little new mail to process. Wide area circuits easily support a few interactive sessions between remote field offices and the central site. And there is no waiting for print jobs when only a few small reports are printed each hour.

At the opposite extreme, we find that full resource utilization results in long queues and lengthy waits. The wait time grows linearly with the number of active users so long as nothing breaks down due to the excessive delays. A session disconnect is a common symptom of a breakdown.

In between these two extremes user response time increases as more users are added and as more resources achieve significant utilization (see Figure 1-2).

The response time curve is very general and somewhat simplified. It applies when the network is not overloaded by only one or two active users. It assumes users perform similar work and have the same steady work habits. It assumes there are a fixed number of active users that have to wait for a response before starting another transaction. It assumes the network is well behaved under saturation conditions as opposed to ill behaved (with users

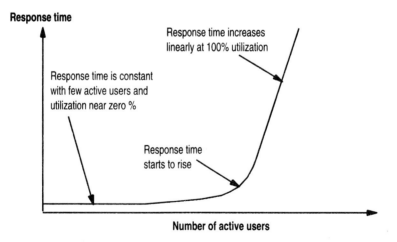

Figure 1-2 Few active users don't interact and response time remains steady at the low end. Response time increases gradually as more users are added. Under saturation conditions the response time increases linearly with the number of active users.

being timed out and disconnected at random). Later in the book in, chapters 7 through 10, we will present methods for computing response time of variously configured networks.

1.5 WHAT SPEED SHOULD A REMOTE NETWORK LINK BE?

The matter of sizing WAN links at design time or at upgrade time is invariably dropped into the lap of the network designer. Users are not interested in bandwidth, collision rates, or CRC errors but these quantities are fairly easy to measure. Available bandwidth varies with the offered traffic load, going to near-zero at saturation. Response time becomes more and more unpredictable at this point. Speaking statistically, the variation of the response time around its mean increases dramatically. Network designers can only provide and control bandwidth to achieve a certain level of service (response time). They can even fine-tune a router's priority queues in an effort to favor interactive traffic over bulk traffic.

Given the network topology, the location of clients and servers and the work habits of the users, the network designer attempts to calculate line speeds that meet both response time and throughput requirements. We assume that the results of an audited requirements analysis is in hand. Using techniques such as mean-value analysis, worst-case analysis, queuing theory, or simulation, line speeds can be mathematically adjusted to meet the requirements.

There is a temptation to simply specify the fastest line speed available from the carrier. The cost of overprovisioning all the WAN links may not be a deterrent to this. But without an analysis to justify, say, 1.544 Mbps T-1 speeds we have crossed our fingers behind our backs again. Choosing parameters for frame relay PVCs involves choosing among committed information rate (CIR), port speed (or clock speed), and burst rate. Simulation tools are well suited to help define the appropriate values for these parameters that will meet all user needs in the foreseeable future.

Modern network management tools provide full access to circuit utilization and traffic patterns. Such data is often plotted and trended to reveal the business cycles. It is tempting to project along the utilization peaks to determine when the 90% saturation point will be regularly reached, and then double the line capacity in time with the hope that the peaks drop back down to about 45%. In practice, the removal of this bottleneck improves throughput and the line utilization remains higher than anticipated. A full analysis that considers traffic sources, traffic destinations, and user work habits will result in correct design parameters. Chapter 2 presents various methods available for collecting network traffic information.

WAN Line Speed Issues

Choose a higher available speed when the network performance is poor.
Base line speed on peak user traffic volume plus an overhead margin.
Existing circuit utilization is easy to measure operationally with SNMP.
User response time is much harder to measure.
Remember the number of hops also effects response time.

1.6 SHOULD A SERVER BE UPGRADED OR SHOULD A SECOND SERVER BE INSTALLED?

User response time includes the delay introduced by the server system. As the workload on the server increases, its utilization will approach 100% and response time degrades linearly. Should we upgrade the server by increasing the number of disks, installing faster disks, replacing the LAN adapter with a 32-bit version, adding more RAM, or upgrading the CPU? If we identify the bottleneck we may double the performance of the server. Another option is simply to purchase a second server and redistribute the user data between them.

These types of considerations apply to other scenarios. Is it better to double the speed of a WAN line or put in a second line of equal speed and do load balancing? Is it better to add a second printer of similar type or put in a faster printer. Is it better to add four 4 PPM printers or one 17 PPM printer? Is it better to hire 10 more customer care agents or train all 50 of them to increase their work speed?

Server Upgrading and Replacement Issues

Component upgrades are generally cheaper.
Two servers are more reliable than one.
Situate servers near their users (in the network sense).
Cannibalize slow server's components for use in its replacement.

Chapter 9 introduces queuing theory. A simple result from queuing theory—a rule of thumb that's often useful—is that it's always better to have one fast server than two half-speed servers. When the single fast server is run at low utilization, its response time will be almost half that of the half-speed server. At high utilization levels, the fast server and the two half-speed servers will provide about equal response time. One fast server is better than two half-speed servers.

1.7 HOW MANY X-STATIONS CAN BE SUPPORTED ON THIS ETHERNET LAN?

An X-station (or X-terminal or X-term) is a display server that consists of a keyboard, mouse, LAN connection, RAM, ROM, CPU, and color monitor. The X-window standard provides a method for host-based applications to communicate with these display servers via TCP/IP sockets. X-terminals are useful low-cost graphics heads for UNIX systems that allow their CPU power to be used amongst a community of users distributed across the enterprise network. X-terminals may be purchased as premanufactured commodity items. X-terminal software is also available for PCs, Macintoshes, and UNIX workstations.

In practice, an X-window application such as FrameMaker, OpenView, or Zmail run on one UNIX host and users located anywhere on the network can access an instance of the application. The question then arises, how many such X-terminal users can be added to the network before response time deteriorates?

> **Figuring the maximum number of X-stations on a LAN**
> Budget 1% utilization per active X-station user.
> Measure X-application traffic or ask the application vendor.
> Maximum allowed Ethernet utilization is 40% (rule of thumb).
> Users say response time is more important than LAN utilization.
> Use the X-station SNMP agent and MIB to measure utilization.

One rule of thumb is that each X-terminal generates about 1% utilization. To keep LAN utilization below 40% (a rule of thumb as well) we limit the X-terminal count to 40 active users. If we know that up to 50% of all users are active at any time, we can install up to 80 X-terminals on the LAN.

Measuring the peak LAN traffic generated by one heads-down user running an X-term application is an improvement over the 1% rule. A LAN analyzer or an SNMP management station can measure this traffic. Experience shows that many applications may generate a fraction of 1% utilization, others may generate 2%. Applications that continuously track mouse movement (as when creating a freehand drawing) can generate a few hundred small packets per second. Applications that move full-screen bitmapped images (about one megabyte) can generate significant traffic, depending on the performance of the UNIX server and the X-terminal.

What about response time? Studies show that as LAN utilization exceeds 25%, X-terminal response time becomes erratic. Another rule of thumb is that response times in excess of one-tenth of a second tend to create dissatisfied users. Queuing theory and simulation methods can provide better estimates of response time versus number of users.

Average response time is an important metric. So is variation. Queuing methods often provide a probability density formula (see Chapter 6). This formula gives us the ability to state, for example, "the probability that the response time is less than one second is 99%."

1.8 CAN WE ADD A NEW APPLICATION TO THE ENTERPRISE NETWORK?

Many enterprise networks are designed and provisioned to support all existing applications and to provide excellent performance. The ability of the network to support additional traffic comes under scrutiny when the prospect of deploying a large new application looms on the horizon. The location of the application and database servers has to be decided. Additional user workstations will be deployed and LAN traffic will increase. The impact on existing WANs must be determined.

A rigorous approach is to benchmark the application on an isolated LAN and measure the LAN traffic of each transaction. A needs analysis is conducted to determine the number and type of transactions at each location. The network topology is determined. Existing network traffic flows are measured. Topology and traffic generators are input to the simulation tool. Then a simulation is performed to provide response time figures for each user site and utilization figures for WANs and LANs. The simulation is usually run several times with

> **Considerations When Adding New Enterprise Applications**
>
> Ensure current traffic levels and response times will not be negatively impacted.
> Determine the location and number of clients and servers at full deployment.
> Estimate or benchmark new application transaction volumes.
> Simulate the network with the additional application traffic loads.
> Include any new sites that will be joined with the enterprise network.

increasing numbers of total users to locate bottlenecks in the network architecture. Additional simulations are usually run to evaluate the effectiveness of topology variations and line speed increases. The best location for the servers can be determined. The net result is a reproducible documented analysis that answers how a new application can be deployed. The simulation approach is detailed in Chapter 13.

A good example of an enterprise-wide application is electronic mail. Each user in the company operates a mail reader that in turn communicates with a mail hub (or post office). The mail hubs move messages among user mail boxes and interface with mail gateways. This application impacts the entire enterprise network. Other commercial enterprise applications are Lotus Notes and SAP.

1.9 HOW SUITABLE IS FRAME RELAY FOR INTERACTIVE APPLICATIONS?

The attractive pricing structure of frame relay service naturally attracts the attention of network designers. Instead of building a private network of meshed point-to-point leased lines, the same functionality is available using permanent virtual circuits (PVCs) within the frame relay cloud. The service provider's network infrastructure moves the data frames along the PVC between the enterprise routers. The network is designed to provide a guaranteed committed information rate (CIR) but round-trip response time will vary because other customer traffic competes on the network. Frame relay certainly proves a good fit for bulk data transfer such as documents and Email, but what about interactive applications?

Some argue that frame relay is inappropriate for interactive applications because users need a consistent response time that frame relay cannot provide. Others report that users routinely login to remote hosts across frame relay lines to run interactive applications. The network designer needs to know how variable the frame relay network performance is and the service provider may have some historical data. Network congestion will vary throughout the day and a business cycle may be apparent. Congestion patterns will vary with the service provider network. Delays vary with the number of hops within the network and the speed of the lines interconnecting these switches (see Figure 1-3).

To characterize user response time we need to analyze the delays that a given frame relay network will add to the application delays. Model the frame relay network as a simple queue with a worst-case response time that corresponds to the CIR. Estimate the arrival rate of user packets and you can calculate the average response time and its probability distribution. Using a simulation tool such as Systems & Networks' PlanNet you can set the

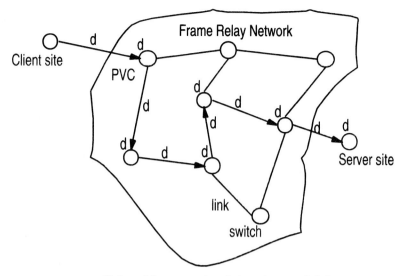

Figure 1-3 Frame relay networks are often drawn as opaque clouds because we don't usually know the underlying topology. Here we see the store and forward path of a PVC. We have add up all the little delays (d) to get the forward delay and add up the reverse delays to get the total network response time.

parameters of the frame relay module, draw the network topology, position the users and the server systems, and determine average response time on a per-transaction basis. A transaction typically requires several packet exchanges between client and server systems.

The above technique lets the designer predict how response time will vary with the number of interactive users, the number of hops, and the CIR of the network. For analysis details, check out the queuing theory and simulation methods in Chapters 9 and 10.

1.10 WILL AN FDDI BACKBONE FOR THE FILE SERVERS SUPPORT FUTURE NEEDS?

We all know that networks grow additional segments and subnets as needs dictate. Servers are initially placed at appropriate locations and user habits evolve as they discover these new resources on the network. LAN utilization increases imperceptibly over time until local users start noticing the occasional hesitation. Once it becomes apparent that servers attract considerable client traffic, then alternative topologies are considered to improve client response time. One is to put FDDI cards into each server and place them all on a new subnet (see Figure 1-4). A multiport router connects the other networks that support the clients. Other solutions might be CDDI, 100VG-AnyLAN, and Ethernet switches.

Will the FDDI subnet solve the response time problem? To find out, traffic measurements are made at each server. Chapter 2 goes into detail about data collection methods. Client counts are made. An analysis is done to calculate server and FDDI utilization and

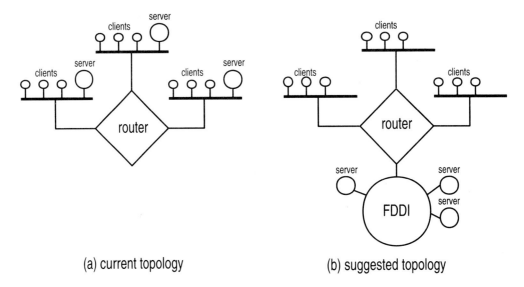

Figure 1-4 The existing network topology (a) has three subnets and allows all users to access all servers. Users complain about erratic response time. We want to analyze the potential response time improvement of moving all three servers to an FDDI subnet topology (b). Using a simulation tool will allow us to predict the response time for current usage levels as well as future levels.

client response time. The calculation is repeated for increasing numbers of clients to locate the bottlenecks for this configuration, which may be the servers, the FDDI ring, or the router. The analysis results may or may not support the FDDI topology. If not, then other topologies can be analyzed and the cost, inconvenience, and embarrassment of implementing the FDDI solution is avoided.

2

Collecting Network Performance Data

2.0 INTRODUCTION

Capacity planning requires us to measure or estimate network traffic volumes. This chapter is devoted to appropriate tools and techniques that vary in cost, scope, accuracy, simplicity, and practicality. These tools include SNMP, LAN analyzers, segment monitors, UNIX commands, and the interview process.

This chapter reviews the need for good benchmark performance data. We go into the details of using SNMP, LAN analyzers, RMON, and HP EASE traffic probes. For the UNIX system we go into tools such as on-line packet tracing, *ping,* and *netstat.* We even review *awk* as an aid in processing the ASCII trace files many of these tools generate.

Next we introduce the statistical properties of network traffic, but leave the mathematics to a later chapter. Collecting network performance data may overwhelm us, so we go into sampling frequency considerations. In the absence of measured data we delve into traffic estimation methods.

2.1 THE NEED FOR BENCHMARK PERFORMANCE DATA

Benchmark performance data is taken with a traffic tracing tool while a client-server application undergoes heads-down testing. One user executes the same transaction type repeatedly, either a fixed number of times or over a fixed time interval. These parameters are recorded and the user is categorized as being a light, medium, or heavy user. The network traffic of this session is traced and recorded packet for packet. This data is the most valuable type for capacity planning because it is reproducible, supportable, and documentable. It can

Benchmark Data
Results are reproducible if test procedures are followed.
Performance measurements can often be reused.
Avoid contamination from nonbenchmark LAN traffic.
Extract statistics are good for all methods of analysis.

be processed using most of the tools discussed in this book. The traces can be played back in a simulation or the traffic statistics can be extracted for analysis.

A few benchmarking guidelines should be observed. The transaction trace is ideally free of other LAN traffic to preserve the accuracy of the packet timing data. This means that an isolated LAN should be used for benchmarking. The client and server systems should be on the same LAN segment to avoid contaminating the interpacket timing with delays introduced by bridges, routers, and any intervening segments. Errors in timing around one millisecond result because the frame has to be retransmitted onto the remote LAN segment after being received by the bridge or router.

The transaction traces can be reused as long as the conditions of the benchmark still apply. For example, suppose we benchmark a WordPerfect user who loads a 75 Kbyte file from a Novell file server over a LAN segment. That trace can be used a year later for another capacity planning exercise if the same word processor, network operating system, LAN type, and file size are appropriate. Substituting AmiPro for WordPerfect or LAN Manager for Netware will compromise the accuracy of any capacity projections. Substituting Token Ring for Ethernet requires care in reprocessing the original traces because of differences in the frame format, contention protocol, and media speed. Substituting SMB/NetBEUI for IPX/SPX results in substantially different packet interchanges even for the same word processing package.

Applications that may be benchmarked in this manner include SAP, network printing (both inspooling and outspooling), network virtual terminal (telnet and rlogin), Email, Lotus Notes, pharmacy support, File Server, and the Domain Name System (DNS).

Statistics that can be extracted from transaction traces are the transaction duration, the total number of bytes, the average LAN utilization, the total number of frames, the average packet rate, the number of frames sent by the client, the average client packet rate, the number of frames sent by the server, the average server packet rate, the average client think time, the average client request length, the average server response length, and the average server response time.

2.2 SNMP HISTORICAL DATA COLLECTION

The nineties are the decade of the Simple Network Management Protocol (SNMP). It is the basis for managing all open network architectures. Hubs, switches, bridges, routers, terminal servers, X-stations, network printers, protocol translators, PCs, Macs, and file servers all support SNMP. SNMP can be used to collect performance information from network devices for purposes of capacity planning.

SNMP is truly simple. There is a manager and an agent. The network management application (NMA) runs on the network management station (NMS). It builds an SNMP GET request and transmits it as a UDP datagram into the IP network, which delivers it on a best-effort basis to the managed device (which is often referred to as the managed object). The SNMP agent in the device decodes the request, calculates the necessary return value(s), and builds an SNMP GET response which makes its way back to the NMA. The SNMP protocol always includes a community name for authentication purposes. This requires the NMA to know the agent's community name, which is often the default string `public`. The other SNMP operations are SNMP SET and SNMP TRAP and they will not be discussed further.

SNMP agents perceive management information base (MIB) data as a tree structure grouped in functional branches. The interesting branches are the interface, IP, TCP, and UDP groups because they contain performance counters we can read. The industry standard MIB-2 is supported by all modern network devices. Additional MIBs have been developed for hubs, terminal servers, FDDI, and ATM. To keep up with the latest MIB developments, subscribe to *The Simple Times* by sending Email to `st-subscriptions@simple-times.org` with the word `help` in the text.

Vendors often provide enterprise-specific MIBs to support their products. The system `venera.isi.edu` on the Internet contains a repository of vendor MIBs. Network management applications often come with a set of vendor MIBs. Network management stations provide MIB compilers which accept the ASCII MIB files and provide a GUI called a MIB browser to navigate and study the MIB tree structures. This browser is a valuable tool for learning what performance parameters a given MIB supports.

SNMP distinguishes between GAUGE and COUNTER variables. GAUGE variables work like your car's speedometer and return rate information. CPU utilization is an example of a GAUGE variable. COUNTER variables always increase monotonically. They never

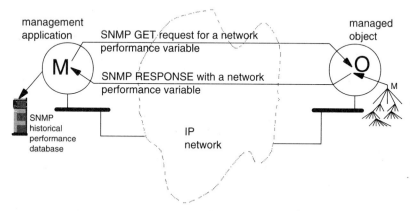

Sampling Network Performance Data Using SNMP

Figure 2-1 A network management application (M) builds a UDP datagram containing an SNMP GET request for some performance MIB variable, transmits it, sets a time-out, and waits for a response. The managed object (O) SNMP agent receives the SNMP GET, calculates a return value, and transmits an SNMP RESPONSE back to the requester.

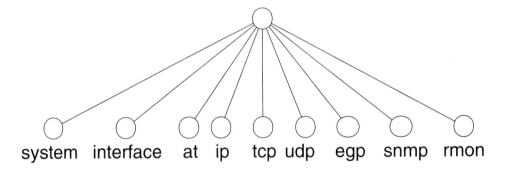

MIB-2 Tree Structure

Figure 2-2 The industry standard MIB-2 tree structure contains hundreds of performance variables organized into logical groups. The interface group contains the most interesting performance information about the LAN adapters while the IP group has information about routing performance.

go down except when they reach their maximum value and drop back to zero (they wrap). The number of octets received by an interface is an example of a COUNTER variable.

Note that SNMP provides only numbers to indicate performance. The numbers count things like octets or packets or events such as collisions. No transaction information, packet information, or timing information is available. SNMP doesn't know the source or destination of the data. It is true that the MIB-2 TCP group can deliver a list of active TCP connections and that the AT group can deliver a list of active IP/MAC addresses, but statistics for each active TCP connection are not available.

The NMS provides a GUI to set up historical data collection of SNMP variables. You specify the name of the network device, the MIB variable to poll, which MIB instances (the number of the interface, for example), and how frequently to take a sample (the polling interval). After a few months of collecting this data to disk, you can pull up the data grapher and discern the daily, weekly, and monthly cycles in the network performance data for a device or group of devices (see Figure 2-3).

The SNMP data can also be exported to an ASCII file for inclusion in performance reports. The data is usually in comma separated variable (CSV) form. Interface performance data is one of those COUNTER variables that increases monotonically, so plotting the throughput of a serial line in bits per second involves a few spreadsheet operations to take differences between successive samples and scale these to get bits per second numbers.

With hundreds of MIB values to choose from and a lot of different devices on the network, which should be measured? Table 2-1 will help you decide.

For command-line fans, the usual syntax for issuing an SNMP GET request to a managed device is `snmpget device-name MIB-variable`. Table 2-2 provides a list of interesting MIB-variable names taken directly from RFC 1213.

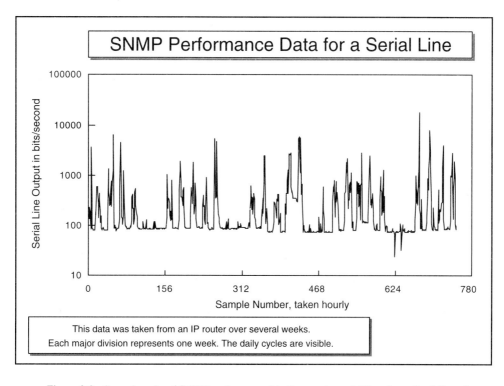

Figure 2-3 Several weeks of SNMP performance data for a router serial line shows the daily and weekly business cycles. Insufficient data is present for trending and a few spikes are visible. The y-axis has been scaled logarithmically to better show the noise floor in the data. Since SNMP data are generally COUNTER variables, successive samples are differenced and scaled to convert octets per hour to bits per second.

TABLE 2-1 CHOOSING USEFUL SNMP MIB VARIABLES FOR MEASURING NETWORK PERFORMANCE

Classification	Functional description of MIB variable	Device
performance indicators	interface octets in and out	hub, switch, bridge, router, server
	interface unicast frames in and out (directly addressed)	
	interface nonunicast frames in and out (broadcasts/multicasts)	
	CPU utilization	
	forwarding rate	bridge, router
performance degradation indicators	Ethernet transmit collisions	hub, switch, bridge, router, server
	Ethernet deferred transmissions	
	TCP retransmissions	server
connectivity and data transmission problem indicators	interface CRC errors in and out	bridge, router, server
	interface lost carrier	
	interface disconnect	
	Ethernet excess retries (16 consecutive collisions)	

Sec. 2.2 SNMP Historical Data Collection

TABLE 2-2 FORMAL NAMES OF SOME USEFUL SNMP MIB VARIABLES

Formal name	Description
ifInNUcastPkts	The number of nonunicast (i.e., subnetwork broadcast or subnetwork multicast) packets delivered to a higher-layer protocol.
ifInUcastPkts	The number of subnetwork-unicast packets delivered to a higher-layer protocol.
ifInOctets	The total number of octets received on the interface, including framing characters.
ifInDiscards	The number of inbound packets that were chosen to be discarded even though no errors had been detected to prevent their being deliverable to a higher-layer protocol. One possible reason for discarding such a packet could be to free up buffer space.
ifInErrors	The number of inbound packets that contained errors preventing them from being deliverable to a higher-layer protocol.
ifOutErrors	The number of outbound packets that could not be transmitted because of errors.
ifOutQLen	The length of the output packet queue (in packets).
ipForwDatagrams	The number of input datagrams for which this entity was not their final IP destination, as a result of which an attempt was made to find a route to forward them to that final destination. In entities that do not act as IP gateways, this counter will include only those packets that were Source-Routed via this entity, and the Source-Route option processing was successful.
ipOutDiscards	The number of output IP datagrams for which no problem was encountered to prevent their transmission to their destination, but which were discarded (e.g., for lack of buffer space). Note that this counter would include datagrams counted in ipForwDatagrams if any such packets met this (discretionary) discard criterion.
tcpRetransSegs	The total number of segments retransmitted—that is, the number of TCP segments transmitted containing one or more previously transmitted octets.

2.3 LAN ANALYZER TRACING AND STATISTICS MONITORING

LAN analyzers consist of a LAN interface (such as Ethernet, Token Ring, FDDI), a programmable hardware filter, RAM buffers, a node list, a keyboard, a mouse, a display, decode software, statistics software, a disk for file storage, a floppy disk to export data, an operating system, an "analyzer" application to control all this hardware, a remote control facility, and often a complete set of TCP/IP utilities. These instruments are often based on the PC architecture running MS-DOS and are portable. Examples include the Network General Sniffer, HP 4972A, HP Network Advisor, HP Internet Advisor, and a variety of telecommunications instruments that can measure WAN interfaces such as T-1, frame relay, and X.25.

The analyzer LAN interface operates in promiscuous mode. It receives all LAN frames regardless of the destination address, the CRC correctness, or the presence of a collision. The hardware filters examine certain fields in the frame such as the source and/or destination address or other protocol fields such as the TCP port number. Frames matched by the filter are passed into RAM and buffered there before being written to the disk drive. The data is later examined using a protocol decode package that breaks out each frame's fields in a longhand ASCII form (see Figure 2-4). This ASCII form is useful for further performance analysis.

To use a LAN analyzer for benchmark tracing, the Ethernet (MAC, layer 2, LLA, link, hardware) addresses of the client and server systems are put into the hardware filter. This ensures that only frames of interest are captured to disk. This is a practical way to prevent frame losses when a lot of other LAN traffic is present and the capture buffers would otherwise overflow. When client-server traffic is very high, the LAN analyzer can be set to capture only the first N bytes of the frame to disk. This reduces the amount of captured data significantly. This works because the frame headers contain all the important information about the frame.

When a LAN analyzer is used to monitor and capture all frames on a LAN, the disk file will grow rapidly and about ten minutes worth of traffic is all that can be saved. This trace can be a gold mine of information if it is taken at the right time because it contains many conversations. To find these conversations, the trace file is first converted to ASCII form using the analyzer's own conversion utility. Then it is processed with an *awk* script, which identifies conversational pairs, counts the number of packet exchanges between each pair, and identifies the top talkers in the ten-minute interval. This top talker pair can be taken as a worst-case conversation and used for further network performance analysis.

The *awk* utility is available on all UNIX systems and versions of it exist for the MS-DOS environment. The MKS Toolkit is a commercially available product from MKS in Ontario, Canada. An excellent text on *awk* is the O'Reilly bug book *sed & awk*.

LAN analyzers also come with statistics packages that keep a record of utilization, frames, collisions, CRC errors, runts, jabbers, and oversize frames. The information can be displayed as histograms, line graphs, tables, and pie charts. Such data can be used for trend analysis for an individual LAN segment. The data can also be used to detect unacceptable performance conditions. But note that packet traces are more useful than operational statistics for capacity planning purposes.

Tables 2-3 and 2-4 provide some rules of thumb on how to interpret LAN analyzer statistics. On a multiprotocol multiapplication network operation, experience is often used to adjust these values to reflect operations norms. On networks that have been fully analyzed, these values are often set to correspond with the onset of response time degradation.

Frame number: 25
Frame Date: May 13 1994
Frame Time: 13:01:48.890212300
Receive Length: 109
Stored Length: 109
Preamble Bits: 64
Frame Errors: none
Frame Data: 08-00-09-88-F8-9E-02-60—8C-B9-5F-5F-08-00-45-00
<THE REMAINING DATA IS MERCIFULLY NOT DISPLAYED>
CRC: C06A422BH

Figure 2-4 This is an HP Network Advisor decoded display. The Frame Time stamp and Receive Length are useful for further analysis. The destination MAC address 08-00-09-88-F8-9E and the source MAC address 02-60-8C-B9-5F-5F are in the Frame Data field.

TABLE 2-3 ETHERNET PERFORMANCE METRIC RULES OF THUMB

Ethernet metric	Threshold	Rule of thumb notes
Packets per second (PPS)	n/a	Can vary from ~800 to 14,881 PPS on Ethernet.
Collisions per second	n/a	Collisions have to be compared with packets.
Percent collisions	2–5	Collisions per packet.
Percent utilization	40	An arguable value. Some say 25% and others 50%.
Broadcasts per second	20–30	Over 80 per second can crash low-end PCs.
Percent CRC errors	0	CRC errors indicate induced noise on the LAN.
Percent alignment errors	2	Many collisions cause alignment errors.

TABLE 2-4 WAN PERFORMANCE METRIC RULES OF THUMB

WAN serial link metric	Threshold	Rule of thumb notes
Percent utilization in	90	Queue wait times are ten times the norm.
Packets per second in	n/a	Varies with line speed and frame size.
Percent erred packets in	1	Retransmitted frames reduces WAN performance.

2.4 SEGMENT MONITORS, RMON, AND HP EASE

Segment monitors operate in promiscuous mode (just like LAN analyzers do) and collect LAN performance information. This information is stored in RAM until it is either retrieved by a network management application or transmitted to one. Examples of segment monitors include the HP LanProbe III, the Network General Distributed Sniffer, the Novell LANalyzer, and the HP Traffic Probe. Some hub vendors even build RMON engines right into their products. Both devices can provide valuable network performance information.

The Remote Monitoring MIB (RMON) provides an industry standard data structure and command structure for controlling segment monitors. Standard SNMP SET and GET commands allocate buffers, control data gathering, and retrieve information from the segment monitor. The complexity of the RMON MIB makes the MIB browser GUI, the *snmpget* and the *snmpset* commands impractical. Hewlett-Packard's OpenView Probe Manager (see Figure 2-5) and NetMetrix products offer GUIs for configuring the LanProbe III and retrieving the complex RMON MIB data structures for display and storage.

The RMON MIB is documented in RFC 1271. It defines various measurements called groups (see Figure 2-6). The following text taken directly from the RFC describes the contents of these groups:

> The **statistics group** contains statistics measured by the probe for each monitored interface on this device. This group currently consists of the etherStatsTable but in the future will contain tables for other media types including Token Ring and FDDI.
>
> The **history group** records periodic statistical samples from a network and stores them for later retrieval. This group currently consists of the historyControlTable and the etherHistoryTable. In future versions of the MIB, this group may contain tables for other media types including Token Ring and FDDI.

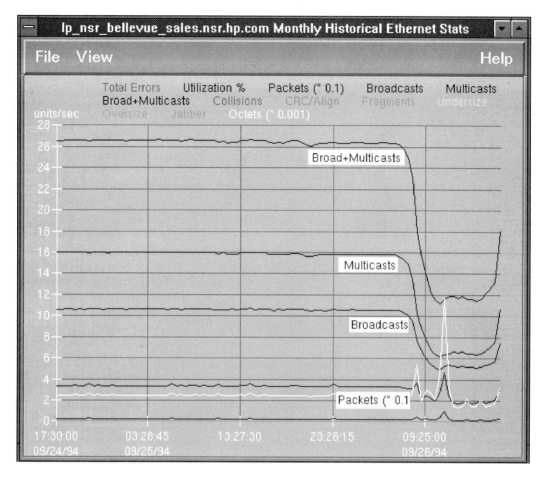

Figure 2-5 This OpenView Probe Manager displays the RMON history group statistics. Performance statistics include Utilization %, Packets, and Octets. Problem statistics include Total Errors, Broadcasts, Multicasts, Collisions, and Fragments. Pathological statistics include CRC/Align, Undersize, Oversize, and Jabber.

The **alarm group** periodically takes statistical samples from variables in the probe and compares them to previously configured thresholds. If the monitored variable crosses a threshold, an event is generated. A hysterysis mechanism is implemented to limit the generation of alarms. This group consists of the alarmTable and requires the implementation of the event group.

The **host group** contains statistics associated with each host discovered on the network. This group discovers hosts on the network by keeping a list of source and destination MAC Addresses seen in good packets promiscuously received from the network. This group consists of the hostControlTable, the hostTable, and the hostTimeTable.

The **hostTopN group** is used to prepare reports that describe the hosts that top a list ordered by one of their statistics. The available statistics are samples of one of their base statistics over an interval specified by the management station. Thus, these statistics are rate based. The management station also selects how many such hosts are reported. This group consists of

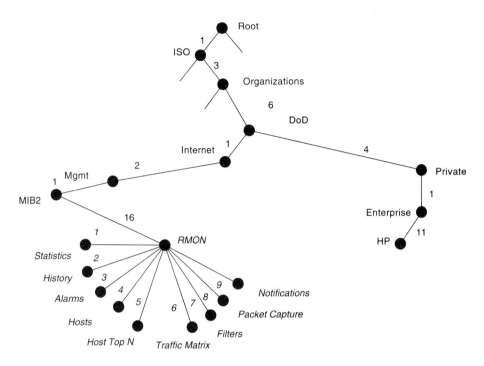

Figure 2-6 The RMON MIB is attached to the MIB-2 tree structure and contains nine somewhat interdependent groups of variables. The statistics, history, and packet capture features provide excellent data for predicting the performance of existing networks. The remaining groups are better suited for operational use.

the hostTopNControlTable and the hostTopNTable, and requires the implementation of the host group.

The **matrix group** stores statistics for conversations between sets of two addresses. As the device detects a new conversation, it creates a new entry in its tables. This group consists of the matrixControlTable, the matrixSDTable and the matrixDSTable.

The **filter group** allows packets to be matched by a filter equation. These matched packets form a data stream that may be captured or may generate events. This group consists of the filterTable and the channelTable.

The **Packet Capture group** allows packets to be captured after they flow through a channel. This group consists of the bufferControlTable and the captureBufferTable, and requires the implementation of the filter group.

The **event group** controls the generation and notification of events from this device. This group consists of the eventTable and the logTable.

RMON probes typically contain four to eight megabytes of RAM, which is not enough to store long-term performance statistics. HP Probe Manager running on an HP-UX system periodically uploads the history group buffers to a disk file to provide long-term history statistics. Long-term statistics should be retained for several business cycles. Many businesses have quarterly milestones and this pattern of activity is visible in the monthly data. Enough disk space must be made available to keep this much performance data on line.

The RMON packet capture feature can be used to record client-server conversations between two nodes. Probe manager uploads the packets (or the first N bytes of each one), decodes them, displays the ASCII, and stores the data to disk. This trace information can be used to extract client-server statistics and to drive a simulation tool. System & Networks' PlanNet tool will accept HP LanProbe II and III decoded traces and use them to generate simulated traffic.

HP's Embedded Advanced Sampling Environment (EASE) is built into HP hubs, bridges, routers, LanProbe III, and Traffic Probes. The EASE engine pseudo-randomly samples every 400th frame (a configurable parameter), encapsulates its header in an SNMP trap, and transmits it to an EASE server (see Figure 2-7). The EASE server writes the frame's time, length, source, destination, and protocol into the EASE database. HP's

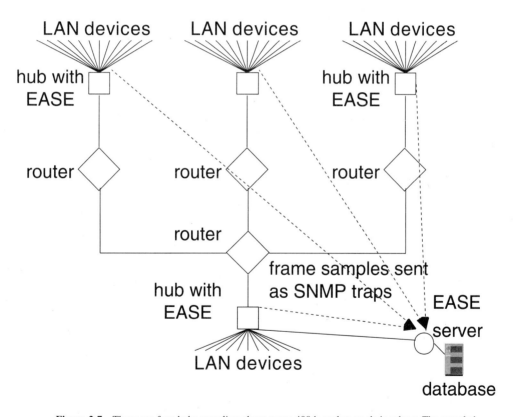

Figure 2-7 There are four hubs sampling about every 400th packet on their subnet. The sampled frames may be any protocol and their headers are sent as SNMP traps over the IP internet to the EASE server. The EASE database is accessed using HP's History Analyzer, Traffic Monitor, and Traffic Expert, applications that display network performance data graphically.

History Analyzer (HA), Resource Manager (RM), and Traffic Expert (TE) applications use the EASE database to display network performance information is useful ways.

Sampled data contains statistical uncertainties that can be averaged out by taking sufficient samples. History Analyzer and Traffic Expert averages performance data over one-hour intervals. This reduces the sampling error and provides reasonable accuracy. Unfortunately, short duration traffic spikes are not visible in a one-hour average. Note that the 1995+ version of Resource Manager is now called Traffic Analyzer.

To instrument the enterprise network, EASE engines are located on all collision domains. They forward their samples to one EASE server where a performance is history maintained. This data can be accessed from any UNIX system running HA, RM, and TE. History Analyzer offers smoothed long-term statistics for each or all protocols on a subnet. Consistently high levels of traffic may suggest changes to the topology. Traffic Expert is used to decide how to change the topology and which source-destination pairs to move to another subnet. The rest of this chapter is devoted to the displays and features of the three HP EASE traffic display tools (see Figures 2-8 to 2-15).

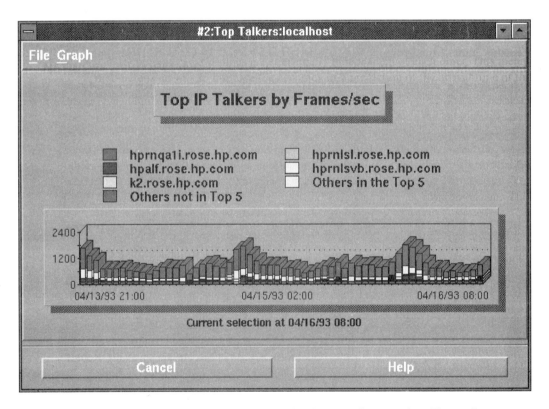

Figure 2-8 This History Analyzer report is showing the top IP talkers on a subnet. The top talker may be used to characterize a typical conversation in a worst-case performance analysis to determine how many such systems can be safely co-located on one subnet.

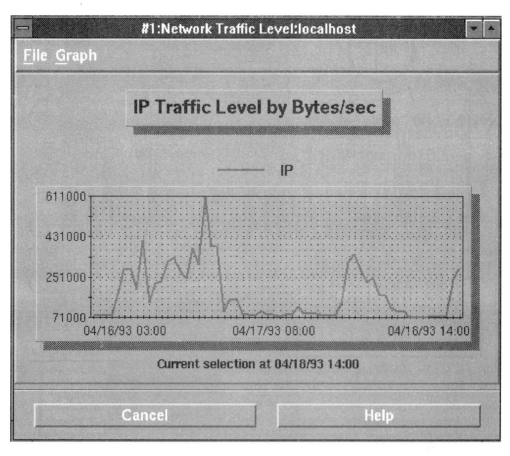

Figure 2-9 This History Analyzer report is showing IP traffic in bytes per second on a LAN. Assuming an Ethernet medium of 10 Mbps gives a peak utilization of 6.11% over a one-hour period.

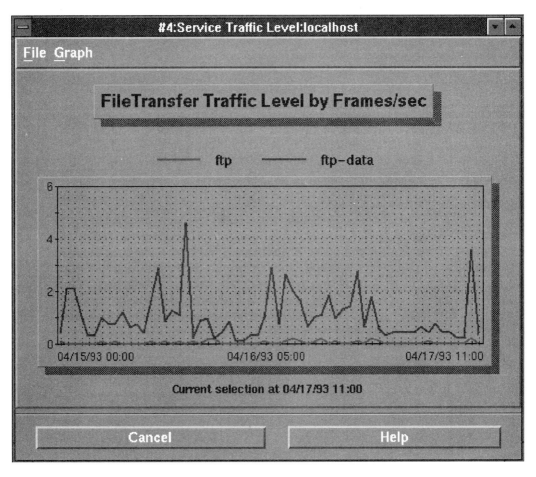

Figure 2-10 A History Analyzer report showing the level of FTP data and FTP control frames on a LAN. The ftp-data packet rate dwarfs the ftp control packet rate.

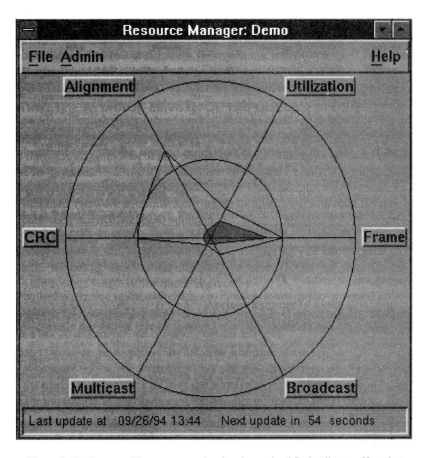

Figure 2-11 Resource Manager report showing the top-level Radar diagram. Note that Frame and Utilization, Broadcasts and Multicasts, and Alignment and CRC statistics are like groups and are located next to each other for maximum clarity. This diagram is updated automatically once a minute, pushing out any high-water marks.

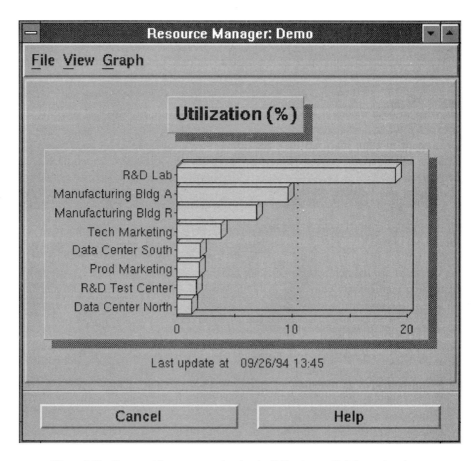

Figure 2-12 Resource Manager report showing the Utilization on all eight monitored segments for the previous one-minute time slice. Clicking on the Utilization button on the Radar diagram (Figure 2-11) opens this window.

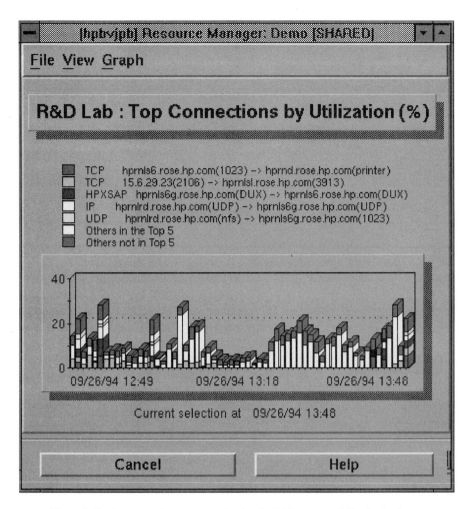

Figure 2-13 Resource Manager report showing the R&D segment Utilization by the top communicator pairs over the last 60 seconds. Clicking on the R&D segment label (from Figure 2-12) opens this window.

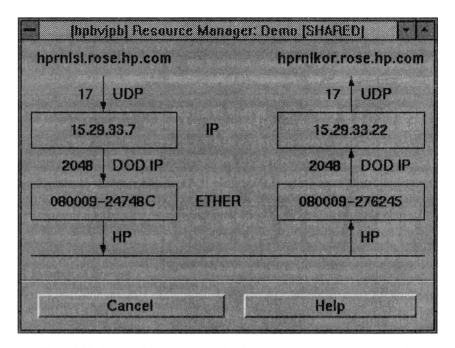

Figure 2-14 Resource Manager decode of a single packet header that was captured in the database. It shows the layer 2, 3, and 4 protocol addresses for both sides of the conversational pair. Clicking on one of the colored buttons of Figure 2-13 will create this type of display.

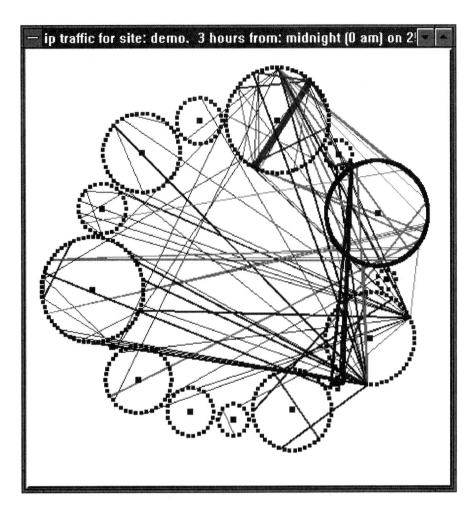

Figure 2-15 This is a Traffic Expert traffic diagram. Traffic within a subnet is normally displayed on the CRT in red, traffic between subnets in blue, and traffic to an unmonitored segment in yellow. The EASE sampling device is represented by the dot at the center of each circle and the points around the center represent nodes on that subnet that have sent or received packets. The thicker lines represent more traffic than thinner lines do. When a lot of lines converge on one node, it usually indicates a server attracting a lot of client traffic.

2.5 UNIX TRACING FUNCTIONS

UNIX systems are found wherever enterprise-wide applications require a robust, bullet-proof and time-tested secure multiuser multitasking operating system. UNIX packet tracing functionality can be used to characterize the network performance of these applications. So long as the client or the server application is UNIX-resident, packets will be moving in and out of the system's network interfaces and can be captured, filtered, decoded, and saved to disk (see Figure 2-16). Processing these trace files results in both statistical and scriptable information useful in queuing analysis and network simulations.

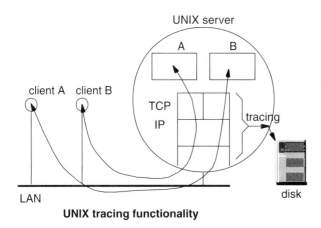

Figure 2-16 UNIX tracing can capture multiple conversations between remote clients and local server programs (denoted as A and B). The role of client and server may be reversed and both programs may even reside inside the UNIX system. Broadcasts and multicasts received on the LAN adapter can also be traced.

UNIX tracing functionality

The following limitations should be understood. As stated, the UNIX system must be a participant in the client-server communication. Merely installing a promiscuous-mode driver into some computer does not make it a LAN analyzer. There will be packet loss at higher utilization as LAN adapter buffers, operating system buffers and the file system buffers overflow. This is true for 10 Mbps Ethernet, even more true for 16 Mbps Token Ring, and doubly true for FDDI, 100 Mbps Ethernet (100-BASE-T or 100VG-AnyLAN), and ATM. Finally, since the UNIX system is already doing real work, the additional overhead of packet capture will introduce timing jitter on the capture data. Results will be more accurate when the UNIX system is less busy.

The benefits of using UNIX tracing functions is that it's free, all the packets are time-stamped, source-destination conversations can be observed, and the *awk* tool is on-line for postprocessing the trace data. Multihomed systems (those with multiple LAN adapters) can trace packets on all interfaces concurrently.

2.6 THE UBIQUITOUS ping COMMAND

The *p*acket *i*nter *n*et *g*roper (*ping*) program is distributed with UNIX systems and can usually be found on PC and Macintosh implementations of TCP/IP software. IP routers usually provide one too. `ping` is used for troubleshooting purposes. For example, it can be used to bounce a packet off a remote system to verify that it is reachable. The program merely constructs an Internet Control Message Protocol (ICMP, per RFC 792) loopback request packet for a target IP address and injects it into the local area network interface. The network passes the datagram along from router to router until it reaches its destination. The receiver accepts the loopback request and issues a loopback response to the initiator (the `ping` command). After checking the sequence number of the reply, `ping` prints the round trip time. `ping` sends a loopback packet once a second heedless of any previous replies (see Figures 2-17 to 2-19).

An operational network's performance can be monitored by running background pings continuously between various legs of the network. This directly measures the network response time at all times during the day. Processing this volume of ASCII data falls to *awk* and plotting the data is a job for a spreadsheet.

```
ping hppad.waterloo.hp.com: 1500 byte packets
1500 bytes from 15.4.2.1: icmp_seq=0. time=655. ms
1500 bytes from 15.4.2.1: icmp_seq=1. time=648. ms
1500 bytes from 15.4.2.1: icmp_seq=2. time=827. ms
1500 bytes from 15.4.2.1: icmp_seq=3. time=646. ms
1500 bytes from 15.4.2.1: icmp_seq=4. time=647. ms
1500 bytes from 15.4.2.1: icmp_seq=5. time=644. ms
1500 bytes from 15.4.2.1: icmp_seq=6. time=645. ms
1500 bytes from 15.4.2.1: icmp_seq=7. time=649. ms
1500 bytes from 15.4.2.1: icmp_seq=8. time=649. ms
1500 bytes from 15.4.2.1: icmp_seq=9. time=667. ms

—hppad.waterloo.hp.com ping Statistics—
10 packets transmitted, 10 packets received, 0% packet loss
round-trip (ms) min/avg/max = 644/667/827
```

Figure 2-17 Output from the command `/etc/ping hppad 1500 10`. The correct number of bytes (1,500) are returned in each echo reply, hppad's IP address is shown as 15.4.2.1, the ICMP sequence number of each reply increments from zero, and the round-trip time in milliseconds is fairly consistent. No packets were lost during the ten-second interval and the minimum, average and maximum round-trip times are given at the end of the display.

```
ping hppad.waterloo.hp.com: 64 byte packets
64 bytes from 15.4.2.1: icmp_seq=0. time=364. ms
64 bytes from 15.4.2.1: icmp_seq=1. time=374. ms
64 bytes from 15.4.2.1: icmp_seq=2. time=160. ms
64 bytes from 15.4.2.1: icmp_seq=3. time=178. ms
64 bytes from 15.4.2.1: icmp_seq=4. time=164. ms
64 bytes from 15.4.2.1: icmp_seq=5. time=165. ms
64 bytes from 15.4.2.1: icmp_seq=6. time=163. ms
64 bytes from 15.4.2.1: icmp_seq=7. time=209. ms
64 bytes from 15.4.2.1: icmp_seq=8. time=335. ms
64 bytes from 15.4.2.1: icmp_seq=9. time=574. ms

—hppad.waterloo.hp.com ping Statistics—
10 packets transmitted, 10 packets received, 0% packet loss
round-trip (ms) min/avg/max = 160/268/574
```

Figure 2-18 Output from the command `/etc/ping hppad 64 10` using a 64-byte packet typical of telnet traffic. The round-trip time now averages much less but it shows more variation.

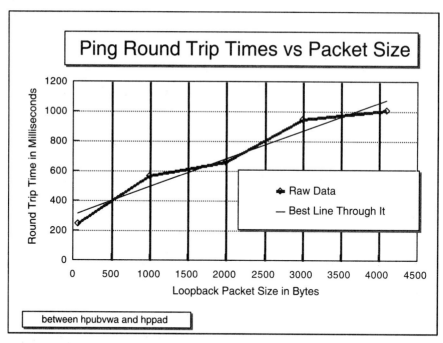

Figure 2-19 ping can be used to measure response time for different packet sizes. It reports the min/avg/max round-trip times, the number of packets sent, the number received, and the number lost. Ten pings were sent to the system hppad for a variety of frame sizes with the results plotting out linearly. The system is 9 hops away for a round-trip of 18 hops.

The following command line options apply to the UNIX (BSD4.3) version of `ping`:

```
ping [-r] [-v] [-o] host [packetsize] [count]
```

Parameter	Description
`-r`	Ignore the routing table and send the packet on the LAN.
`-v`	Report all ICMP packets seen, not just the ICMP echo replies.
`-o`	Force intervening nodes to record their IP address to the packet (9 max).
`host`	The name or IP address to be pinged.
`packetsize`	The size of the loopback packet (16–4,096 bytes), defaults to 64.
`count`	The number of loopback responses `ping` will receive before stopping.

Not all implementations of `ping` are created equal. Some PC versions often report only that the round-trip time is less than 50 milliseconds—scarcely useful. LAN analyzers can be programmed to send out ICMP loopback packets and measure the round-trip time.

Timing data from `ping` can be used in elementary queuing theory to analyze network performance. The network is taken as two queues in tandem, the remote system's service time (the time to actually perform the ICMP loopback) will typically be less than a few milliseconds. Assuming roughly equal loading in the forward and reverse directions lets you assign half the round-trip delay to each direction. See Chapter 9 for more details.

2.7 USING PERFORMANCE INFORMATION FROM THE UNIX BSD netstat COMMAND

UNIX systems as well as some PC versions of TCP/IP usually provide a version of `netstat` that extracts kernel statistics about the LAN adapters, IP, ICMP, TCP, and UDP protocol layers. The statistics provided by `netstat` for each OSI protocol layer are the total for all applications that participate in TCP/IP communications. No finer resolution is available.

Output from the command `netstat -s` is shown in Figure 2-20. The command `netstat -i` provides LAN interface statistics.

Like all good protocols based on the OSI model, TCP/IP/Ethernet add headers and trailers around their data. Each OSI layer may have a different maximum transmission unit (MTU) requiring fragmentation and reassembly. This suggests how the performance data gathered at a given OSI layer should be adjusted to compensate. Table 2-5 provides the necessary terminology and header/trailer data for TCP/IP.

Let's compute the protocol overhead of a TCP/IP/Ethernet example. Suppose 16,384 bytes of user data is sent to TCP. Let TCP have a maximum segment size of 4,096 bytes. Four segments (16,384/4,096) will be sent, each with a 20-byte TCP header added. IP notes that Ethernet's MTU is 1,500 bytes of data and fragments the 4,116-byte datagram into three packets of 1,480, 1,480, and 1,156 bytes. IP now adds its own 20-byte header and passes 1,500, 1,500, and 1,176 bytes to Ethernet, which frames the data with an additional 18 bytes and injects 1,518-, 1,518-, and 1,174-byte frames into the medium. The same happens for the remaining three TCP segments. Thus 16,840 bytes and 12 frames are actually

```
tcp:
    57758939 packets sent
        45334534 data packets (831226678 bytes)
        18356 data packets (20651810 bytes) retransmitted
        11230996 ack-only packets (10253230 delayed)
        24 URG only packets
        9484 window probe packets
        454033 window update packets
        711785 control packets
    34647013 packets received
        19760872 acks (for 1141199184 bytes)
        167583 duplicate acks
        0 acks for unsent data
        16974178 packets (2115956587 bytes) received in-sequence
        74245 completely duplicate packets (24437159 bytes)
        304 packets with some dup. data (192663 bytes duped)
        205290 out-of-order packets (125705208 bytes)
        2210 packets (125 bytes) of data after window

ip:
    78221988 total packets received
```

Figure 2-20 The command `netstat -s` executed on an HP 9000 model 750 UNIX workstation that has been up for 31 days produced the above output (mercifully shortened). After executing the `netstat` command periodically, say once a minute, and concatenating the output into a file, an *awk* script can be written to take differences between samples and compute performance statistics. The most useful are the TCP statistics for packets and bytes sent and received.

TABLE 2-5 OVERHEAD IN THE OSI MODEL PACKET HEADERS

Protocol name	OSI layer name	OSI layer number	Header overhead in bytes	PDU name	Comments
TCP	transport	4	20	segment	see RFC 793
IP	network	3	20	packet	see RFC 791
Ethernet	link	2	14	frame	6-byte source, 6-byte destination, 2-byte type field
IEEE 802.2	link	2	15	frame	6-byte source, 6-byte destination, 3-byte LLC field
Ethernet	physical	1	4	bit	32-bit CRC trailer
IEEE 802.30			8	bit	64-bit frame preamble

Note that both Ethernet and IEEE 802 enforce a 64-byte minimum frame size. If user data plus protocol headers won't fill a frame, the LAN adapter pads the frame to the 64-byte minimum.

transmitted on the Ethernet, not counting the 64-bit preamble and mandatory 9.6 microsecond interframe gap.

2.8 PROCESSING PACKET TRACES USING UNIX'S awk

This section will touch on the basics of `awk` programming. The name `awk` is simply the first letter of each author of the language. It comes with UNIX systems and can be purchased for PC platforms from MKS systems in Canada. This section will introduce only the basics of `awk`—refer to the examples here and to the commercially available books such as the O'Reilly bug book called *sed & awk*.

Network traces may come from LAN analyzers, RMON segment monitors, and UNIX tracing. Users of the Systems & Networks' PlanNet tool already have the `csv2trc` `awk` scripts built in for converting Network General Sniffer and HP LanProbe III traces. With just a little effort other ASCII trace formats can be converted and used for network performance analysis.

All raw ASCII trace files contain four fields of important information that have to be extracted before any performance analysis can proceed. These fields are described in Table 2-6 and shown in Figure 2-21.

Network traces will consist of any number of similar line groups, one line for each frame. The task at hand is to write an `awk` script that processes each line, identifies the packet boundaries, does the necessary arithmetic (to calculate the delta-time between packets), and writes an output file. The output file format is one line per packet with fields for

TABLE 2-6 INFORMATION FIELDS FOUND IN TRAFFIC TRACES NEEDED FOR PERFORMANCE ANALYSIS

Field needed	Description	Examples
source	packet sender	Ethernet, IP address, or node name:
destination	packet receiver	08-00-09-12-34-56, 15.4.2.1, hppad
length	packet bytes	60 bytes. Often excludes the 4-byte CRC, but caution!
time	time stamp	13:01:48.890212300

Frame number: 25
Frame Date: May 13 1994
Frame Time: *13:01:48.890212300*
Receive Length: *109*
Stored Length: 109
Preamble Bits: 64
Frame Errors: none
Frame Data: *08-00-09-88-F8-9E*-02-60—*8C-B9-5F-5F*-08-00-45-00
<THE REMAINING DATA IS MERCIFULLY NOT DISPLAYED>
CRC: C06A422BH

Figure 2-21 In this decoded ASCII frame format for the HP Network Advisor, the four fields described in Table 2-6 are underlined and italicized.

delta-time, source, destination, and length. The fields are separated by white space and terminated with a semicolon (see Figure 2-22).

```
0.00000 Client Server  64;
0.05262 Server Client  64;
0.00380 Client Server 101;
0.00675 Server Client 189;
0.43194 Client Server  64;
2.24765 Client Server  64;
0.10980 Server Client  64;
0.00301 Client Server 101;
```

Figure 2-22 Example of a trace file. These files are used in Systems & Networks' PlanNet simulation tool and have the *.trc* extension. The very first delta-time should be zero. Raw packet trace data can be converted to trace file format using *awk* scripts.

The **awk** script executes the BEGIN statement before reading the data input file. Every time **awk** reads in a new line, it attempts to match each pattern in the line, executing the statements if successful. If no pattern is present the statements are executed unconditionally. Each line of input data is broken into fields denoted as $1, $2, and so on. The default field separator is white space. Upon reaching the end of the data input file, **awk** executes the END statements.

The formal outline of all **awk** scripts is as follows:

```
BEGIN
{ statements}
pattern 1
{ statements}
pattern 2
{ statements}
      ..............
pattern N
{ statements}
END
{ statements}
```

The **awk** command is invoked as follows (from the MKS PC version):

Usage: `awk [-f programfile] [-Fs] [program] [var=value...] [file...]`

`-f`   'programfile' contains the awk program

-Fs   's' is the field separator string (equiv. to FS=s)

Use 'program' for **awk** program only if no -f specified.

If no 'file' is specified, use standard input.

For example, to invoke **awk** on the command line to process a **ping** output file pingtime.txt:

```
awk -F = '{print $2 $3}' < pingtime.txt | sed 's/[a-z]//g' >
pingdata.txt
```

The equals sign is the field separator. **awk** reads the standard input (redirected from pingtime.txt) and prints the second and third fields to the standard output. This is piped to the streaming editor, **sed**, which removes all occurrences of alphabetic characters to leave simply the sequence number and the round trip time. **sed**'s output is redirected to **pingdata.txt** for later spreadsheet processing.

The challenge in processing LAN traces is to find ASCII patterns in the data input file and write statements that correctly process and output the trace data. The following is a working UNIX shell script with an **awk** script in it that will accept an HP Network Advisor (HP 4980) trace and produce a .trc file. It has an optional STATISTICS mode for computing elapsed time, total bytes, average data rate, and the number of frames processed. This mode allows the network manager to calculate operational statistics from the packet trace, which can be used to validate a subsequent performance analysis.

```
# Shell and awk script to convert 4980 ASCII data to trc data
# Usage: 4980-trc ASCII_file_name > file_name.trc
# ASCII data comes from the CONV.EXE program that comes
# with the Network Advisor.
#
# Strip off the DOS line feed, Control-M first
# and feed that into an awk script:
#
cat $1 | sed 's/^M//' |
awk -F:'
BEGIN { STATISTICS_MODE = "off";
    frame = 0;
    frame_number = 0;
    time_stamp = 0;
    last_stamp = 0;
    data_length = 0;
    frame_length = 0;
    total_bytes = 0;
    delta_time = 0;
    total_time = 0;
    flag = 0;
    source = "source";
    fixed_frames = 0;
    destination = "dest";
```

```
        }
#
# start of body part
#
"Frame number "==$1 {frame_number = $2}
"Frame Time "==$1 {
            decimalp = index($4, ".");
            seconds  = substr($4, 1, decimalp - 1);
            fraction = substr($4, decimalp + 1);
            time_stamp = fraction/1000000000.0 + seconds \
                                               + $3*60 \
                                               + $2*3600;
            delta_time = time_stamp−last_stamp;
            if (frame_number==1)
                {delta_time = 0};
            last_stamp = time_stamp;
            total_time += delta_time;  }
"Receive Length"==$1 {
            data_length = $2;
            total_bytes += data_length;  }
{ if (flag==1) {
        destination = substr($1,1,17);
        source      = substr($1,19,18);
        flag = 0}                                }
"Frame Data"==$1 {flag = 1}
"CRC" ==$1 {    printf("%10.5f %6s%11s %17s %4d;\n",
                delta_time,
                substr(source,1,6),
                substr(source,8,11),
                destination,
                data_length);
                frame++}
#
# end of body part
#
END { if(STATISTICS_MODE == "on") {
    print "\nElapsed time in seconds =" total_time,
          "\nTotal transmitted bytes =" total_bytes,
          "\nUtilization (bits/sec) =" total_bytes*8/total_time,
          "\nTotal number of frames =" frame,
          "\nLast frame number was =" frame_number;
                    }
    }
'
#end of shell script
```

2.9 SAMPLING FREQUENCY OF PERFORMANCE DATA

How frequently should performance data be sampled and stored? Most instrumentation is capable of taking one-second samples. The volume of performance data collected at this rate is prodigious if long-term data is kept and if the network has a lot of performance collection points.

The sampling frequency determines the resolution of the data and its storage requirements. A LAN analyzer reporting one-second utilization averages adds up all the bytes it sees during the second and saves that number. Given that over 14,000 frames per second may be encountered during that one second, short-term measurements offer the highest resolution and possesses the greatest variation between samples. Averaging data over a minute results in considerably reduced variation between samples—about one-eighth as much, but gives us 1/60 the volume of data. Averaging data over an hour provides very smooth performance data with 1/60 the variation between samples and 1/3,600 the volume of data.

Statistical performance data taken from client-server benchmarks should be as faithful as possible and be taken once per second. This ensures the most accurate standard deviation estimate. It's the variability of data rates that creates all the interesting behavior in networks. Users do not work in lockstep. Packets arrive in bursts separated by variable time gaps. Packets form queues in routers and wait for transmission. Queuing analysis depends on variation in packet arrival times, as do simulation methods. Mean value performance techniques are inherently insensitive to variability of data rates..

The down side of sampling frequently (especially with SNMP, UNIX tracing, and UNIX `netstat`) is that it takes a good fraction of a second to take the measurement. At one second sample intervals this latency creates jitter and an occasional missed sample. The jitter increases the apparent standard variation of the data.

Network performance statistics may have a periodic component. If so, the data sampling period should be less than half of that. The data period should not be divisible by the sampling period. Otherwise the samples will consistently be taken at the peaks, midpoints, or low points of the data. The sampling error is called aliasing and results will be unacceptable. The Nyquist Sampling Theorem is the basis for this. For example, if there is a 20-minute regular cycle in a serial line's utilization, samples should be taken less than ten minutes apart. Seven seconds would be a good choice because it does not divide evenly into 20.

Network managers using SNMP to measure Internet performance don't want network management traffic to swamp regular traffic. The Heisenberg Uncertainty Principle from physics states that we disturb the object we measure and the more precisely we try to measure it the more we disturb the object. At some point no further improvement in measurement accuracy is possible. An analogous situation exists with SNMP measurements since they disturb the network being measured. To get a handle on how much SNMP sampling traffic impacts the network, we can use the calculation shown in Figure 2-23.

$$\text{NumberOfSamplingPoints} := 1000$$

$$\text{PacketsPerSample} := 2$$

$$\text{TimeBetweenSamples} := 60 \quad \text{seconds}$$

$$\text{SizeOfPacket} := 85 \quad \text{bytes}$$

$$\text{MediaSpeed} := 256{,}000 \quad \text{bits per second}$$

$$\text{SampleRate} := \frac{\text{NumberOfSamplingPoints} \cdot \text{PacketsPerSample}}{\text{TimeBetweenSamples}}$$

$$\text{SampleRate} = 33.333 \quad \text{packets per second}$$

$$\text{Utilization} := \frac{\text{SampleRate} \cdot \text{SizeOfPacket} \cdot 8}{\text{MediaSpeed}} \cdot 100$$

$$\text{Utilization} = 8.854$$

Figure 2-23 A calculation that shows how to compute the packet rate and line utilization incurred by an SNMP management station situated on the remote side of a WAN serial line. A rule of thumb is to keep SNMP traffic overhead below 10% utilization for the medium.

2.10 TRAFFIC CHARACTERISTICS: PACKET SIZE DISTRIBUTION AND ARRIVAL RATE

Other sections in this chapter covered various data collection methods ranging from LAN analyzers to synthetic methods. Various network performance analysis methods will work if only average or worst-case information is known about the offered traffic. Other methods such as queuing theory require information about the traffic's variability. For that reason the network designer needs to understand what characterizes network traffic. The distribution of packet sizes may follow several idealized probability curves. All packet sizes between an upper and a lower limit may be equally likely. The uniform probability function best describes this characteristic. Packet sizes may follow a bell-shaped curve. The normal (Gaussian) distribution is suited for this. In many situations packets arrive in a consistent but random bursty manner. The exponential distribution ideally models this behavior.

In practice, packet sizes may be fixed or take on a limited number of sizes, conforming to no convenient statistical pattern. When determining traffic patterns in the interview process, it is best to ask questions that shed light on the variability of data patterns. When there is doubt about the packet size distribution, assume it is exponential. This provides a healthy degree of randomness and the mean value and standard deviation are equal. LAN analyzers can provide packet size distributions. So can the RMON MIB, which provides packet counts for 64, 65–127, 128–255, 256–511, 512–1,023 and 1,024–1,518 bytes.

Packet Size Distributions
Uniform.
Exponential and Poisson is often assumed.
Normal, or approximately so except for the tails.
Bimodal is often seen in practice.
Measure with RMON and EASE probes.

Packet arrival rates may be characterized like packet sizes. When in doubt, assume the interarrival times are exponentially distributed. This won't fit all situations. For example, the Routing Information Protocol (RIP) sends its routing tables on all interfaces every 30 seconds. LAN Manager server announcements are sent by default every minute. While a client application may read information from a network drive according to the exponential distribution, the returned data may be closely spaced fixed-size packets. For example, an NFS client may request a logical record only to have the server hand over a full 8,192-byte disk block (fragmented into 1,518-byte Ethernet frames). LAN analyzers are able to provide information about the interarrival times between packets. Note that the business cycle defines how the average packet rate fluctuates and the peak value should be used in performance analysis work.

The average packet size and the average packet arrival rate should be multiplied to calculate the average bandwidth requirements. Should the product be close to (say 75% of) the maximum speed of the LAN/WAN medium, this is a warning flag that performance calculations are going to be very dependent on the quality of the traffic information.

2.11 SYNTHESIS AND ESTIMATION OF TRAFFIC

When traffic traces are not available and pinpoint accuracy is not required, performance analysis has to be done with synthetic data. Skilled staff may not be at hand to take the desired traffic traces, or the equipment to gather the traces may simply be unavailable. A methodology is needed to collect the necessary traffic flow information.

First, determine the network topology. Locate all the LAN segments and document how they communicate via the interconnecting hubs, switches, bridges, and routers. Record all the media speeds for LAN segments and WAN serial lines. Document any performance-related parameters such as bridge/router latency and forwarding rates, buffer sizes, media MTU, and distances. Also be aware of which media are half duplex or full duplex.

Second, collect traffic information. Identify the location and number of transaction sources (users at client systems) and servers. There may be system-to-system activity to be considered, such as mail being moved between mail hubs. Find out what kinds of transactions users submit, how much transaction data moves around, and how frequently they are submitted. There will be times when certain workloads peak out, such as Monday morning, the end of the month, and the end of the fiscal quarter. Traffic information should be characterized by both packet counts and byte volumes.

Third, take the network topology and traffic information and construct a data flow diagram. Add up the data flows at each junction to find the average value, the variation, and the peak values. Also do a sensitivity analysis to determine the impact of uncertainty in the traffic information.

Finally, use a network performance methodology such as mean-value, queuing, or simulation analysis to determine user response time.

A Network Printing Example

Network printers are located at the main office and the users are located at a branch office. The branch office file server drives the printers over the WAN link, a 56 Kbps fractional T-1 serial line. Consider network print performance. Suppose that on the last day of the month, 20 users prepare and print 50-page documents at the rate of one to three (average two) per user per hour. The reports are printed on two Ethernet-attached 17 PPM LaserJet printers. Each document page contains text and illustrations and is between 5,000 and 15,000 bytes in size, averaging 10,000. Assume 1,500-byte packets and ignore protocol details.

The mean-value throughput analysis is straightforward. Multiplying 20 users by 50 pages by two documents by 10,000 bytes by eight bits per byte and dividing by 3,600 seconds gives us 44,444 bits per second average data rate. At the low end users print 5,000-byte pages and one document per hour minimum for a rate of 11,111 bits per second. At the high end, users print 15,000-byte pages and three documents per hour maximum for a rate of 100,000 bits per second. This exceeds the line capacity. From time to time the 56 Kbps line will slow productivity.

From a printer performance perspective, if all users are printing one document per hour, they generate 20 users times 50 pages divided by 60 minutes per hour equals 16.7 pages per minute. At two documents per hour they generate 33.3 pages per minute and keep both printers going full-time. At three documents per hour they generate 50 pages per minute, more than the two printers can accommodate.

Interestingly, we have two performance bottlenecks here. Adding a third printer will provide enough printing capacity but without an increase in line speed the users won't be able to take advantage of it.

Estimating network printing data volumes is difficult because the size of the document on disk has little bearing on the amount of data sent to the printer. For example, a 16-color, 336 $\times$ 457, 41,095-byte GIF file is expanded to 226,509 bytes when sent to a 300 DPI HP LaserJet IIIsi PostScript printer by Paint Shop Pro. The TCP/IP/Ethernet protocol overhead is not included in these numbers.

An Interactive Network Applications Example

Consider interactive network applications on an Ethernet LAN. Suppose that PC users login to a UNIX server and run a character-mode application using the TCP/IP `telnet` command. Estimating network traffic based on what users type is more straightforward. Each keystroke becomes a three-packet exchange of 64-byte Ethernet packets. The keystroke generates one byte of data, TCP/IP wraps 40 header bytes around it and Ethernet pads this out to the 64-byte Ethernet minimum. The UNIX application receives the character and typically echoes it back to the user (along with a piggyback TCP ACK of the original packet), creating a second packet. The client TCP will usually ACK this character with a third packet. Happily, when the application returns a multiline result to the user, it is generally carried in a single packet.

To estimate worst-case typing traffic, remember that a 100-words-per-minute user typing six-character words generates only 10 characters per second of input. That's about half the speed of an auto-repeating keyboard. One hundred such users will generate 1,000 characters times three packets per character times 64 bytes per packet times 8 bits per byte equals 1,536,000 bits per second. This utilization level is well below Ethernet's maximum rate and can be comfortably carried.

A Client-Server Application Example

Consider client-server applications on an Ethernet LAN. A typical transaction sends 250 bytes to the server and gets 3,000 bytes in return. One user generates 20 transactions per minute. The server average response time is 40 milliseconds, due entirely to CPU processing. Assume 50 active users are engaging the server. Using TCP/IP/Ethernet will add 58 bytes of overhead to the 250-byte request for a 308-byte request. The response will be fragmented into three segments of 1,460, 1,460, and 80 bytes of user data. Each will be padded with 40 bytes of TCP/IP header and 18 bytes of Ethernet framing to yield 1,518-, 1,518-, and 138-byte packets. Each transaction actually generates a 3,482-byte response, ignoring TCP ACK overhead.

The total data rate is 50 users times 20 transactions per minute per user times 3,482 bytes per transaction times 8 bits per byte divided by 60 seconds per minute equals 464,267 bits per second—a very low value for Ethernet. The transaction rate is 50 users times 20 transactions per user per minute divided by 60 seconds per minute equals 16.7 transactions per second. The CPU utilization will average 16.7 transactions per second times 40 milliseconds per transaction equals 667 milliseconds per second or 66.7%. This value is significant. A response time analysis should be done to see if this server utilization is acceptable to the user community. Refer to Chapters 9 and 10 on queuing and simulation.

There is considerable value in keeping benchmark traffic traces in a library for future reference. They can be modified for reuse in new performance studies. When trace data is lacking, Systems & Networks' PlanNet product includes Scribe, a tool for generating application traffic generator scripts for their simulator.

3

Quality of Network Performance Data

3.0 INTRODUCTION

In collecting network performance data, questions arise about its accuracy, validity, applicability, appropriateness, quantity, and properties. Is enough data being collected to provide a statistically valid sample? Will the real network actually experience the type of traffic being measured? Have all the necessary traffic samples been taken and can we ignore some of it? This chapter addresses these issues.

After focusing on how measurement data becomes comes contaminated we'll turn our attention towards methods for defining user profiles and their workloads. We take a graphical look at the daily and weekly cycles of measured network traffic.

3.1 DEALING WITH CONTAMINATION OF THE DATA DURING MEASUREMENT

Suppose that benchmark traffic traces are taken of client-server traffic. Contamination may result from the LAN not being quiet. Other devices not part of the benchmark may be generating traffic that competes with the benchmark traffic. This effects the interframe timing of the benchmark traces, usually by increasing it and occasionally causing a collision or a transport layer retransmission. The traffic capture tool should be set to filter out all packets on the LAN except those between the client and the server under measurement. This won't correct the interframe timing jitter of course, but it simplifies the postprocessing of the data. The severity of unexpected background traffic is minimal if it occupies only a few percent of the available bandwidth.

Traffic measured on one LAN medium has different properties than on another. For example, measurements taken on an Ethernet should not be applied directly to FDDI or IEEE 802.5 token ring. Differences due to the number of framing characters and MTU should be compensated for, as should the media speeds.

Benchmarking a word processing package using, say, LAN Manager provides performance information that is difficult to extrapolate to Banyan Vines, Novell NetWare, AppleTalk Filing Protocol, or Sun's Network File System. The file system redirector protocols are different, the frame formats and sizes are different, and the transport and network protocols differ drastically.

All benchmark traffic measurements should be taken at the server. That way the server response time is accurately captured. If there is a link (bridge, router, or serial line) between client and server, and traffic is measured at the client, the apparent server response time is increased due to the propagation delay across the link. Assuming no other traffic is moving across the link, the propagation delay can be subtracted from the server response time. If there is other link traffic and its magnitude is known, then a simple queuing analysis can be done to calculate the additional delay caused by it.

If the client system or the server system are performing other work besides the application being benchmarked, the traffic traces will not be representative of the application. The client and server systems should be otherwise idle.

The client think times used during the benchmark should not be so short that the server becomes significantly utilized. This will exaggerate the server response time measurements. Any stress testing done on the server usually provides sizing information for the system that will ultimately be deployed for production. Such data should not be used for network performance analysis.

Benchmarking with a 50 MIP server and analyzing the network performance for a 150 MIP server requires some adjustments to the packet traces. Systems & Networks' Plan-Net provides an `awk` script called `trc2atg` which takes a client-server trace file and computes the average server response time (as well as the average client think time, the average client request size, and the average server response length). The server response time figure should be scaled to one-third (50/150) of that measured in this benchmark.

Sources of Measurement Contamination

Target and measurement media are different.
Network Operating Systems are dissimilar.
Applications are similar but not identical.
Queues existed at servers and network links during the measurement.
Target and measurement system configurations are different.
Disk I/O delays are lumped in with CPU instruction delays.
The LAN carried other traffic not related to our benchmark.
Measurements were taken remote from the server system.
The server is doing other work in addition to our application.
The benchmark network and systems are already highly utilized.

Server response time is the sum of disk I/O latency and CPU instruction execution latency. Their exact values are not evident from LAN traces. A knowledge of the disk cache hit ratio and the amount of data written to and read from the disk is needed for the transactions being benchmarked. Without this knowledge, an arbitrary portion of the server response time has to be assigned to disk and CPU. To determine the sensitivity of network performance analysis to this portion, an analysis should be done that takes the portion of disk I/O from zero to 100%.

In general, statistics derived from contaminated data should be subjected to a sensitivity analysis to check how much the performance results depend on changes in this data. For example, if the average server response time is found to be 2.0 milliseconds, repeat the performance calculations at ± 50% of this. The results should lie approximately on a line.

A common misconception is that benchmarking must be done under the same conditions as final deployment. Validation testing should be done under these conditions. But if two dozen clients are to be deployed at a remote office connected via a 56 Kbps line to the central server, benchmarking must still be done with one client and the server on the same LAN. Measurements taken here can be used to calculate network performance for any network topology—especially using a simulator.

3.2 NUMBER OF LIGHT, MEDIUM, AND HEAVY USERS DURING TESTING

Benchmarking client-server applications is often done using real users behind the keyboard. It helps to characterize the light, medium, heavy, and heads-down user. By definition, the heads-down user generates the highest transaction rate. Heavy users generate transactions at 90% of the heads-down rate, medium users 50%, and light users 10%. Since network response time calculations depend on the so-called number of active users, it is essential to calibrate this in terms of real mixtures of light, medium, heavy, and heads-down users. For example, suppose heads-down users can generate ten transactions per minute. There are 40 light, 16 medium, and 10 heavy users. They are equivalent to 21 heads-down users and generate 210 transactions per minute, as shown in Table 3-1.

TABLE 3-1 PROJECTING A TRANSACTION RATE BASED ON A MIXTURE OF USER PROFILES

	Type of User		
	Light	Medium	Heavy
Number of users in this category	40	16	10
Percentage of traffic corresponding	10	50	90
Contribution from these users	4	8	9
Sum of contributions	21		
A heads-down user transaction rate	10		
Projected transaction rate of our users	**210**		

This method of analysis gives the most realistic values for the interarrival time between packets and transactions and on average data and packet rates used in downstream performance analysis.

3.3 UNDERSTANDING THE BUSINESS CYCLE IMPACT ON NETWORK TRAFFIC

The daily utilization cycle on a LAN or WAN link is like a signature and the network administrator should be familiar with this signature at each point of the network. Traffic signatures during the so-called prime shift exhibit the greatest traffic. Weekend signatures generally show low usage levels. A 24-by-7 business may exhibit three distinct peaks during a given 24-hour period (see Figure 3-1 to 3-3).

These graphs reveal interesting information. Where the utilization is low it may be said that "It doesn't get any better than this." When the utilization is at its greatest it may be said that "It can get as bad as this." The daily utilization data for one or more weeks may be overlaid on the same plot to show the variations from day to day.

The data in these examples is taken from SNMP performance data taken hourly with the HP OpenView Network Node Manager's historical data collector. Such data can be exported to an ASCII file, copied to a PC with the file transfer protocol (FTP) command, and imported into Lotus 1-2-3 or some such spreadsheet as structured text.

Hourly performance data may be evaluated weekly, monthly, or quarterly. The impact of multiple time zones will be visible as early peaks, and Europe and Asia traffic will also be evident. Special spikes should be noted. The evening backup, the 30-minute "mail trucks," and the morning "build" will be evident. The increasing number of builds as a software release looms will be visible on the Engineering LAN. Near the end of the business quarter, sales activities shift as more billings occur, more quotations are generated, and more management reports are generated, and the Marketing LAN will see its busiest times. Long-term utilization graphs provide an understanding of what and when the worst case really is on the network. This case should be analyzed to evaluate the network's performance.

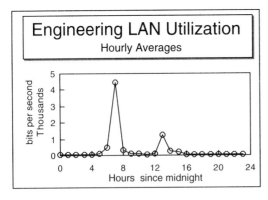
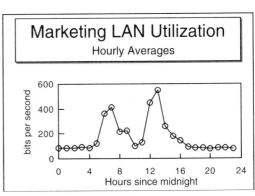

Figure 3-1 The business cycle on an Engineering and Marketing LAN shows distinct peaks in the morning and in the afternoon. Low utilization is seen early morning, lunch time, and late afternoon. The Engineering LAN's morning peak is very high. There is one prime shift for this business.

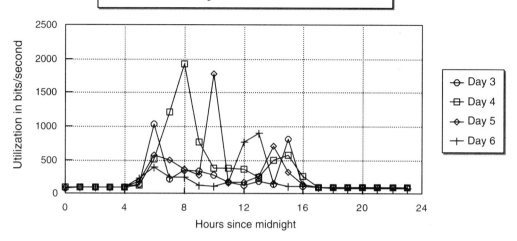

Figure 3-2 Plotting four days of raw utilization data on the same *x*-axis reveals that the daily business cycle for this company shows strong morning utilization peaks and weaker afternoon peaks. A strong dip in utilization still occurs at lunch time.

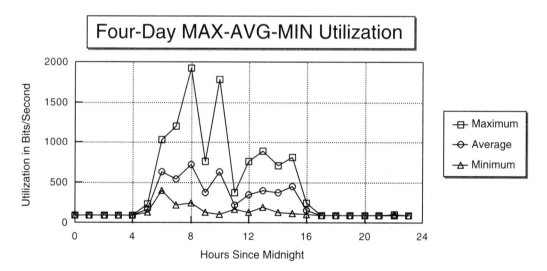

Figure 3-3 The same four days as above are presented again. Instead of the raw utilization data, each hourly maximum, average, and minimum value is plotted. Notice how widely different these three measures are. Clearly the network designer should predict network performance using the peak values. Note the dip in utilization around the lunch hour.

Sec. 3.3   Understanding the Business Cycle Impact on Network Traffic

Measuring the network utilization will reveal the usage cycles of existing applications under current business practices. To predict the performance of the network when a new application is to be deployed, or when a completely new set of business practices are to be implemented, conventional utilization measurements will not be available. Information about traffic patterns will have to be determined by conducting a needs/requirements analysis.

This process generally begins by developing a set of very open-ended questions designed to expose all facets of the business. Interviews at various levels of management are conducted using customized questionnaires appropriate to the interviewees. After collating the information and asking any follow-up questions for clarification, the document is reviewed by the interviewees for accuracy and acceptance. Finally the information is translated into data flow estimates. Volumes, peaks, averages, response times, arrival rates, and delays are derived. The impact on the network can then be evaluated using techniques such as mean value, queuing, and simulation (given later in the book).

3.4 MIXTURES OF DIFFERENT USER WORKLOADS

There are two other methods for determining what traffic a heads-down worst-case user might generate. Suppose that it is not possible to secure the cooperation of a typical user. We have access to the LAN and can measure anything we want. We have no information about the number of users active at the time or what protocols are in use.

The first method is to pick a (hopefully) representative client system (by its MAC address, for example) and capture all conversations it has with various servers during the day. Identifying the client's busiest period of the day provides the worst-case packet rates and utilization data needed to extrapolate worst-case network performance. The volume of data collected using this method is not prohibitive. The down side of this method is that the user may not be typical and the day-long trace will not really contain a good peak.

The second method entails capturing all LAN traffic over a fixed time span of say ten minutes. The time limit is determined by the storage capacity of the LAN analyzer, and 10–30 megabytes of packet headers can easily be captured during the ten minutes. The captured data is then studied to locate the busiest client-server pair (measured in packets, packets per second, bytes, or bytes per second). This conversation is taken as the worst case traffic. For a large user population (500–1,000), the odds are good that one of them will generate the necessary traffic spike during the ten-minute sample. There may in fact be several client-server conversations to choose from that qualify as worst-case.

The client-server statistics derived from either method are used to predict the network performance when all the clients are as active as the busiest one identified using one of the methods above. The target network utilization and user response time should be acceptable under the worst-case condition. Otherwise topology changes will be indicated, such as segmentation of users onto smaller subnets, moving servers to isolated segments, using an Ethernet switch, deploying an FDDI ring, or considering ATM or 100VG-AnyLAN.

4

The Performance Properties of Network Devices and Topologies

4.0 INTRODUCTION

The performance of data networks depends on the performance properties of the network electronics as well as on the topology chosen to interconnect it. In this chapter we the study hubs, switches, bridges, and routers and learn how to tune routers for performance. Next we learn how the location of the client and server impacts user response time. Since the generic server is a critical part of any network, we study how servers impact the network, study a generic server model, and look at the NFS server as a reality check

The type of medium used to interconnect systems also effects overall performance and so we examine the design curves for Ethernet, Token Ring, and FDDI and dispel a few myths about Ethernet versus Token Ring. Likewise we study the performance of wide area network technologies such as T-1, X.25, and frame relay.

Vendors of network electronic equipment achieve success by differentiating their products from the competition, and one way to do that is by demonstrating superior specifications. Some of these specs correspond to important features while others produce little real performance benefit. We look at specifications normally found in the literature from a performance perspective.

The last section provides a methodology for making complex decisions, with an example on choosing among a variety of routers.

4.1 HUB, BRIDGE, ROUTER, AND SWITCH PERFORMANCE CHARACTERISTICS

Hubs

Hubs connect together LAN devices at the physical layer (OSI layer 1). Moving data bits at media speeds demands low latency, and Ethernet hubs only have one small elastic buffer, about 32 bits long, to hold data bits for retiming purposes. All bits received on one port are retransmitted on all the other active ports. This bit-copying operation is done at the hardware level, so there is no software overhead such as SNMP or HP EASE firmware to slow the hub's operation.

Ethernet hubs may typically be cascaded with a maximum of four between LAN devices (see Figure 4-1). The reason? Transceivers in each port require five bit times to synchronize on the data bit stream. Two bits may be lost on each retransmission. The frame preamble starts out as 64 bits long at the data source and is truncated by up to 7 bits as it passes through each hub. The destination device requires at least 32 bits to properly synchronize on the frame preamble or the data frame may not be detected at all. These tiny performance and timing issues do not usually impact network performance but lost frames do cause performance problems.

Large LANs may be constructed by cascading hubs and the resulting high traffic levels often limit their growth. Each hub is responsible for propagating collisions to all of its segments. Every device transmission is propagated to every LAN segment. Every broadcast and multicast packet is also heard in all corners of the LAN.

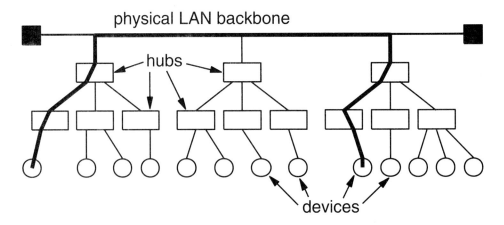

Figure 4-1 Hubs will support full Ethernet speeds provided that the topology obeys the technical specifications. Here a path between two devices passes through four hubs, the maximum legal limit. Increasing the depth of this balanced tree will result in packet losses and directly impact performance.

Bridges

Bridges connect LAN segments together at the link layer (OSI layer 2). Moving data frames incurs latency because they are completely copied into memory before being either forwarded or filtered and discarded. Bridges require considerable memory to store frames for forwarding onto another link. Frames received on all ports are examined to see if the destination MAC address corresponds to another port. If the destination is on the same segment as the frame was received on, the bridge updates its port table and discards the frame. If the destination is on another segment, the bridge queues the data on that port and retransmits it with a MAC header appropriate for that medium. Ignoring bridge overhead, the latency of the forwarding operation equals the time it takes to retransmit the frame on the target LAN segment. Large frames experience more latency. The maximum frame sizes are 1,518 bytes for Ethernet, 4,096 or 16,384 bytes for token ring, and 4,500 bytes for FDDI. These technologies clock at 10, 4 or 16, and 100 megabits per second respectively. Forwarding latency is calculated from these parameters using the formula

$$ForwardingLatency = \frac{FrameSize \cdot 8}{MediaSpeed}$$

Bridging has no provision for fragmentation and reassembly—dealing with frame size differences. A bridge that has to forward a 4,000-byte frame to an Ethernet will not be able to do so and will drop the frame instead. There is usually no problem between bridging Ethernet LANs with IEEE 802.3 LANs even though the frame formats are different. This form of transparent bridging is successful. Otherwise proprietary encapsulation bridging methods are required, which limit interoperability possibilities with other vendors' equipment.

Bridges have to obey the rules of the LAN. A frame to be forwarded to another segment has to wait its turn. If the segment is busy, the frame must wait according to the media access rules (see Figure 4-2). A very congested target LAN causes significant queuing delays in the bridge. If the media speed of the target segment is lower than the source segment, the queuing delay will be greater.

LAN segments that are already congested with traffic are often connected together with bridges because their filtering operation isolates traffic and allows only intersegment traffic to cross. Only complete error-free frames are processed. Collision fragments, frames with CRC or alignment errors, runts, giants, and jabbers are not forwarded. Bridges "clean up" physical layer problems that hubs must pass on. But because they operate at the link layer, bridges must pass all broadcast and multicast frames, since these are never learned. Port tables may be manually configured to filter or forward specific MAC addresses for security purposes. Typical bridge "switching" latency is 100 microseconds once the entire frame has been input.

Large LANs may be constructed by cascading bridges and the resulting broadcast/multicast levels often limit their growth. Bridges may not be placed more than seven in a row. Every bridge regenerates a complete frame, so preamble truncation is not an issue. Bridges running the IEEE 802.1(d) spanning tree protocol may be placed in mesh configurations to improve LAN reliability. The protocol constructs a tree from the mesh to avoid circulating loops. The redundant bridges do not carry traffic, other than the spanning tree protocol. Performance analysis of such LANs is more of a challenge because the exact structure of the spanning tree may not be readily apparent.

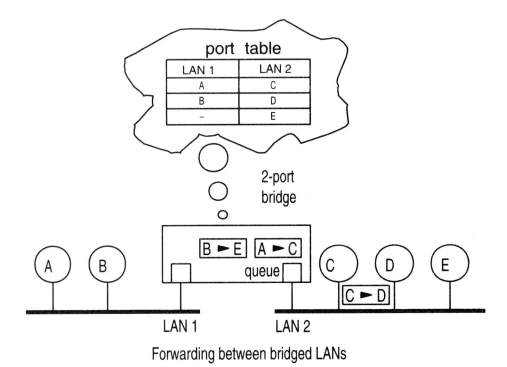

Figure 4-2 The bridge has learned that nodes A and B are on LAN1 and that nodes C, D, and E are on LAN2. Two frames are shown queued for transmission on LAN2, one destined for node C and one destined for node E. The packet B>E will incur additional latency because of the queuing delay. Both queued packets will wait until the present transmission C>D on LAN2 has ended.

Routers

Routers connect together LAN devices at the network layer (OSI layer 3). Moving packets incurs latency because they must be copied into memory before being forwarded. Routers are typically equipped with several megabytes of memory to buffer packets because routers often have many ports and a variety of port speeds to contend with. When a router receives a frame on an interface, the header is examined (such as the Ethernet Type field or the IEEE 802.2 DSAP) to determine the network protocol for the packet. The router compares the packet's destination network with its routing table and queues the packet onto the appropriate output port. The routing decision may take longer if there are packet filters configured, if multiple output queues have to be managed, if other packets on other ports are being processed, if routing table information is being processed (via RIP, OSPF, or IGRP updates), if SNMP requests are being handled (although these may be assigned lower priority), or if compression has to be done (on slower serial lines).

From a performance standpoint, each packet will encounter port latency on reception, some CPU latency due to processing in the router CPU, queuing delays, and output port latency on transmission. Note that for certain network protocols such as IP, some router vendors are able to "fast switch" the packet, incurring very little CPU time. This will not work if packet filtering is enabled, since this requires the router to decode the packet IP and TCP headers to find the source/destination IP addresses and the source/destination TCP port numbers. Some vendor equipment can route packets faster between ports attached to the same LAN adapter than between ports on different LAN adapters. Typical router latency is 200 microseconds. Router vendors characterize the performance of their hardware in terms of packet forwarding rate given at various packet sizes summed over all ports.

Routers perform fragmentation and reassembly when dealing with packets too large to fit on the target medium (see Figure 4-3). LANs with arbitrary properties may be connected together with routers because the entire MAC header is stripped from the frame, leaving just the packet. Modern routers are able to route multiple network protocols such as IP, DECNET, AppleTalk, OSI, Banyan IP, and IPX. Many can encapsulate nonroutable protocols such as LAT, NetBIOS, and SNA inside IP datagrams using a method called IP tunneling.

Routers have to conform to the LAN access methods and wait their turn before transmitting a packet. Any congestion is handled by queuing the packet for transmission

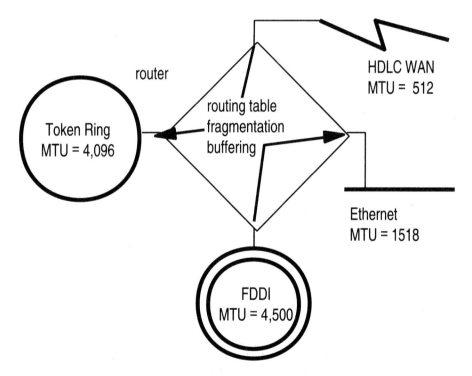

Figure 4-3 Routers can connect dissimilar LAN/WAN technologies together and compensate for frame size differences (MTU) using fragmentation and reassembly. Speed differences are overcome using multimegabyte buffers, which may be partitioned into priority queues on each port. Priority queues are helpful when routing or tunneling time-sensitive protocols like AppleTalk and SNA. Broadcasts are stopped by routers unless bridging is turned on to accommodate nonroutable protocols like NetBIOS and LAT.

and waiting for an opening. The lower the line speed, the longer the delay in forwarding the packet.

LAN segments that are congested with traffic can be connected by routers without fear of broadcasts being passed through it. Collisions, CRC errors, and other physical layer problems are similarly filtered out. Routers are the ultimate LAN interconnect device. Because routing is network protocol dependent, routers may have to be operated in bridged mode as well, to pass nonroutable protocols. Since bridges work in promiscuous mode, the CPU has to process all frames on all bridged LAN segments. CPU utilization increases accordingly.

Ethernet Switches

Ethernet switches connect LANs together at the physical layer (OSI layer 1) and combine the best features of hubs, bridges, and routers. They have the speed of a hub and operate at media speed. They filter like a bridge but have far less latency. They have the multiport concurrent forwarding performance of a router but don't route. A frame received on one port is compared to a port table and sent to the target port only—all within 40 microseconds or so. This means the frame is still being received on one port even as it is being retransmitted out the other port. The forwarding is done in hardware, leaving the CPU free for network management purposes such as SNMP. The term *cut-through* describes this feature. Ethernet switches provide some "cleansing" of physical layer "garbage" but collision fragments still pass between source and destination ports, and broadcast/multicast traffic is propagated to all ports.

Ethernet switches may be cascaded and each vendor specifies the rules. In general, switches may be cascaded from a root switch to one more level. Some vendors provide a standard Ethernet AUI connector, some provide a full-duplex Ethernet connection, while others provide an FDDI connection supporting "translation," a proprietary encapsulation scheme to cascade the switches. Port counts typically vary from 4 to 16 (see Figure 4-4).

ATM Switches

ATM switches are used to create high-speed LANs. ATM Network Interface Cards (NICs) generate 53-byte cells that are forwarded by the switching fabric to the target system at high speeds. Considering that many applications generate datagrams much larger than the 53-byte MTU (48 bytes of payload and 5 bytes of MAC framing), the ATM Adaptation Layer (AAL5) will fragment the packets using a method called LAN Emulation.

ATM enjoys a wide range of line speeds and physical layer interface specifications. Table 4-1 lists the speeds and interfaces available.

Stations connected to an ATM switch do not interfere with each other provided there is no blocking or queuing in the inputs and outputs of the switching fabric. Unlike Ethernet, IEEE 802.5 token ring, and FDDI, each station can generally obtain bandwidth on demand. There is no CSMA/CD or token-passing access method to delay a transmission.

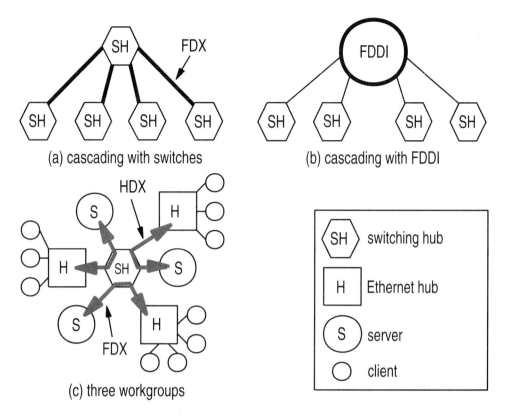

Figure 4-4 (a) Ethernet switches (switching hubs) are cascaded to accommodate more systems. (b) Some vendors provide a proprietary high-speed backbone for connecting switches. (c) Three independent work groups can share a single six-port Ethernet switch. Servers are connected to the switching hub using the full-duplex (FDX) Ethernet configuration while the Ethernet hubs use standard Ethernet. The three concurrent packet transfers shown result in a peak aggregate data rate of 30 megabits per second.

TABLE 4-1 ATM PHYSICAL LAYER SPEEDS

Megabits per second	Interface description
25	full-duplex level-3 UTP (an IBM/Chipcom special)
45	full-duplex DS3 ports used for WAN ATM
51	full-duplex OC-1 or Cat-3 UTP
100	full-duplex multimode fiber (TAXI interface for FDDI)
155	full-duplex SONET OC-3c MM fiber, Fibre Channel, or Cat-5 UTP
622	full-duplex SONET OC-12c on SM/MM fiber
1,244	full-duplex SONET OC-24 on SM fiber
2,488	full-duplex SONET OC-48 on SM fiber

Note: OC-1 runs at 51.840 Mbps. Other defined OC speeds are OC-3, OC-9, OC-12, OC-24, OC-36, and OC-48. All are multiples of the OC-1 speed.

4.2 TUNABLE PARAMETERS ON ROUTERS: PRIORITY QUEUES AND COMPRESSION

Priority Queues

Mixed protocol traffic such as IP, AppleTalk, and DECNET can be routed without difficulty so long as utilization levels are low. When a serial WAN circuit is operating at any significant utilization level, the protocols sensitive to timing delays will cause session disconnects. This is especially true of AppleTalk since it was designed for LANs. TCP/IP conforming to Van Jacobson TCP adjusts itself very nicely to changes in available network bandwidth.

By default, routers store and forward packets in the order they are received and each packet experience similar delays regardless of network protocol. To provide for time-sensitive protocols, many router vendors include output priority queuing based on network protocol, packet size and service (see Figure 4-5). SNA and AppleTalk are examples of time-sensitive protocols. The queues may be designated as low, medium, normal, and high priority, or they may be numbered from (say) 1 to 31. A variation of this theme is to assign a guaranteed percentage of bandwidth to each protocol. Dealing with output priority queues places an additional CPU load on the router and further suggests that the method is appropriate and necessary only for low-speed circuits and not for Ethernet, Token Ring, and FDDI.

Suppose that a network routes AppleTalk, DECNET, and IP. On a serial circuit, a router may be configured to give AppleTalk high priority, DECNET medium priority, and IP low priority, based on the protocol's sensitivity to timing variation. This allows AppleTalk to dominate the link and starve out the other protocols. Another approach is to

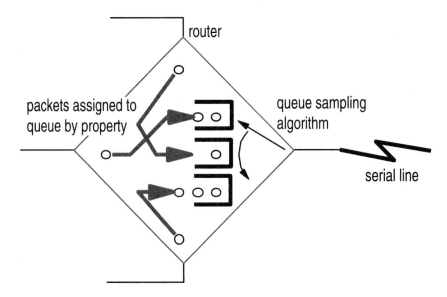

Figure 4-5 Routers may assign packets to priority queues based on properties such as protocol, service, and size. The queues may be drained into the serial line by sampling each one based on a percent bandwidth or queue priority.

assign, say, 50% of the bandwidth to AppleTalk, 25% to DECNET, and 25% to IP. The router attempts to guarantee each protocol this percentage. Now, if, say, IP needs more than 25% and the other protocols don't need their allotment, then IP can get more bandwidth. One way to implement this is to have the router sample the AppleTalk queue two times for each sample taken from the IP and DECNET queues. A more accurate implementation is to have the router compute the actual bandwidth used by each protocol over some time interval and to adjust the sampling rate of each queue to fine-tune the bandwidth percentages actually allocated. Routers may enforce a maximum queue size and discard packets that arrive when the queue is full.

How does the network administrator decide what packet attribute to prioritize on? Interactive application traffic generally consists of small request packets, small ACK packets, and various-sized reply packets. The packet rate is fairly low and contributes only a small fraction of the total bandwidth used. Response time is important so these packets are assigned to a high priority queue. For interactive traffic over IP, telnet (using TCP port 23), rlogin (using TCP port 1023), and X-windows (using TCP port 6000) are the most common.

At the opposite end of the scale are the bulk data transfers such as file transfer protocols and Email. These can consume much of the network bandwidth and generate large packets but are not time critical and can be assigned to a low-priority queue. Bulk transfers over IP include FTP (using TCP ports 20 and 21) and SMTP (using TCP port 25).

In between are client-server applications that generate mostly small-to-medium packets, not as many as the interactive applications do, and which can be assigned to a medium-priority queue.

Many network managers will find that the above tuning guidelines require that they experiment on their live networks to find the best settings. Balking at this approach suggests a better planning approach, such as simulation, to determine the best settings beforehand. See Chapter 10 for guidance here.

Priority queuing is not perfect. Even though an AppleTalk packet is sent to the high-priority queue, the serial line may already be transmitting a large IP or DECNET packet and the AppleTalk packet will have to wait. Routing and link maintenance protocols are usually given higher priority than data is. Queues that give priority to small AppleTalk packets also carry TCP ACK packets, which contain only 40 bytes of data.

Compression

Compression can be used to improve the performance of serial lines. The slower the line speed the greater the benefit. Since compression and decompression are router-CPU intensive, the network administrator would be prudent to monitor how much overhead compression incurs, especially if there are more than a few 56 Kbps lines coming into the router, or if a high-speed circuit is involved. Multi-CPU router architectures may specify an aggregate effective bit rate for all ports on a WAN card. This means that additional WAN cards can also take advantage of compression because the central CPU is not used for this purpose. Router CPU utilization is generally measurable as an SNMP vendor-specific MIB value that can be monitored using a network management station. For example, Cisco routers provide the *BusyPer* MIB variable for CPU busy percentage.

Compression algorithms take time to execute, so there is additional latency before forwarding a packet. The reduced time to transmit a compressed packet more than compensates for this. This assumes the packet can in fact be compressed. If the compression algorithm determines that the packet cannot be compressed, the time taken to come to this conclusion is wasted.

Text data sent in large packets can generally be highly compressed. Smaller packets will not benefit from compression as much because there is less opportunity to squeeze out redundancies in small amounts of data. Routers will assign a default maximum transmission unit (MTU) to a serial interface. Typically, this is 1,500 bytes. Smaller values will render the compression algorithm less effective. Binary files such as DOS executables may or may not compress and some file types, notably GIF files, certain kinds of TIFF files, and compressed archive files such as the PC **.ZIP,** UNIX **.gz** and Macintosh **.sit** are already compressed and will not compress further.

What compression levels are reasonable? Using the MKS compress utility to characterize compression efficiency, we find that compressing a 95,799-byte PostScript file reduced it to 45,365 bytes, a 52.64% reduction. Compressing a 5,100-byte ASCII file containing 1,000 instances of the word "john" reduced it to 370 bytes, a 92.74% compression! Compressing the 54,619-byte file COMMAND.COM reduced it to 43,110 bytes, a 21.07% drop. Compressing a 325,267-byte GIF file increased it to 439,026 bytes, a 34.97% increase. MKS's compress utility has the advantage of being able to take out the redundancies of the entire file in one pass. Routers are stuck with the MTU of the serial line—typically 1,500 bytes of data.

4.3 CLIENT LOCATION IMPACT ON PERFORMANCE

Client systems located on the same LAN as their server will get the best performance. This architecture is hard to analyze when there are many servers on a distributed network with clients located at many different sites. Client-server applications tend to be the least sensitive to network delays because they already incur processing delays at both the client and the server side, and this masks the network delays to some extent.

Some Tuning Tips

One important rule is to avoid loading applications from a network drive located on a server that is many hops away—especially if a WAN is involved. Swapping to a file on a network drive on a remote server isn't a recipe for high performance either. Including network drives in the PATH environment variable may cause each network drive to be checked before the operating system locates the command. A "temp" directory on a network drive may reduce performance as well. Clients using Serial Line Internet Protocol (SLIP) or Point to Point Protocol (PPP) over dial-up lines should follow these rules explicitly.

Computing Delay

Clients separated from their servers by one or more congested serial lines will certainly see reduced performance, but the amount of reduction depends on how many packets it takes to compete a transaction. A transaction that normally takes three seconds to complete may require ten packet exchanges with the server. The network time is only 52 milliseconds (see Figure 4-6).

Compute the turn-around delay on a WAN link

NumberOfPackets := 10

LineSpeed := 1,544,000

PacketSize := 500

$$\text{RoundTripDelay} := \frac{2 \cdot \text{NumberOfPackets} \cdot 8 \cdot \text{PacketSize}}{\text{LineSpeed}}$$

RoundTripDelay := 0.0518

RoundTripDelay := 0.520

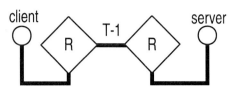

Figure 4-6 A calculation to find the network delay due to ten 500-byte packet exchanges on a T-1 serial circuit. Protocol headers and trailers are included in the 500 bytes. The delay is fixed as long as the packet size is constant and there is no other traffic to share the line with.

If the serial line is 90% utilized, simple queuing theory calculations show that the average network wait time is ten times worse, or 520 milliseconds. Even this only extends our average transaction response time from 3.0 to 3.5 seconds, which is not that bad. But statistically, this 520 milliseconds is exponentially distributed. This means the probability of actually having to wait up to 520 milliseconds is 0.63 and the probability of having to wait longer than 520 milliseconds is .37 (see Figure 4-7).

Instead of allowing a client and server to be separated by a congested or low-speed serial circuit, bring the data closer to the client. Either move the data onto a local server or move the remote server to the client-side LAN. This solution may not be very appealing to

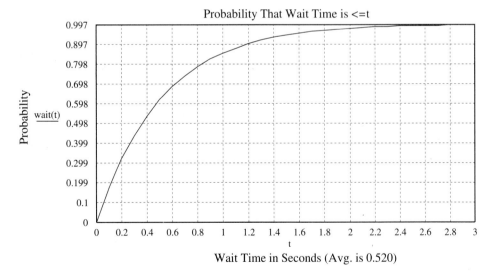

Figure 4-7 The graph for the cumulative probability function of the network queue delay time. It shows, for example, that the chance the wait time is less than or equal to 1.2 seconds is 0.9 or 90%. This means there is a 10% chance the wait time will exceed 1.2 seconds. Stated another way, one out of every ten transactions will be delayed at least 1.2 seconds.

users located at other locations because it may increase the network delays they see. A better approach to relocating the data or the server is to conduct a networkwide traffic matrix study to determine location, number, and traffic load for all client systems. Just looking at the matrix may suggest an obvious solution. Conducting a few simulations, moving the data/server around, will provide good performance figures from which to choose the best server location.

A client located on a busy LAN segment may appear to perform poorly. Moving it to quieter LAN segment should improve client performance.

4.4 HOW SERVER PERFORMANCE CAN IMPACT THE NETWORK

A server's maximum performance is governed by the most narrow of all bottlenecks built into it (see Figure 4-8). Server performance may be increased by adding RAM, which allows more of a file to be loaded into the server's memory, and by configuring read-ahead to take advantage of it. By locating the File Allocation Table (FAT) in memory, directory search time will be reduced. Configuring disk striping allows the server to do disk I/O to multiple disk spindles concurrently and may improve throughput considerably. Using the fast-and-wide SCSI interface bus may improve the performance of disk I/O transfers. The most effective way to improve the server's performance is to identify which bottleneck is responsible for limiting performance and widening that one bottleneck.

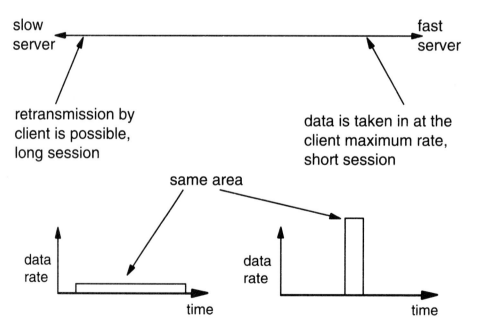

Figure 4-8 The peak level of the network traffic is always limited by some performance bottleneck. A fast server shifts that bottleneck to the client. Here we see we see how the server speed effects the client-server data rate. Faster servers result in higher traffic spikes of shorter duration. Slow servers result in lower traffic levels that last longer.

Total client response time equals

> time to transmit the client request (network limited)
> +time to service the request (server limited)
> + time to transmit the response to the client (network limited).

The network and server components are shown graphically in Figure 4-9.

A fast server can attract higher sustained traffic, and users are naturally attracted to high-performance servers. This results in more bursty traffic and greater variation in network response time.

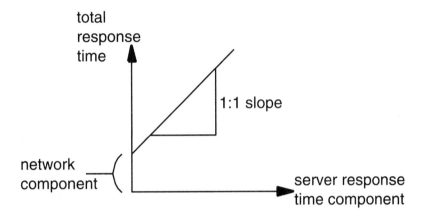

Figure 4-9 The client-server total response time depends on both the network latency and the server response time. Reducing the server response time to zero bottleneck will only reduce the total response time to that of the network component.

4.5 A GENERIC MODEL FOR A FILE SERVER

The network manager needs to understand the performance aspects of file servers since it is a major resource on the network. A fundamental model for a file server is shown in Figure 4-10.

CPU cycles are needed whenever a packet moves around inside a file server. When there are no queuing delays (because the request rate is low or requests can be satisfied from the buffer cache), server CPU time is still needed—usually a fixed quantity plus a transfer time proportional to the packet size. Without a queue delay, random disk I/O is still needed to get the data into RAM.

The model shows that increasing the disk I/O subsystem's performance will reduce the queuing delay. A faster disk drive will increase performance. So will adding a parallel disk and "sprinkling" the files between them. Configuring "immediate ACK" in the disk driver allows the disk controller to buffer the data and return an immediate completion indication, which in turn allows an immediate write completion indication to be returned to the client. The NOS may also provide an option to buffer the data and return an immediate completion to the client. In both cases, the client receives the write completion indication early and can request another operation sooner.

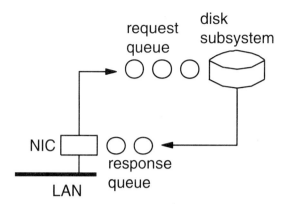

Figure 4-10 A simple file server model consists of a NIC to accept client requests and transmit server responses, RAM to buffer these packets, and a disk to provide file I/O services. The request queue is generally longer than the response queue.

Some protocols allow multiple outstanding writes to be posted before waiting for a completion indication. The Network File System (NFS) client may be configured to write 8-Kbyte blocks to the server. The IP layer will fragment this datagram into several LAN frames, all of which are sent in a rapid burst to the server, which reassembles them before writing the datagram to disk. Novell Netware's "burst mode" provides a similar ability. The basic theory is to send as much data during the network round-trip time as possible.

The file server request buffer may overflow and cause a loss of request packets. The client will detect this with a time-out and retransmit the request. It is tempting to increase the file server request buffer to reduce overflows, but this will simply increase the queuing delays under busy conditions even further to the point where the client will time out and retransmit the request. Two identical requests will be queued up. It is better to keep the queue shorter so that the second request is discarded. Indeed, it may be better to shorten the queue to reduce queuing delays. See Chapter 9 for details on this.

4.6 REALITY CHECK—NFS SERVER PERFORMANCE AND TUNING PARAMETERS

Because NFS figures so prominently in the high-end UNIX file server arena, it is appropriate to review its performance properties here.

Basic Network File System (NFS) Operation

The NFS client performs an operation on a remote file or directory by issuing a remote procedure call (RPC) using the User Datagram Protocol (UDP). If no response arrives from the server within a time-out period, the client retransmits the request. Because NFS uses Internet Protocol (IP) as its networking protocol, the request may be fragmented to accommodate the maximum transmit unit (MTU) of the LAN medium. NFS will work over a wide area network with some tuning to accommodate the slower speed of the links. Both client and server have various tunable parameters that impact the performance obtained (see Table 4-2). The server parameters are normally established at boot time and the client parameters are normally set at mount time.

TABLE 4-2 TUNABLE PARAMETERS AVAILABLE UNDER NFS

Parameter	Location	Description
read/write block size	client	request size of the disk I/O buffer
-async	server	server returns immediate completion on writes
number of nfsd processes	server	number of concurrent nfsd programs spawned at bootup
socket size	server	size of the UDP buffer area that queues NFS requests
time-out value	client	number of seconds the client will wait for a response
number of time-outs	client	number of times a client will retry before giving up
file system block size	server	size of one physical I/O disk block, an indivisible value

When NFS is used over a WAN, an occasional IP datagram may be discarded due to congestion. This will prevent the complete UDP datagram from being reassembled. The client will retransmit the entire UDP datagram after the time-out period and hopefully none of the fragments will be lost this time. On congested networks, this behavior can prevent clients and servers from communicating all but the smallest files. The solution is to reduce the read/write block size at the client to about 1,024 bytes to avoid the fragmentation/reassembly problem. This solution increases the response time a bit, since only 1,024 bytes of data is exchanged per network round-trip time.

Another performance anomaly is seen when the server file system has a natural block size that differs from the read/write block size specified by the client. These parameters should be set equal to maximize performance. Otherwise the server has to perform multiple physical disk I/O operations per logical NFS I/O—assuming the server handles this properly.

NFS Performance Metrics

Modern RISC-based UNIX NFS servers are capable of performing thousands of NFS I/O Operations (NFS IOPS), a term has become a de facto standard for rating NFS servers. The server data rate typically exceeds the capabilities of Ethernet, even of IEEE 802.5 token rings clocking at 16 Mbps. The solution is to install additional LAN cards in the NFS server, or use a faster LAN medium to obtain additional LAN bandwidth. Placing servers on Ethernet switches, and using full-duplex Ethernet adapters also provides performance gains.

The performance of an NFS server is given by the formula

$$IOPRate = \frac{MediaSpeed \cdot MediaUtilization}{IOPSize \cdot 8}$$

where:

IOPRate	is the rate of NFS I/O Operations per second
MediaSpeed	is the media speed in bits per second
MediaUtilization	is the target fractional utilization of the LAN medium
IOPSize	is the number of bytes in each I/O operation

An IOPSize of 4,096 is used in Table 4-3. It's a common default and represents half a typical disk track of 8,192 bytes. Thus the number of disk I/Os per second is about half the number of NFS IOPS. The disk drive average throughput should be matched to the LAN medium throughput to avoid bottlenecking the NFS server. To this end, Table 4-3 gives the available IOPRate for common LAN media.

TABLE 4-3 MAXIMUM NFS IOPS AVAILABLE WITH SOME STANDARD LAN TECHNOLOGIES

Medium	MediaSpeed in bits/second	% Media utilization	IOPSize in bytes	IOPRate IOP/Sec
4 Mbps Token Ring	4,000,000	70	4,096	85
10 Mbps Ethernet	10,000,000	40	4,096	122
16 Mbps Token Ring	16,000,000	70	4,096	342
100 Mbps FDDI	100,000,000	70	4,096	2,136
155 Mbps ATM	155,520,000	70	4,096	3,322
622 Mbps ATM	622,080,000	70	4,096	13,289

Server and client NFS performance is measured using the UNIX `nfsstat` command. The `netstat` command is used to detect UDP socket overflows. To determine the operational performance of an NFS server, the `nfsstat` command is executed periodically from a UNIX `cron` script and the output is collected for later processing using an `awk` script. Figure 4-11 shows output from `nfsstat`.

```
Server rpc:
calls           badcalls        nullrecv   badlen     xdrcall         nfsdrun
546323          0               0          0          0               2057933

Server nfs:
calls           badcalls
546323          0
null            getattr         setattr    root       lookup          readlink        read

292 0%          301595 55%      1968 0%    0 0%       149975 27%      945 0%          47766 8%

wrcache         write           create     remove     rename          link            symlink

0 0%            33931 6%        1514 0%    853 0%     30 0%           5 0%            4 0%

mkdir           rmdir           readdir    fsstat
9 0%            8 0%            6628 1%    800 0%

Client rpc:
calls           badcalls        retrans    badxid     timeout         wait            newcred
79735           2               9          0          11              0               0

Client nfs:
calls           badcalls        nclget     nclsleep
79689           0               79721      0
null            getattr         setattr    root       lookup          readlink        read

0 0%            5808 7%         106 0%     0 0%       12926 16%       26808 33%       10692 13%

wrcache         write           create     remove     rename          link            symlink

0 0%            21262 26%       106 0%     58 0%      32 0%           9 0%            0 0%

mkdir           rmdir           readdir    fsstat
1 0%            0 0%            1813 2%    68 0%
```

Figure 4-11 Output from the UNIX `nfsstat` command.

Tuning nfsd

One important tunable parameter on the NFS server is the number of nfsd processes, the daemons that perform the actual disk I/O (see Figure 4-12). A rule of thumb recommends setting this to twice the number of disk spindles available to NFS clients. The idea is to provide enough copies of nfsd to satisfy one I/O on each disk and have a second one standing by for the next request. The default is four.

If there are not enough copies of nfsd to keep up with client demands, then the file systems will remain underutilized because not enough disk I/O requests can be posted. As long as the file system utilization is kept high, the server will provide excellent throughput. A generous number of nfsd processes will ensure this. But if an excessive number of nfsd processes are configured, then the server CPU utilization may become excessive. This is because each time an NFS request enters the server, all copies of nfsd waiting for data on the socket are sent to the UNIX run queue. The first nfsd gets the request and processes it. All remaining copies of nfsd, in succession, will complete their socket read operation with a no-data indication and simply reissue the get request. Considerable CPU cycles are wasted if too many copies of nfsd are configured.

Under heavy server load, all copies of nfsd are waiting for disk I/O and new client requests accumulate in the UDP socket buffer. This buffer can overflow, dropping requests that will be retransmitted after the client times out (see Figure 4-13). Increasing the socket

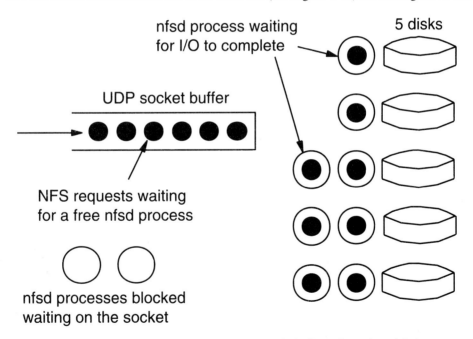

Figure 4-12 Each NFS client request entering the socket buffer can be used to satisfy the socket-get request by a copy of nfsd. The nfsd program that gets the NFS request examines it, posts an I/O request on the appropriate file system, and waits for its completion. Then it posts another socket request. Here we see two of the file systems with one I/O request and three file systems with two I/O requests pending. Two copies of nfsd are shown blocked on the socket—a condition that will be remedied at once since there are now six NFS requests in the socket buffer.

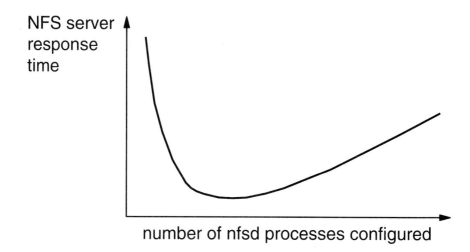

Figure 4-13 NFS server response time is minimized when there are approximately two copies of nfsd for each file system exported. When in doubt, it is better to have too many copies of nfsd than too few, based on the slope of the curve. If all copies of nfsd are waiting for too long on the disks, incoming NFS requests will accumulate in the UDP socket buffer, possibly overflowing it and causing new requests to be discarded.

buffer size will avoid loss of NFS requests. If the queue gets too long, the average queue wait time may exceed the client time-out interval and the client will issue another request. There will be two identical requests in the queue and the server will process both of them. See Chapter 9 on queuing theory for methods to help set the buffer sizes properly under these conditions.

Other NFS Tuning Options

NFS servers may be further tuned using vendor-specific features. HP-UX provide a server option, -async, which can be configured on a per-file system basis to allow asynchronous NFS write operations. The NFS client receives a response after the disk write is queued and before the physical write is performed. This frees the client from waiting for the server to complete the write and allows it to issue the next write operation that much sooner—increasing performance significantly (see Table 4-4).

TABLE 4-4 NFS SERVER WRITE PERFORMANCE INCREASE USING THE HP-UX -async OPTION IN /etc/exports

File size in bytes	Time (seconds) to write the file to the server		Performance factor increase
	Standard NFS write	Using -async option	
1,250,000	8.37	1.61	5.2
2,500,000	11.07	2.43	4.56
12,500,000	65.27	12.62	5.17
25,000,000	130.2	23.53	5.53

Modern SCSI disk controllers contain buffers to enhance performance and the UNIX drivers can be configured to take advantage of this. Kernel tunable parameters usually exist to enable this feature.

4.7 LOCATING SERVERS FOR BEST PERFORMANCE

Section 4.3 provides information about locating clients for optimum performance that applies equally well to locating servers (and network printers and any other resource on a LAN shared by many users). Let's look at several alternative server locations and discuss the performance implications of each one (see Figures 4-14 and 4-15).

To support enterprise-wide access to servers, the limited bandwidth of wide area links has to be considered. For existing servers and clients, traffic matrix measurements can be made with tools like HP's OpenView Traffic Expert. On simple WANs, the router IP traffic matrix may be used. A user interview process may be necessary if no measurements are available for the traffic matrix.

The server may be situated optimally using several methods. The simplest method is to locate it on the subnet whose clients generate the greatest volume of server traffic. This provides superb performance for one client location and may provide terrible performance for many other client sites.

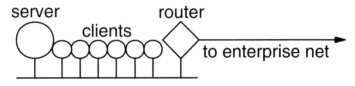

Clients and server are on one LAN

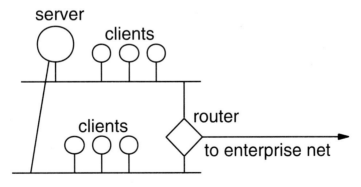

dual-homed server reduces LAN traffic

Figure 4-14 Servers should be located on the same LAN as the clients whenever possible. If too much LAN traffic results, adding a second NIC to the server (multihoming) allows clients to be distributed on two LANs, with the router still providing IP routing to allow all clients access to the corporate network.

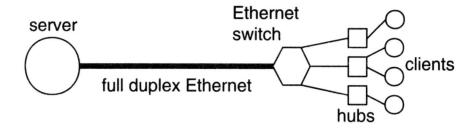
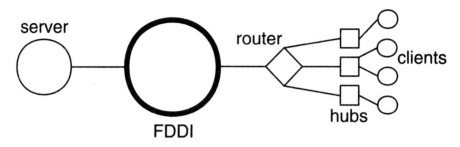

Figure 4-15 LAN solutions for dealing with high traffic are Ethernet switches (see Section 4.3) and FDDI rings for the server. The Ethernet switch solution has the advantage of requiring no subnetting but does not offer the performance of FDDI and requires a proprietary full-duplex Ethernet NIC for best performance. ATM and 100VG-AnyLAN can be used instead of FDDI to get a similar performance boost.

The next best method is to position the server to minimize the maximum number of hops. A refinement on the hop count method is to consider the line speed of each hop in the cost (see Figure 4-16).

The cost of each hop is usually measured in milliseconds, the propagation delay experienced by a packet of typical size on a Ethernet. For the NFS protocol, 1,500-byte packets is an excellent choice. An example topology is shown in Figure 4-17.

The best way to position a server on a network is to determine the worst-case data flows generated by the clients and perform a simulation that plays back that traffic flow. Move the server location in successive simulations to create a set of client response times. The maximum response time from each simulation is noted, and the simulation with the smallest maximum response time has the best server location.

$$\text{PacketSize} := 1{,}500 \quad \text{bytes}$$

$$\text{LineSpeed} := 256{,}000 \quad \text{bits/second}$$

$$\text{Delay} := \frac{\text{PacketSize} \cdot 8}{\text{LineSpeed}} \cdot 1{,}000 \quad \text{milliseconds}$$

$$\text{Delay} = 46.875 \quad \text{milliseconds}$$

Figure 4-16 Calculation for finding the packet forwarding delay over a WAN hop.

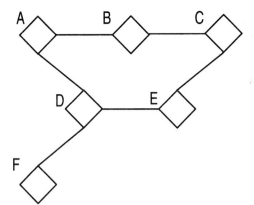

Figure 4-17 The optimum location for a server is computed by first counting the number of serial line hops between each location and all the others. The result is a table like Table 4-5. It is generally symmetric unless asymmetric routing is used on the WAN. The numbers below the diagonal need not be recomputed due to the symmetry of the array. The maximum hop count for each server location is written down in the rightmost column. In this case the server locations that minimize the maximum hop count are A, D, and E with a hop count of two so these should be chosen.

TABLE 4-5 NUMBER OF SERIAL LINES TO TRAVERSE BETWEEN CLIENT AND SERVER

Server location	Number of serial lines						
	A	B	C	D	E	F	MAX
A	0	1	2	1	2	2	**2**
B	1	0	1	2	2	3	3
C	2	1	0	2	1	3	3
D	1	2	2	0	1	1	**2**
E	2	2	1	1	0	2	**2**
F	2	3	3	1	2	0	3

4.8 ETHERNET, TOKEN RING, AND FDDI SIMULATION DESIGN CURVES

The PlanNet simulator can be used to characterize the behavior of Ethernet, Token Ring, and FDDI under load. To this end, a simulation was performed for each LAN technology. The basic model is shown in Figure 4-18.

Simulation Setup

A very fast server responds to client packets and we vary the client count between 1 and 200. Each client attempts to generate 1% LAN utilization by sending exponentially distributed packets to the server at exponentially distributed think times and waiting for a response packet. The client simulation traffic generator is calibrated to generate 1% utilization on an otherwise quiet LAN.

The simulator concurrently executes an identical script for each traffic generator. Parameters for the script have to be calculated. We want each traffic generator to produce 1% utilization and this can be obtained by many combinations of think time and packet size. For Ethernet, the method shown in Figure 4-19 accurately calculates the average think time. The distribution of packet sizes is shown in Figure 4-20.

Simulation Model for a Data Source and Sink

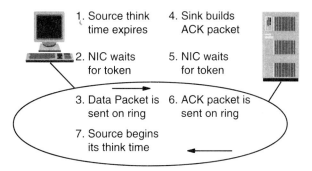

Figure 4-18 The simulation for each LAN topology (a ring is shown here) is based on a packet exchange between client and server as shown in steps 1 to 7. High utilization on the medium results in longer response time, which effectively reduces the client data rate. If the data or response packet is lost, the client will time out and start over. If the response returns too late to the client, the client also times out and starts over.

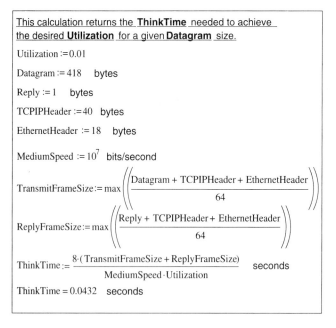

Figure 4-19 Calibration of the PlanNet simulator traffic generator requires an average think time. This calculation details the Ethernet version of the arithmetic. Note we've considered Ethernet's minimum frame size of 64 bytes. The average datagram size has to be adjusted if we truncate the exponential distribution to limit packet sizes between two limits such as 20 and 1,480.

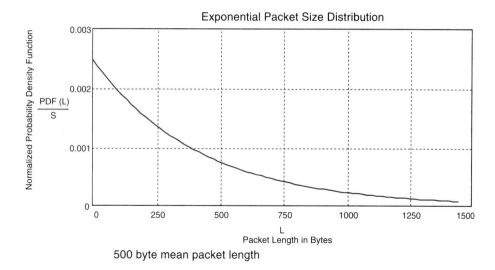

Figure 4-20 For the simulation, the packet size is constrained to be less than 1,500 bytes (for Ethernet) and at least 1 byte. While the simulator will properly fragment any packet larger than the LAN medium's MTU, it disturbs the accuracy of the traffic generator. Note the excellent range of packet sizes generated by the exponential distribution—a good random mix.

Simulation Design Curves

For the simulation design curves that follow (Figures 4-21 to 4-23), the parameters in Table 4-6 were used for the traffic generators. PlanNet was used to produce the data and the results are presented as Lotus 1-2-3 graphs. Note that each traffic generator is calibrated to produce 1% utilization on the target LAN medium when that medium is otherwise unutilized. The purpose of simulating up to 200 users is to explore the complete range of performance properties of the LAN medium.

TABLE 4-6 SIMULATOR SCRIPT PARAMETERS FOR EACH LAN TOPOLOGY

	LAN		Packet size parameters			Think time (msec)
Type	Max frame	Bit rate	Minimum	Mean	Maximum	
Ethernet	1,518	10,000,000	20	500	1,480	43.2
IEEE 802.5	17,900	16,000,000	20	500	1,480	27
FDDI	4,500	100,000,000	20	500	1,480	4.32

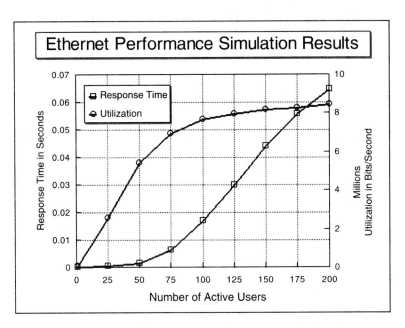

Figure 4-21 Simulation design curve for Ethernet showing client response time and medium utilization. Note the dual axes. Response time increases linearly as we enter the saturation region of utilization, and there is no collapse of any kind—no meltdown as predicted by certain mythology about Ethernet.

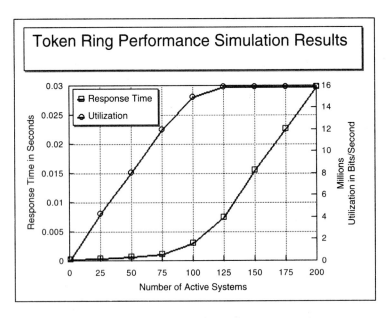

Figure 4-22 Simulation design curve for 16 Mbps IEEE 802.5 token ring. The curves are similar to Ethernet. Client response time increases linearly as the ring's utilization increase into the saturation region. Note the dual axis display.

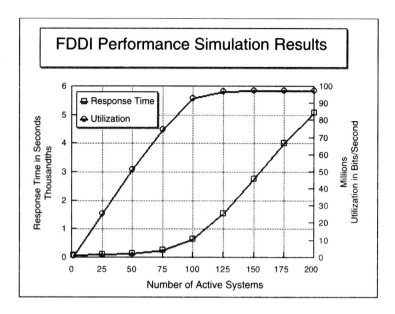

Figure 4-23 Simulation design curve for 100 Mbps FDDI. Client response time increases linearly as the medium approaches saturation. Note the dual axis display.

4.9 PERFORMANCE MYTHS ABOUT ETHERNET AND TOKEN RING

The previous section demonstrated that Ethernet, Token Ring, and FDDI have similar performance curves for utilization and response time. This is contrary to some commonly held beliefs, or myths. These commonly held misconceptions about Ethernet include

1. *Misconception:* collisions are bad and cause both packet loss and a loss of bandwidth.
2. *Misconception:* Ethernet should run at low utilization not to exceed 40%.
3. *Misconception:* Ethernet will collapse if pressed near its saturation.
4. *Misconception:* Ethernet is not deterministic, unlike the token ring.

Antidotes to these misconceptions are found in the professional literature and in the simulation results in the previous section. To wit

1. Collisions are a natural aspect of Ethernet's media access protocol (CSMA/CD). The colliding nodes wait a pseudo-random number of slot times before retrying. Recall that an Ethernet slot time is 51.2 microseconds. This is really done in the NIC. This slows down the overall transmission rate into the LAN. Only after 16 consecutive collisions (excess retries) will a NIC drop a frame. The transport layer (for example, TCP) will retransmit the datagram after a time-out. Actual bandwidth loss is not severe—per the simulation results.
2. Ethernet may be run at high utilization provided that the users can accept the response time degradation that comes with it, and provided that the transport protocols are robust enough to accommodate variable network delays. Van Jacobson TCP is an

example of a transport protocol that adjusts its time-out value dynamically. See RFC 1185, "TCP extension for high-speed paths," and RFC 1323, "TCP extensions for high performance."

3. Ethernet will not collapse under heavy load because the increasing response time slows down all transmitting nodes. A lot of early attempts to mathematically model Ethernet often included simplifying assumptions that were later found to be unsupported. The value 1/e, about 36.8% was often quoted, with best of intentions, as Ethernet's maximum utilization. Not so.

4. Determinism has to do with predictability. Can Ethernet guarantee to deliver a packet to its destination in a given time? Let's look at the worst case—the transmitting node has to defer its transmission for a maximum length frame, plus 15 consecutive collisions in a row and the transmitting node waits the maximum number of slot times before retrying (see Table 4-7).

Each deferral corresponds to a delay of $1{,}518 \cdot 8 / 10{,}000{,}000 = 1.2$ milliseconds, ignoring the 9.6 microsecond interframe gap, so 16 such attempts adds 19.4 milliseconds to the 366.9 milliseconds for a total of 386.3 milliseconds. This analysis does not account for Ethernet nodes deferring transmissions due to collisions caused by still other nodes. Still, if there are 16 consecutive collisions, the transmitting NIC aborts the frame, and the transport protocol must time out and attempt a retransmission. Conclusion: Ethernet performance can be quantified just like token ring performance can. (Notice that the Ethernet simulation in the previous section gave us about 60 milliseconds average response time and about 85% utilization for 200 active users. Compare 60 milliseconds with the 367 milliseconds we just calculated and you conclude that losing a packet due to excess retries is indeed a rare event.)

TABLE 4-7 CALCULATING ETHERNET WORST-CASE MEDIUM ACCESS TIME

Collision number	Maximum number of slot times
1	2
2	4
3	8
4	16
5	32
6	64
7	128
8	256
9	512
10	1,024
11	1,024
12	1,024
13	1,024
14	1,024
15	1,024
Total delay in slot times	7,166
Total delay in milliseconds	367

4.10 T-1, FRAME RELAY AND X.25 AS DESIGN BOTTLENECKS.

Basic WAN Performance Issues

Except for relatively modern WAN technologies such as SMDS and ATM, point-to-point T-1, frame relay, and X.25 line speeds are bottlenecks between LANs. T-1 line speeds vary from 56,000 to 1,544,000 bits per second, while X.25 circuits are limited to 56,000 bits per second. A robust transport layer is essential over WANs to allow for the large swings in available bandwidth (see Figure 4-24). Application and transport protocols that take advantage of full-duplex streaming mode and windowing schemes improve end-to-end performance by allowing applications to send multiple packets before waiting for acknowledgment. The HDLC protocol between the routers also provides for windowing, but the small overhead for windowing is ignored here.

To understand the performance gains from streaming, suppose a client sends packets continuously as fast as it can, using TCP/IP, to a server which replies with one ACK per data packet. The network is point-to-point fractional T-1 at 56,000 bits per second. Assume HDLC encapsulation on the WAN, which adds six bytes or 48 bits of overhead, and ignore Ethernet framing. The throughput is based on how much data the client sends in one network round-trip time. The calculation in Figure 4-25 (represented graphically in Figure 4-26) gives WAN throughput as a function of the available parameters.

Note that serial line compression would reduce the apparent amount of data transmitted and improve throughput. Use of the Point to Point Protocol (PPP) instead of HDLC will change the calculation somewhat due to header size differences. For dial-up routers using Serial Line Internet Protocol (SLIP) or Compressed SLIP (CSLIP), there are also header differences. Smaller headers can increase throughout.

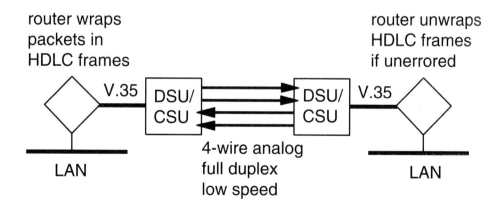

Figure 4-24 Routers join remote high-speed LANs with low-speed, full-duplex, analog serial lines. These lines are "nailed connections" between telephone switches that may traverse the country. Packets are encapsulated in an error-detecting protocol such as HDLC or PPP, increasing their size. The originating router retransmits a packet if the receiving router detects a CRC error. A packet that traverses multiple hops suffers greater delays than the one-hop scenario given here, so streaming transport protocols are used to improve throughput.

$$\text{LineSpeed} := 56{,}000 \quad \text{bits/second}$$

$$\text{LineUtilization} := 0.1 \quad \text{fraction of the line in use by other traffic}$$

$$\text{BandWidth} := \text{LineSpeed} \cdot (1 - \text{LineUtilization}) \quad \text{bandwidth available}$$

$$\text{TCPIPHeader} := 40 \text{ bytes}$$

$$\text{WANHeader} := 6 \text{ bytes}$$

$$\text{DataSize} := 500 \text{ bytes}$$

$$\text{ACKSize} := 50 \text{ bytes}$$

W_0 number of packets that can be sent before waiting for a reply

$$\text{SendTime}(W) := \frac{W \cdot (\text{TCIPHeader} + \text{DataSize} + \text{WANHeader}) \cdot 8}{\text{BandWidth}}$$

$$\text{ACKTime} := \frac{(\text{ACKSize} + \text{TCIP Header} + \text{WANHeader}) \cdot 8}{\text{BandWidth}}$$

$$\text{RoundTripTime}(W) := \text{SendTime}(W) + \text{ACKTime}$$

$$\text{ThroughPut}(W) := \frac{W \cdot \text{DataSize} \cdot 8}{\text{RoundTripTime}(W)}$$

$$W := 1.10$$

Figure 4-25 Calculating the throughput of a WAN circuit requires estimates of the protocol overhead and existing congestion levels. The formulas given here are derived in terms of W, the window size, measured as the maximum allowed number of outstanding packets a transmitter can send before stopping to wait for an ACK from the receiver.

Analog transmission impairments can reduce throughput. A single-bit error requires an entire frame to be retransmitted. In such situations, the network manager may choose to reduce the MTU of the serial circuit to improve throughput (see Figure 4-27).

Enter Frame Relay

Frame relay improves upon the point-to-point WAN by removing all but the local loop from the network manager's perceptions. The router requires a frame relay adapter. The network is engineered and managed by the service provider. The routers use a preconfigured permanent virtual circuit to communicate with their peers (see Figure 4-28).

There are several frame relay performance parameters (see Figure 4-29). The port speed is the clock speed for the circuit and ranges from 56,000 to 1,544,000 bits per second. The committed information rate (CIR) is the minimum guaranteed bit rate the customer

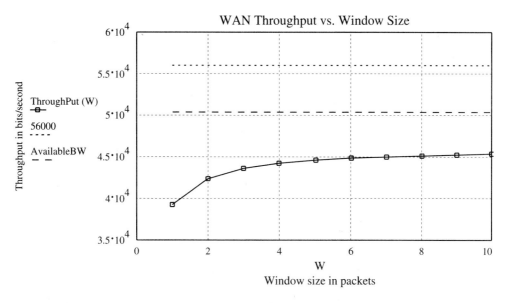

Figure 4-26 This is the graphical representation for the calculation given in Figure 4-25. The improvement in throughput due to even modest windowing is apparent. If windowing is not available, improvement can be achieved by an equivalent increase in the data packet size. Due to protocol overhead, throughput does not approach line speeds for any degree of windowing.

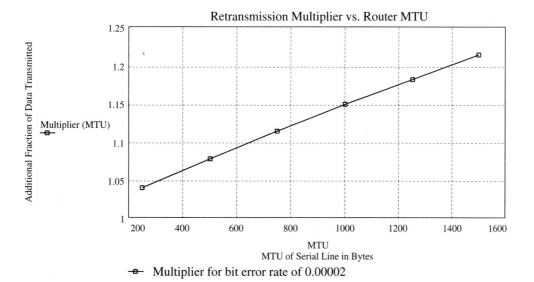

Figure 4-27 Varying the serial line MTU can reduce the chances of a single-bit error destroying the data and forcing a complete retransmission. Here we see that for a bit error probability of 0.00002, using 1,500-byte HDLC frames on the WAN link causes over 20% of the traffic to be retransmitted. Bear in mind that HDLC frames incur 6 bytes of framing overhead, so reducing the MTU too much will be counterproductive.

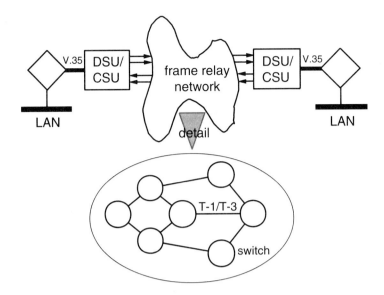

Figure 4-28 Frame relay networks are drawn as clouds because their internal structure is unimportant to the customer. Speeds up to T-1 are available and the routers communicate with each other using the frame relay link layer protocol (LLC). A permanent virtual circuit (PVC) is established to allow the routers to exchange packets. End-to-end performance depends on the number of switches and the network congestion created by other customers.

pays for on a per-PVC basis. The committed burst size B_c is the corresponding number of bits that the PVC can send in the T_c time interval. B_e is the excess burst size above B_c the network tries to deliver but marks discardable. Oversubscription occurs when the sum of the CIRs for all PVCs exceeds the port speed. While the maximum frame size must be at least 262 bytes, per RFC 1294, it is typically 1,600 bytes.

Frame relay networks are often provisioned to accommodate corporate traffic flows. Topologies vary between fully meshed and hub-and-spoke (see Figure 4-30). Hub-and-spoke topologies tend to have full T-1 speeds at the hub and 56,000 bit per second speeds at the spokes. Frame relay service providers may recommend a ratio less than or equal to 4:1 between the hub and the spokes. For TCP/IP networks this is not necessary because TCP's window-based flow control will prevent the transmitter from overrunning the receiver buffer. This is especially true where Van Jacobson TCP is used.

The hub-and-spoke topology has the side effect of requiring spoke sites to route through the hub site to communicate with each other. The fully meshed topology provides the best performance but costs more because each PVC has to be provisioned from the service provider. The performance differences are worth a closer look.

The hub-and-spoke topology requires packets to travel through the frame relay network to the hub, encountering some switches, various line speeds between them, and different levels of congestion. The latency due to the first spoke line speed and the hub line speed are cumulative. The hub router, likely a busy one, has to switch the packet onto its destination, adding more latency. The final journey from the hub to the target spoke will encounter additional network switches, links, and congestion. Figure 4-31 represents an

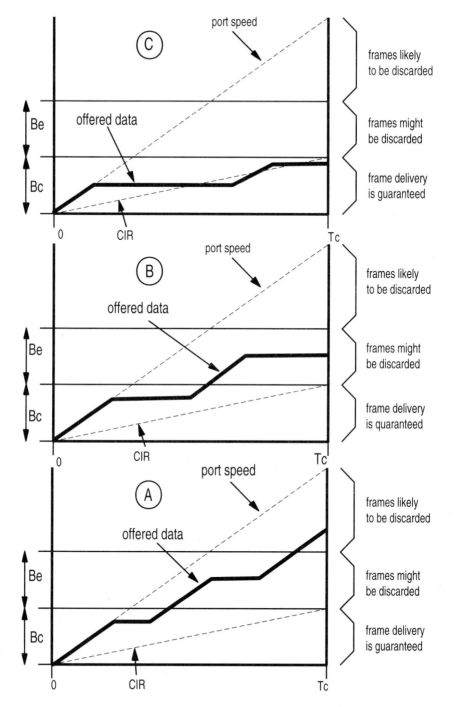

Figure 4-29 Frame relay performance parameters. Drawing A shows three packets sent faster than the excess burst rate $B_e + B_c$ during the measurement interval T_c. Drawing B shows two packets sent within the burst rate level. Drawing C shows two packets sent within the CIR rate for the PVC. Note that $T_c = B_c/\text{CIR}$ for nonzero CIR.

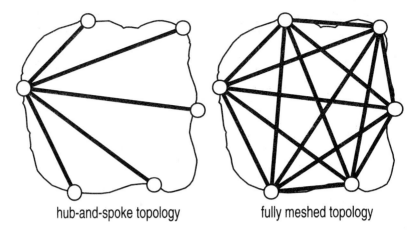

Figure 4-30 Six sites connected to a frame relay network all have just one local drop to the service provider network, regardless of how the logical topology appears. A minimum of five PVCs to the hub site are needed to provide full connectivity. Spoke sites communicate between each other via the hub router, with some performance degradation. A fully meshed topology among N sites requires $N \cdot (N-1)/2$ PVCs, so six sites require 15 PVCs.

OSI model perspective of all delay points in a frame relay network. Figure 4-32 gives an analysis for packet delay versus subscriber line speed.

X.25 Networking

X.25 is a packet switching technology. Components consist of packet switches, packet assembler disassemblers (PADs), and systems with X.25 adapters (see Figure 4-33). Line speeds up to 56,000 bits per second are available. The X.25 standard encompasses three OSI layers.

Layer one is usually RS-232-C for speeds up to 19,200 bits per second and V.35 for speeds up to 56,000 bits per second. Layer 2 is the Link Access Protocol version B (LAP-B), a synchronous protocol that includes a sliding window scheme for flow control, a frame check sequence (FCS) for error control, and six bytes of framing overhead. A bit-stuffing feature is necessary to support the transmission of transparent (binary) data, which may increase the number of bits sent by a few percent. Layer 3 is the X.25 network protocol, which also includes a sliding window protocol for flow control and adds a three-byte packet header.

The standard maximum packet contains 128 bytes of user data. By taking advantage of a large sliding window of, say, seven, 896 bytes of data can be transmitted into the network before the remote end has to ACK the data. At the link layer, LAP-B can be configured with a large window size for similar purpose, except this window applies only to the two controllers at each end of the physical connection.

X.25 networks may be private or public. Routers are available that support the X.25 interface and they operate much like frame relay, in that the router interfaces on the network are configured to know the X.121 addresses of remote routers. Since X.25 supports switched virtual circuits (SVC), routers may establish a connection with a peer, move traffic, and close the connection.

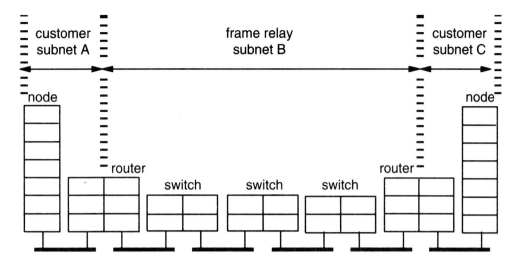

Figure 4-31 Viewed from the seven-layer OSI model, we see that the frame relay subnet moves frames between switches at the layer 2—the link layer. Subnet A routes packets into the frame relay subnet, which propagates them to the router at subnet C. The routers are configured to communicate with each other over preconfigured PVCs in a point-to-point fashion, much like the point-to-point private leased-lines WANs. The IP address of the frame relay side of each router is associated with the DLCI address of its peer.

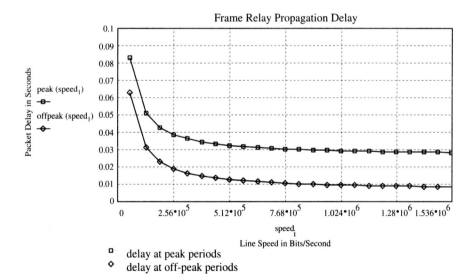

Figure 4-32 End-to-end delay of a 200-byte packet in a two-switch frame relay network. For off-peak periods a fixed 5.2 millisecond delay is incurred. For peak periods an additional 10 milliseconds per switch is added to this. The remainder of the delay is calculated directly from the port speed at each end, which is assumed to be same. The 6-byte frame relay encapsulation is included in the 200 bytes, and RFC 1042 and RFC 1294 encapsulation issues are ignored. Network protocol overhead for forward (FECN) and backward (BECN) explicit congestion notification isn't considered here.

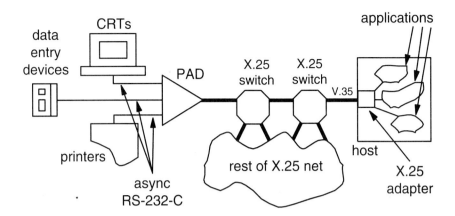

Figure 4-33 Serial devices such as CRTs, printers, and data entry devices are multiplexed using a PAD. The X.25 network moves packets between the PAD and the host using LAP-B link layer protocol. The X.25 network protocol provides end-to-end flow control and acknowledgment between the PAD and the host applications. The V.35 connection's 56,000 bps maximum may support 256 concurrent PVCs. Each PVC becomes a fixed path through the array of X.25 switches.

The X.25 switch performance rating is in packets per second (see Figure 4-34). For an eight-port switch, five ports may be receiving packets, seven may be transmitting. Because LAP-B is a full-duplex protocol, each port may be transmitting and receiving concurrently. Packets may be queued up in the switch's memory due to traffic patterns, line

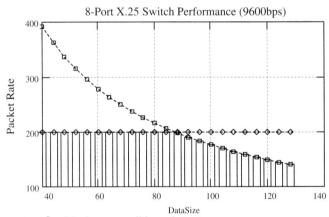

Figure 4-34 The performance of an X.25 switch is limited by both the switch's own top end and the limit imposed by the packet size. Here we have an eight-port switch operating full duplex on all ports at 9,600 bits per second. This calculation really counts each packet twice because it has to enter and then exit again. If the switch has to deal with a call setup or a line error, maximum performance necessarily drops until this transient condition subsides.

speed differences, and packet sizes. The media speed is one limiting factor for performance. It affects the rate that frames can be transmitted, and not all frames carry packets because LAP-B also depends on acknowledgment packets for flow control purposes. Another performance limitation is the maximum aggregate forwarding rate of the switch on all ports—in packets per second, a quantity that is usually specified by the switch vendor. The switch has to execute a certain number of instructions to identify the logical channel number identifier (LCNI) of the virtual circuit (VC), consult the routing tables, and forward the packet out the correct port.

The flow control mechanism found both in the LAP-B link layer and the X.25 network layer work independently. The LAP-B flow control is strictly between any two connected devices and the X.25 flow control is strictly between the end nodes. In both cases, the receiver advertises its window information to the transmitter, indicating which packet/frame numbers it has received successfully, which ones it has not yet processed, and also which ones it is ready to receive (see Figure 4-35).

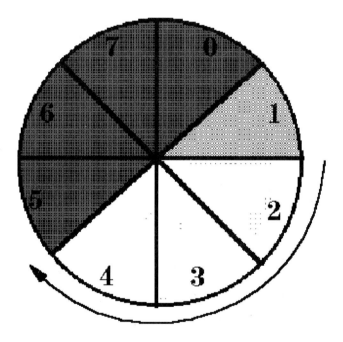

Figure 4-35 This example of the sliding window flow control mechanism used by X.25, its link layer protocol LAP-B, and by HDLC, indicates that windows are numbered zero to seven. The window will only open far enough to admit up to four packets. Here packet number one has not been acknowledged by the receiver, so the transmitter may send only packets number two, three, and four. Implicit is that the transmitter must buffer all unacknowledged packets (packet one in this case). Should the transmitter send packets two, three, and four, it must then wait until the receiver acknowledges at least frame number one. Performance increases when the maximum window size is larger. So does latency.

4.11 SPECMANSHIP BY EQUIPMENT VENDORS

Regardless of the vendor's specifications, the conditions under which network electronics operate in real life rarely duplicates those on the test bench. The network manager is not likely to acquire a variety of routers and plug each one, in turn, into the network to see which one works best. Certainly some set of features, the number of ports, product availability, and price will qualify the vendor of choice, but those performance specifications come into play too. RFC 1242 defines some performance parameters to guide both vendors and customers.

Tables 4-8 to 4-11 indicate some of the more common performance-related specifications for various network electronics such as switches, bridges, and routers.

TABLE 4-8 SPECIFICATIONS FOR ETHERNET SWITCHES AND SWITCHING HUBS

Performance feature	Typical value	Notes, cautions, caveats, and humbug
Latency	40 microseconds	The cut-through time applies only if the target port is clear. If this number is 512 microseconds (64 bytes) then collision fragments are filtered out. Larger latencies occur when store-and-forward bridging is being done. Switch vendors often compare this parameter with a bridge's latency of around 1 millisecond, but streaming transport protocols like TCP are immune to latency values this low.
Total packet switching rate	38,000 packets/sec	The ideal case is where each port streams one-way traffic out to another port with no contention across ports. This value is approximately proportional to the number of ports in this case.
RAM	4 megabytes	Large buffers can increase queuing latency. Check if this RAM is shared among the ports or if it is fixed on a per-port basis.
MAC table	4,096	That many nodes per segment would generate both excessive utilization and broadcast storms. There is also an aggregate table size. Some switches allow only one device per port. Ethernet specifies a maximum of 1,024 devices in a collision domain.
FDX/HDX	yes/no	Full-duplex Ethernet is not a standard. It benefits servers most if there are almost equal read and write rates (the norm is 80% reads and 20% writes).
CRC filtering	yes/no	Bridging accomplishes this, as does holding a packet or a fragment for one Ethernet slot time of 512 bit times (64-bytes Ethernet) before forwarding it. This feature's true benefit is arguable.
Interswitch FDDI link	yes/no	Proprietary encapsulation prevents using FDDI-capable systems on the ring, and broadcast traffic passes between the work groups unimpeded. The entire frame has to forwarded between the switches.
Virtual LANs	yes/no	Segment switching, port switching, or cell switching may be used to create these virtual LANs, so performance will vary.
Port count	16	Switches can be cascaded to increase the port count, but the cascading link is a bottleneck too. This favors the bigger switches. An FDDI link between hubs is better than a 10 Mbps full-duplex Ethernet link or a 100-BASE-T link.

TABLE 4-9 SPECIFICATIONS FOR ATM SWITCHES

Performance feature	Typical value	Notes, cautions, and caveats
Number of ports	24	Is there a provision for connecting switches together to increase the capacity of the ATM LAN? There should be an Ethernet DB-15 connector for management purposes.
Port speed	155 megabits per second	Class of Service (A, B, C, D) is more important depending on the data type (from fixed-bit-rate video to TCP data).
Latency	<10 microseconds	The host adapter typically interrupts after receiving N 53-octet ATM cells, so switch latency is not an issue for larger packets consisting of many cells. For isochronous data latency is guaranteed via the Grade of Service (GOS). Queuing on an output port increases latency. Note that a coast-to-coast trip in the USA takes 32 milliseconds.
Aggregate bandwidth	2.5 gigabits per second	This is the full-duplex speed of the switch fabric itself and represents the upper performance limit obtainable if input and output port traffic does not contend with any other traffic for a given port.
Call setup time	<10 milliseconds or 100 calls per second	Calls are set up either by the switch's own call-handling module or by an external management station. Setting up calls through an array of switches takes longer and the call setup time may not be specified.
Buffer space	512,000	Each VC setup may be allocated a fixed amount of this buffer space. A shared buffer pool of fixed 53-byte chunks may be implemented instead. Since multiple cells destined for the same output must all be buffered, some will be dropped if buffer space is unavailable. The higher the switch utilization, the more buffers are needed to maintain the same packet loss ratio.
Number of concurrent VCs	4,000	ATM provides a 16-bit virtual channel identifier (VCI) and an 8-bit virtual path identifier (VPI) that together form a 24-bit protocol connection identifier (PCI) used to route the cell to its destination. Both permanent and switched virtual circuits should be supported by the switch management software.
Traffic type	constant bit rate	Required by isochronous data such as fixed-bit-rate packetized video.
	variable bit rate	Variable-bit-rate video and audio applications.
	available bit rate	Can be used for data with a robust transport such as Van Jacobson TCP, which adjusts dynamically to the available bandwidth.

TABLE 4-10 SPECIFICATIONS FOR BRIDGES

Performance feature	Typical value	Notes, cautions, and caveats
Filtering rate	14,880 PPS	Does this figure apply when security and filtering is turned on?
Forwarding rate	14,880 PPS	Assumes the target LAN is devoid of any other traffic except that being forwarded, and is for 64-byte frames.
RAM	256 Kbytes	Too much RAM increases queuing latency when one LAN is very busy or has a reduced speed, such as a WAN. Too little RAM may cause frame loss due to buffer overflow.
MAC table size	1,024 addresses	This many nodes will create performance and broadcast problems on the LAN, and the bridge will forward the broadcasts.
Compression	1.5:1	Software overhead limits this for low-speed lines and the compression may not be realized for small packets or packets carrying precompressed binary data.

TABLE 4-11 SPECIFICATIONS FOR MULTIPROTOCOL ROUTERS

Performance feature	Typical value	Notes, cautions, and caveats
Forwarding rate	any	Usually quoted for Ethernet encapsulation, it may be much slower for IEEE 802.3. Forwarding between different cards is usually slower than between ports on the same card. The test is often unidirectional, which is not typical in the real world.
Compression	1.5:1	This software feature also competes with SNMP and routing protocol execution overhead. The compression obtainable depends on the data.
Bridging	yes	Software bridging require router CPU cycles
Multiple CPUs	4	Another feature that is not a direct benefit. For WAN modules, this can be a plus because compression software can be run on more WAN lines concurrently.
RAM	5 megabytes	Too much queuing delay will cause packet retransmissions at the host end, so keep the size of queues down. If an interface uses X.25, memory is used for the buffers needed to support the windowing feature of LAP-B.
Multiple protocols	IP, IPX, DECNET, AppleTalk, OSI	Aggregate CPU utilization may go up with the number of independent routing protocols that have to operate concurrently.

4.12 USING DECISION ANALYSIS TO SELECT AMONG ALTERNATIVE SOLUTIONS

When the network administrator has to choose among several alternative solutions, a robust methodology for making the best choice is appreciated. A common mistake is to choose a product or solution based on price or performance alone.

Suppose we're looking for router vendors and we have all the specifications in hand. We should begin by retaining routers that have all the "must-have" features, and then compare the "wants" of the remaining choices by comparing them analytically by computing a weighted sum of features and rejecting low-scoring routers. Finally we evaluate the risk factors and choose the router with the lowest risk. A step-by-step method is given in Table 4-12.

TABLE 4-12 DECISION ANALYSIS—CHOOSING THE BEST SOLUTION METHODICALLY

Phase	Step	Decision making activity
Eliminate potential solutions without all "must-haves."	1	List all the features that the solution must possess.
	2	Keep the potential solutions meeting all these needs.
Determine the cream of the crop by assessing how much of all "wants" each potential solution brings to the table. Eliminate solutions that score the lowest overall in the "wants." Remaining solutions are passed to the last phase.	3	List all the features the solution may possess.
	4	Rank the wants in order of importance, from 1 to 10.
	5	Rate each solution (1–10) on how well it meets the wants.
	6	Multiply the rate times the rank for each solution feature.
	7	Add up these weighted scores for each potential solution.
	8	Discard potential solutions that have low weighted scores.
	9	Keep the top few potential solutions that stand out.
Determine what can go wrong if a potential solution is implemented. Assign the importance and probability of this, and keep the solution that shows the lowest weighted risk.	10	Determine what can go wrong with each potential solution.
	11	Rank the importance (1–10) of each potential problem.
	12	Assign a probability (0–1) to each potential problem.
	13	Multiply the rank times the probability for each solution.
	14	Add up these weighted scores for each potential solution.
	15	Choose the solution with the least adverse risk.

In the following example we apply this method to choosing a router. This is our list of "must haves"

- SNMP support
- at least six Ethernet ports
- at least one frame relay or T-1 port
- MTBF over 6,000 hours
- hot swappable modules
- local hardware support
- OSPF support

Suppose that the only routers that meet these requirements are Router A, B, C, and D. We next make the list of "wants"

- low cost (10 being cheap and 1 being expensive)
- ease of expansion (10 being easy to expand and 1 being limited)
- support quality (10 being excellent and 1 being poor)
- has either frame relay or T-1 (8 for FR and 6 for T-1)
- performance (10 for high packet rates and 1 for poor packet rates)
- easy to configure (10 being easy and 1 being hard)
- bridging support (10 for good support and 1 for poor support)

The spreadsheet in Table 4-13 is constructed to formally document the method for rating each potential router solution.

Router C is clearly trailing the pack so we reject it. Routers A, B, and D are clustered around 398 ±16, meaning their scores are similar.

TABLE 4-13 SPREADSHEET WORKSHEET FOR CALCULATING THE WEIGHTED SCORES OF FOUR ROUTERS BEING EVALUATED

Weight	Feature	Router A		Router B		Router C		Router D	
		Score	Weighted	Score	Weighted	Score	Weighted	Score	Weighted
10	cost	5	50	7	70	10	100	8	80
10	expansion	8	80	8	80	4	40	5	50
9	support quality	10	90	8	72	5	45	9	81
8	frame relay or T-1	8	64	6	48	6	48	8	64
8	performance	6	48	8	64	4	32	9	72
5	easy to configure	3	15	10	50	7	35	8	40
3	bridging support	10	30	10	30	5	15	5	15
	Weighted scores		377		414		315		402

Next we determine what potential problems are associated with each solution. Our list of concerns is as follows

- router won't interoperate as advertised
- vendor obsoletes the router
- router delivery date slips
- router performance is below expectations
- expansion requirements were underestimated

The three remaining routers are put through another spreadsheet (Table 4-14) to compare their risks.

Router D is the least-risk solution and is clearly differentiated from Router A and B. Router D should be chosen.

TABLE 4-14 WORKSHEET FOR FINDING THE LEAST-RISK POTENTIAL SOLUTION

Weight	Risk	Router A		Router B		Router D	
		Score	Weighted	Score	Weighted	Score	Weighted
10	interoperability	9	90	7	70	1	10
10	obsolescence	4	40	3	30	3	30
9	late delivery	6	54	4	36	6	54
6	performs poorly	3	18	8	48	4	24
5	understimated expansion	2	10	2	10	4	20
	Weighted Scores		212		194		138

5

Indicators of Network Performance

5.0 INTRODUCTION

Because there are quite a few metrics for network performance, it behooves us to review these before plunging ahead and doing analysis. The users on the network have an intuitive notion about response time. It's good when they get the prompt back with the information they were looking for. It is possible to measure response time and what you find is that it really varies, sometimes quite a bit, so that variation in response time becomes an important metric too.

Systems people have tools to measure transaction throughput and generally have a fairly good idea of how many transactions per second their system can sustain. Networks people look at utilization as an indicator of performance, usually looking at the remaining bandwidth. LAN managers measure collision rates on their Ethernets. The higher the collision rate the greater their angst. Efficiency is another indicator of performance, and protocol overhead due to the seven-layer model can be a concern because it is perceived as overhead rather than good data.

The maximum number of satisfied concurrent users that a system or a network can support is uppermost in management's mind—the higher the better.

To the user copying a large file across the network, the time it takes is the only metric of importance. The time it takes to display an image on a screen is of foremost concern to the desktop publisher.

Measurements of performance help correct the direction of finger pointing, as the finger moves round and round from the user to the application, the client system, the network stack, the LAN, the network, the server, and finally to the server application before it swings around again.

More subtle measurements of performance are dropped packets, which seem to get lost due to collisions, overloaded WAN links, and even application servers.

In the following sections all of these performance metrics will explored in detail. Here we go.

5.1 PSYCHOLOGY OF RESPONSE TIME

Users work with applications that execute on client systems, move information across a network, and access server systems. They have expectations that response time be predictable and tolerable. They know there are times when "the system" is heavily used and lower their expectations.. Accordingly, predictable tolerable response time results in a productive, happy user. Unpredictable intolerable response time results in an unproductive, unhappy user who makes mistakes and may even avoid using "the system" altogether.

Users entering data into an interactive application executing on a LAN server expect subsecond response time for character echo. Studies have shown that echo times in excess of 100 milliseconds are annoying, since the user has to pause their typing to let "the system" catch up to them. Type-ahead helps but if the user has to backspace over already buffered characters, data entry errors may occur.

Information entered is usually committed by hitting the ENTER key or mouse-pressing a windows OK button.. The server application processes the information and displays the results for the user. This is the server response time and the user expects it to take longer than 100 milliseconds. Depending on the perceived complexity of the transaction, the user will tolerate a response time of one or more seconds.

If a transaction is particularly complex, the user appreciates the opportunity to place it in the background, freeing up the system for continued use. This is a tolerable workaround when response times are excessive.

Note that when the system is responding poorly, it is also subject to apparent "hangs" and possibly to session disconnects. Session reestablishment under such conditions is difficult. Users want their systems to have long-term predictable response time.

5.2 AVERAGE RESPONSE TIME AND PERCENTILES

Average response time is one indicator of performance and the lower the value the better. Users have a second indicator that's also important to them—consistency. Suppose that nine out of ten responses are 0.5 seconds and one out of ten is 5 seconds. The average response time is $0.9 \cdot 0.5 + 0.1 \cdot 5.0 = 0.95$ seconds and itself may be an acceptable value, but the 5-second response time may be totally unacceptable because it occurs quite often. One solution may be to limit the numbers of users (see Figure 5-1).

Long-term variation in response time is also a factor in user satisfaction. The response time statistics (mean and variation) should be time-invariant or stationary. It is not acceptable to have good response time for seven hours and have unpredictable response times during the eighth hour of the shift, which may be when batch jobs or backups are run.

Users care about total response time and not where it's distributed. They may or may not be aware that response time is effected by user think time, client latency, network delays, and server response time. They want an overprovisioned system that always performs well by their standards (see Figure 5-2).

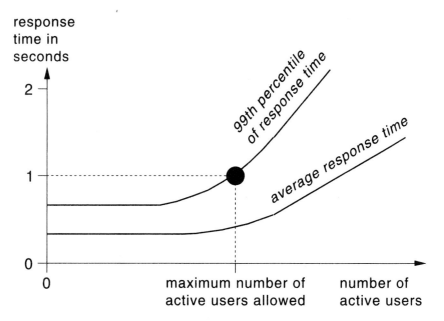

Figure 5-1 This is how average response time increases as the number of active users increases. The curve is very general and applies to networks and servers alike. A good specification for a system is that response time is under one second 99% of the time. Notice that the average response time figure is considerably less than the 99th percentile. If more users are allowed on the system, then response times will become both larger and less predictable. One can entertain the merits of limiting the number of users logged onto the application to some maximum.

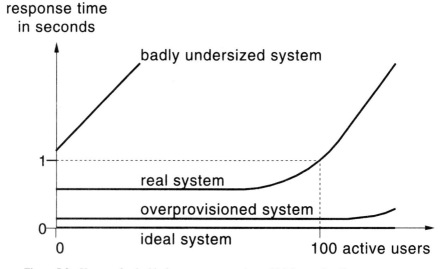

Figure 5-2 Users prefer the ideal system response time which is zero for all user counts. An overprovisioned system is their next choice because response remains low, while the real system is the one users normally deal with. Note the upper curve shows a system whose response time increases directly as users come on line. Such a system has already maximized a resource bottleneck.

5.3 TRANSACTION RATE

Transactions are often measured using benchmarks. Vendors like to advertise their transactions per second (TPS) per dollar cost figures for various configurations of their computer systems. Figures are given for each of the various transactions, usually industry-standard. This provides purchasers with an apples-to-apples comparison, but since real-world transaction mixes vary from site to site and from day to day, "your mileage may vary." Still, a transaction is a useful measure of interactive work.

Application transactions may be configured to have priority over other transactions, or transactions for one application may have priority over transactions from another. The overall transaction rate may not be effected very much even though user response time and its variation may vary greatly.

Transactions are not equal in their use of the classic system resources—CPU instructions, memory space, disk I/O, and network bandwidth. Some transactions move a lot of data between resources while others spend a lot of time waiting for data to become available, freeing up the CPU for other transactions. This means that transactions competing for the same resource may saturate it and limit their completion rate while other transactions with excess resources have not reached a plateau (see Figure 5-3).

The batch job rate is a variation of transaction rate except batch jobs are not interactive transactions. They normally take from minutes to hours to complete, and while the exact completion time may not be critical, they must typically have completed by a certain time of day. When software developers have completed the day's work of writing code, they typically start a "build" operation that may run for hours before the next software version is ready for testing. Electronic mail systems periodically run jobs that move mail between user mailboxes located across the enterprise network.

A final word about batch transactions is that if they compete for network resources they will impact interactive users. Batch jobs are usually configured to run at low priority on systems that also host interactive users, with the intent of not interfering with them.

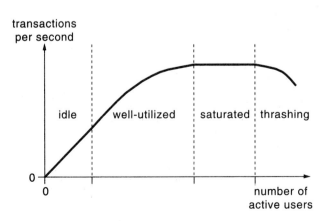

Figure 5-3 Operating regions for a transaction processor begin when few users are on the system and the transaction rate increases linearly. As competition for resources increases the system becomes well utilized and the transaction rate increases more slowly. When the first resource is saturated the transaction rate levels off and would remain so on a well-tuned system. Under overload conditions it is not unusual for a system to start thrashing, when more resources are consumed by the operating system making less available for real work. Thrashing might occur when so many users are logged on that physical memory is exhausted and the virtual memory subsystem has to start swapping processes to disk, quickly bottlenecking this resource as well.

5.4 UTILIZATION PERCENTAGE

A favorite performance metric is percentage utilization for resources such as CPU, disk, memory, and network. Most operating system kernels provide built-in instrumentation that boast hundreds of counters, such as the HP-UX Performance Collection Software (PCS) subsystem. The resulting collection of binary data may be displayed in various ways using tools such as PerfView, Perf/RX, and Glance/Plus. Several programs are often associated with a particular function and the resources used jointly can be reported.

Memory and Disk Utilization

Physical memory is used by the operating system kernel code, its data structures, and buffer spaces. The rest is used by applications for their code, heap, stack, and possibly shared memory data structures. When physical memory is exhausted the virtual memory (VM) subsystem will write some pages of an application's memory to disk, freeing up that memory for another application. The process is called swapping and it occurs when memory is 100% utilized. The VM subsystem paging algorithm tries to swap only those pages that are relatively inactive in order to minimize the amount of VM disk I/O. When there is excessive memory pressure there may be enough disk I/O to saturate this resource too.

Percent of maximum I/O rate is one measure of disk utilization. Disk drives may be specified in physical I/Os per second, average seek time, and sustained data transfer rate. File system buffering attempts to reduce the number of physical I/Os by collecting several small logical I/Os until a physical track's worth of information can be written. The disk is accessed whenever an application is launched from its file image, when it opens, reads, writes, and closes a data file. A database application may cause considerable disk I/O to satisfy a client request. The UNIX Internet daemon `inetd` may spawn a copy of a server daemon process in response to a remote client connection attempt, causing disk I/O. As the disk I/O rate reaches the rated maximum, queues on the disk controller will form in physical memory. Queuing delays will increase application response time and limit transaction rates. High disk I/O rates are not a problem unless the queues are deep.

Percent of storage capacity used is another metric for disk capacity. It impacts performance when the available free space is heavily fragmented across the disk surface, and when existing files are similarly fragmented. This increases the number of seeks needed to read and write the disk and reduces the performance of the disk drive.

CPU Utilization

CPU utilization is measured using either percent utilization or load factor. The O/S kernel counts the number of instructions its idle loop executes when no application is able to execute and no interrupts are pending. When this counter is not incrementing, the CPU is at 100% utilization. But any half-decent O/S time-slices applications, so if two programs are executing an infinite loop and another program needs occasional CPU time, the latter still gets time slices. If any one of three compute-intensive programs can saturate the CPU, then all three running concurrently will still saturate the CPU, but each program will get only one-third of the available CPU.

The load factor is the average number of processes in the run queue, averaged over some time interval such as 1, 5, or 15 minutes (see Figure 5-4). Three compute intensive programs competing for the CPU results in a load factor of three. This is a more useful measure of CPU utilization.

Network Utilization

Network utilization is usually measured in percent utilization or in packets per second. A client or server system is only aware of the amount of network traffic it sends and receives. If the performance collection software indicates the system is sending and receiving at the network's maximum rate, transaction rates will level off and response times will increase. Since the system will not be aware of other traffic on the network, this measurement is not representative of the LAN utilization.

Each of these four resources (disk, CPU, memory, and network) can be considered as a potential bottleneck, each with its own saturation level. Every transaction generally visits each of these resources at least once. If the most narrow of the bottlenecks (the first bottleneck) is reached, widening it will raise the maximum transaction rate to a new plateau. In general, widening any of the four potential bottlenecks will increase the maximum transaction rate somewhat.

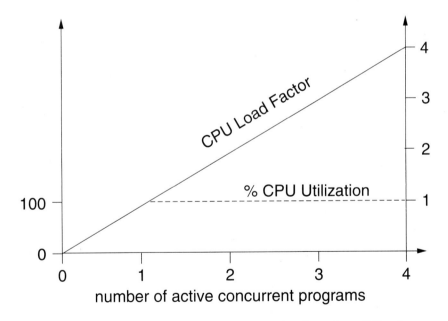

Figure 5-4 CPU utilization measured as a percentage doesn't reveal true CPU performance beyond 100%. It is perfectly acceptable to run a system well into the 100% utilization region, where load factor is the better metric. On a 20 MIP CPU running ten CPU intensive programs, the load factor will be 10.0 and each program will have only 2.0 MIPs available to it. Performance may be unacceptable. But on a 100 MIP CPU the same ten programs still result in a 10.0 load factor but each program now has 10 MIPs available, which may be perfectly acceptable.

5.5 COLLISION RATE

Collision Basics

Myths surrounding the Ethernet collision abound in the Internet notes strings. The quantity is easy to measure with LAN analyzers and segment monitors. Hubs with properly implemented SNMP agents can return collision statistics on each port. Most operating systems can report collisions their Ethernet adapters have participated in. Counting collisions is pointless unless the corresponding number of packets transmitted during the same time interval is also collected for comparison

$$\frac{collisions}{packets\_sent} \cdot 100 = \%collisions$$

When a LAN adapter detects a collision, it transmits a jamming signal of 32–48 bits to reinforce the collision and waits some multiple of 51.2 microseconds (the slot time) before attempting to retransmit the frame. This takes the colliding nodes out of the picture and gives other stations a chance to acquire the medium. Single collisions are a normal aspect of Ethernet operation, don't cause data loss, and don't slow packet delivery times significantly.

Collision Results from a Simulation

See Figure 5-5.

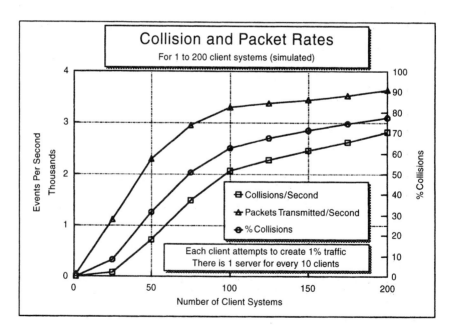

Figure 5-5 Simulation result for a heavily utilized Ethernet segment showing collision and packet rates. Notice the collision rate for 100 users seems a very high 2,000 per second and is at 60%. This is normal operation for Ethernet at these utilization levels.

Potential Frame Loss due to Collisions

Multiple collisions occur when the same frame encounters another collision. The LAN adapter responsible will increment this statistic locally. LAN analyzers don't distinguish collisions this way. Multiple collisions put the LAN adapter into its exponential back-off mode, meaning that no attempt will be made to transmit the packet until 2^2 to 2^{10} slot times have elapsed. Some performance degradation will occur, especially when a frame encounters between 10 and 15 collisions.

Excess retries occur when a LAN adapter encounters 16 successive collisions while attempting to transmit a frame. Ethernet standards require the adapter to discard the frame and move on to the next one in its buffer. Only the LAN adapter is aware of this event and it increments a local statistic to record it. LAN analyzers are not aware of this special event. Since the frame is truly lost, the transport layer is now responsible for detecting the lost data and retransmitting it. The default minimum TCP retransmission timer for HP-UX is one second, so the client-server pair using this transport connection experiences a one-second delay. No data is lost and performance degrades.

Late collisions are collisions that occur after a LAN adapter has transmitted for 51.2 microseconds. They cannot occur when the LAN topology meets the total distance specification for Ethernet and when all nodes do carrier sensing (CS) and collision detection (CD). The LAN adapter experiencing the late collision increments a local statistic. The late collision indicates an Ethernet violation exists and it alerts the network manager to fix the problem.

Practical Collision-related Measurements

See Tables 5-1 and 5-2.

TABLE 5-1 COLLISION-RELATED ETHERNET TRANSMIT STATISTICS KEPT BY THE LAN ADAPTER

Statistic		Description
Frames transmitted		Frames successfully transmitted.
Untransmitted frames	*	Frames not transmitted due to resource limits.
Transmit collisions		Total of all collisions that occurred while transmitting frames.
One transmit collision	*	Transmitted frames that experienced exactly on collision.
More transmit collisions	*	Transmitted frames with two or more collisions.
Excess retries	*	Frames dropped because they experienced 16 collisions.
Deferred transmissions	*	Times the LAN was busy when the adapter had data to send.
Carrier lost when transmitting	*	Times the LAN adapter could not hear its own transmission.
No heartbeat after transmission	*	The IEEE 802.3 transceiver SQE enable is disabled/disfunctional.
Late transmit collisions		Collision detected after 51.2 microseconds had elapsed.

*Indicates a statistic that can only be measured by the host LAN adapter and not by a LAN analyzer.

TABLE 5-2 COLLISION-RELATED ETHERNET RECEIVE STATISTICS KEPT BY THE LAN ADAPTER

Statistic		Description
Frames received		Total of all frames received by the LAN adapter.
Undelivered received frames	*	Good frames not sent up to the host due to resource problems (no space in the buffer).
CRC errors received		Frames received with bad CRC errors are discarded.
Frame alignment errors		Frames received whose number of bits is not divisible by eight.
Unknown protocol	*	Ethernet Type field is for a protocol not registered with the host.
Bad control field	*	The IEEE 802.3 LLC field contained an illegal value.

*Indicates a statistic that can only be measured by the host LAN adapter and not by a LAN analyzer. Note that collisions are often the reason for CRC and alignment errors.

5.6 PROTOCOL OVERHEAD AND EFFICIENCY

Protocol overhead is essential for correct operation of networks but the addition of headers (and trailers at the physical layer) at each OSI layer reduces the data transfer efficiency, especially when only a few bytes of user data is sent in a packet. The handshaking mechanism of reliable protocols also adds additional latency and traffic. Fragmentation and reassembly is necessary to deal with the various maximum transmit unit (MTU) encountered in the network, but it too is overhead.

To help determine protocol overhead, we present in Table 5-3 various protocols and the size of their headers.

The ulterior motive in counting protocol header overhead is to calculate the efficiency of the network. Consider the telnet protocol sending single-byte data packets with TCP/IP over Ethernet. Each keystroke is sent to the server, which echoes the character and includes a piggyback TCP ACK for the original character. The telnet client sends a TCP ACK back to the server to acknowledge the echo character. Ethernet frames have a minimum size of 64 bytes, excluding preamble and interframe gaps, so each of the three frames will be 64 bytes long; the first two contain 1 byte of data and the last has no user data in it. The three frames represent 192 bytes, of which 2 carry data, and the efficiency is only $\frac{2}{192} \cdot 100 = 1.04\%$ but since users cannot send that many packets per second, the pressure on the network remains low.

Handshaking by transport protocols can reduce throughput. Consider the IPX protocol, which is a request-reply protocol. For every request, the client must wait for the server to respond, and the reply is typically 576 bytes. If the packets have to traverse a few routers, the propagation delay reduces throughput even more. Network utilization isn't particularly high but performance isn't great. There is no obvious resource bottleneck. If the transport can be tuned to increase the data payload or if a streaming mode is available, throughput can be increased.

Fragmentation is overhead, but it's necessary when the network protocol has a packet too large for the target medium. Consider an application with 9,000 bytes of data to send.

TABLE 5-3 HEADER OVERHEAD FOR VARIOUS PROTOCOL INFORMATION FRAMES

Protocol	Overhead in bytes	Max frame size in bytes	Description
Ethernet	18	1,518	6 source, 6 destination 2 type, 4 CRC.
IEEE 802.3	21	1,518	6 source, 6 destination 2 length, 3 LLC, 4 CRC.
IEEE 802.5 token ring	28	4,472 & 17,900	6 source, 6 destination 4 misc., 3 LLC, 5 802.2 SAP, 4 CRC. Up to 16 source-routing octets may be added.
FDDI (RFC 1390)	28	4,500	3 802.2 LLC, 5 802.2 SNAP, 4 source, 4 destination, 4 misc., 8 FCS. The source and destination addresses may be 12 bytes.
ATM (RFC 1483)	8	53	4 CRC, 2 length, 1 CPI, 1 CPCS-UU. For AAL-5 multiprotocol encapsulation. The ATM cell header is only 5 bytes.
Frame relay (RFC 1490)	8	n/a	2 flags, 2 Q.922 address, 1 control, 1 NLPID, 2 FCS. For multiprotocol encapsulation.
PPP (RFC 1662)	10	n/a	8 HDLC framing, 2 PPP protocol itself.
HDLC	8	n/a	1 flag, 1 address, 1 control, 4 CRC, 1 flag.
TCP (RFC 793)	20	65,535	8 sequence numbers, 4 ports, 2 window, 6 other. RFC 1106 extends the window size to over one gigabyte.
IP (RFC 791)	20	65,535	8 IP addresses, 12 other.

Note: Frame preambles are not included in these counts, nor are interframe gaps.
MTU = maximum frame size minus overhead.

The FDDI ring MTU is about 4,500 bytes, so IP transmits two datagrams. Suppose this goes through an IP router and onto an Ethernet with an MTU of 1,518 bytes. The router fragments each fragment and six fragments now move on. Finally, another IP router connected to a WAN link with an MTU of 500 bytes breaks each fragment into three for a grand total of 18 IP datagrams. RFC 1191 describes a method for determining the path MTU (PMTU) to avoid sending larger packets that will have to fragmented.

One reason for not fragmenting is to avoid the additional CPU overhead required to fragment and to reassemble the packets. Another is that the risk of losing just one of the fragments requires the sending transport to retransmit the entire datagram, not just the lost fragment.

5.7 MAXIMUM NUMBER OF CONCURRENT USERS

Vendors sell operating system software with "so-many" user licenses. They often provide a small table, such as Table 5-4, to help customers choose the right CPU size at pres-sales time.

Of course the real issue is the user response time when this number of users are pounding the ivory *after* the system and network have been purchased and installed. The

TABLE 5-4 CAPACITY OF THE MYTHICAL ULTRA SYSTEM XL TURBO PLUS

Type of user	Recommended number of concurrent users
light	500
medium	250
heavy	50

number of currently logged-on users is fairly easy to determine. The UNIX command sequence

$$who \,|\, wc \,-l$$

counts the number of currently logged-on users but gives no indication how many are active. The UNIX command `uptime` prints out the system's 1-, 5-, and 15-minute load average.

Users at X-terminals are capable of running multiple shells and applications concurrently. Users with HP Terminal Session Manager (TSM) software can have from three to eight shells active concurrently. Each of these users counts as one user per the O/S but demands considerably more system resources. Users who access a system using telnet or rlogin incur networking overhead that directly attached ASCII terminal users don't.

A final note: Interactive logged-on users are counted as users but users accessing a system using noninteractive services such as the Network File System (NFS), the File Transfer Protocol (FTP), or remote line printing (`rlp`) are not counted as users. The same is true for UNIX systems running LAN Manager/UNIX (LM/X or LM/U) or Portable Netware. Of course these network operating systems (NOS) have their own user license counters, but they are distinct from the UNIX user counter. So while an important performance metric is the number of concurrent users, it's important that we understand how users are actually counted operationally.

5.8 TIME TO PERFORM A LARGE FILE TRANSFER

Users who transfer files believe that the time this task takes out of their busy schedule is an important performance metric. A large file might be a 100-megabyte archive (such as a UNIX `tar` file or a PC ZIP file). Copying this file across an Ethernet will take about 80 seconds at a minimum and probably a lot longer. A 500-Kbyte PostScript file transferred to a network printer may only take a second or so, if the printer's RAM is adequate, but the actual raster image processing (RIP) operation may take half an hour if the document contains complex graphics and mathematical formulas.

A large file might be a word processing file with an embedded bit-mapped graphic such as the draft version of Chapter 4 of this book, which was at one time a mere 311,814 bytes in size, 43 pages long, and contained 11 embedded BMP files and 49,122 characters of text. It took four seconds to save it from memory to disk.

The directory of RFCs is a file called `rfc-index.txt`. It was once 220,088 bytes long and it took 16.07 seconds to copy it from `ftp.uu.net` to `bellevue.hp.com` using anonymous `ftp` over the Internet. Though it's not a large file, anything that takes over 16 seconds to be transferred is large enough.

Any serial WAN will slow a file transfer and reduce performance. The file push and pull times may not be the same either, since serial lines are generally full duplex (FDX) and traffic in one direction is not generally mirrored in the other direction.

The file transfer time may be slowed by file system fragmentation at the sending or receiving system. This is especially troublesome when the disk is near 100% of its storage capacity. There may be other users and applications accessing the same disk drive, competing for disk I/Os. The average disk seek time is the seek time of many random seeks averaged out.

5.9 TIME TAKEN TO DISPLAY A COLOR IMAGE

In the publishing industry it is a routine matter to accesses and view multimegabyte high-resolution true-color images. Fifty megabytes is not considered large. The storage requirements (in bytes) of an image is (roughly) given by the formula below, based on Figure 5-6.

$$FileSizeInBytes = \frac{Width \cdot Height \cdot ColorDepth}{8} + Const$$

The value for `const` in the above formula is 1,074 bytes when curve-fit to the data in Table 5-5. This represents file headers such as the color palette. The file used for this example was a small color image scanned at 24 colors and 100 DPI. It was color-reduced using Paint Shop Pro.

Color image file sizes can be reduced using compression methods. The degree of compression depends on the amount of redundant information in the image, the size of the image, the efficiency of the compression algorithm used, and whether the compression algorithm is lossy. While a file in compressed form takes less time to read from disk and transfer over the network, the decompression time may or may not increase the display time of the image significantly.

Other factors affecting display time of a color image are listed in Table 5-6.

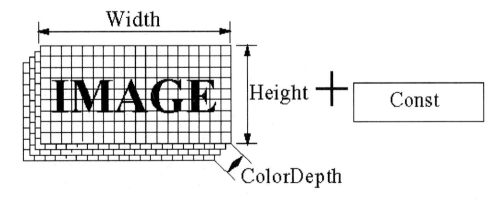

Figure 5-6 This is the basis for the formula for the size of a graphics file.

TABLE 5-5 SIZE OF A SMALL (249 × 245) UNCOMPRESSED TIFF FILE WITH VARIOUS COLOR DEPTHS

Color depth in bits	File size in bytes	Comments
1	8,274	black and white
4	31,168	16 colors
8	62,988	256 colors
24	183,468	17 million colors

TABLE 5-6 FACTORS THAT AFFECT THE DISPLAY TIME OF A COLOR IMAGE

Factor	Attributes	Speed-up methods
File server	Access speed	Faster disk, CPU, bus, LAN adapter (16/32 bit I/O bus).
		Shed users or increase priority of imaging users.
LAN	Medium speed	Reduce file size by compression.
		Install a faster LAN medium.
		Install a switching hub.
WAN	Line speed	Use interlaced GIF images so users can abort partial transfers.
		Use private point-to-point leased lines instead of frame relay.
		Explore SMDS or ATM offerings in the local telecom market.
Network protocol	Latency	Use a streaming protocol with large packet sizes (e.g., TCP).
Client	Performance	Faster processor, more RAM, faster LAN adapter.
Imaging application	Performance	Choose a program optimized for the hardware and NOS.
		If reads are 80%, choose the application that's fastest here.
Image size	Width & height	Use a smaller preview image appropriate to the display size.
Color count	Planes	Use a 16- or 256-color preview image when appropriate.
		Avoid time-consuming display-dithering algorithms.
Decompression	Time	Use a faster algorithm that may be less space-efficient.
Video subsystem	Display rate	Use a faster display subsystem (VRAM memory, 64-bit chips).

5.10 CORRECTING THE DIRECTION OF FINGER POINTING

Bottlenecks

Users have their own personal performance indicators and when they've been exceeded the help desk gets a call: "The network is slow." You see, users are aware they're connected to a network and they're perfectly willing to point an accusing finger in its direction. The help desk will verify the network is involved in the work the caller is doing and proceed to investigate.

To test for performance bottlenecks, each of the following five locations is measured and compared to an existing baseline performance metric

- client system
- client-side LAN
- network in between (LAN/WAN)
- server-side LAN
- server system

These measurements may well point to more than one bottleneck to consider widening (see Figure 5-7).

Methodology for Finding Bottlenecks

However, before plunging into performance troubleshooting it is best to adopt a more methodical approach. It begins by composing a precise problem statement that articulates some deviation from an expected performance goal. For example: "Every day between four and five P.M. the response time of my queries to the sales database from my Macintosh often exceeds ten seconds, and one second is the norm at other times."

Look at each of the five locations listed above and generate questions designed to ferret out information (where, when, how, who, why, what). The theme to all these questions is *change*. For example

- Who else experiences the same problem?
- Which users do not have this problem?
- When does the problem occur?
- When does the problem not occur?
- What has changed on the client system?
- When did the problem first appear?
- Was there a time when this problem never occurred?

The information should then be analyzed by asking questions about differences

- What is different between users who do and who don't have the problem?
- What is different about the problem location?
- What is different about when the problem does not occur?

Figure 5-7 While looking for potential bottlenecks between client and server, there may be more than one to be widened before performance will improve. By analogy there are two narrow pipe sections impeding the flow of fluids through the system. Widening only one of these sections will improve overall fluid flow but until the second bottleneck is also widened, no great improvement will be obtained.

The answers will provide information essential to generating possible causes of the problem. Additional possible causes may be listed from personal experience, from a brainstorming session with others, from the user, from the help desk's problem resolution logs, from the vendors who supplied the hardware, from software and integration services (via their Web server or 1-800 help-line number), and even from a posting to the appropriate news group on the net.

Each possible cause should be consistent with the information available and all other possible causes can be set aside. The remaining most probable causes should then be tested to uncover the true cause.

5.11 DROPPED PACKET RATE AND TRANSPORT RETRANSMISSIONS

Packets are dropped by the link and network layers of the OSI model. The transport layer is designed to buffer unacknowledged data and retransmit it as necessary to maintain the reliable virtual circuits between clients and servers. The rate at which the lower layers drop packets impacts the rate at which the transport layer must retransmit data.

Consider an Ethernet with 100 users and 10 servers transmitting 3,290 good packets per second and experiencing 2,060 collisions per second. These are earlier simulation results. The probability of a data packet experiencing a collision can be expressed as

$$p = \frac{collisions}{collisions + packets} = \frac{2,060}{2,060 + 3,290} = 0.38$$

and the probability of losing this data packet after 16 sequential collisions is

$$p^{16} = 2.355 \cdot 10^{-7}.$$

This is a very small value and it represents the rate at which the transport layer has to retransmit a packet on a fairly busy Ethernet. Other reasons for Ethernet packet loss are CRC errors and lack of resources in the LAN adapters.

Ethernet switches incorporate output queues to buffer packets that contend for the same output port. At high packet rates (with small packet sizes) the switch will discard packets.

ATM switches also incorporate output queues to buffer cells that contend for the same output port. Cells marked as discardable (which is allowed when using TCP transport over AAL5) will be lost when the buffer overflows. The loss of just one 53-octet cell will require the retransmission of the entire data segment submitted to the transport layer. If a TCP transmit buffer of 64 Kbytes is used, the entire 64 Kbytes have to be retransmitted.

Bridges and routers may also drop packets when the internal buffer overflows. This is especially likely when the WAN line is congested and the transport layer times out and retransmits. Transports that continually estimate the round-trip time and its variation can adjust their retransmission timers accordingly. Van Jacobson TCP implements this feature. Note that packets may traverse an extensive internet and experience several bouts of fragmentation. This increases the chances of losing one to them and requiring the retransmission of the entire transport segment.

The actual packet loss rate experienced by Ethernet and ATM switches, bridges, and routers can be estimated using queuing theory or simulation methods, which are covered in Chapters 9 and 10.

6

Network Statistics 101: The Essentials

6.0 INTRODUCTION

Networks carry data with random properties and we have to accept the fact that the network's response time and utilization are going to be random as well. Everything that we measure on our networks are samples from random processes and it's necessary to understand some basic things about statistics. This chapter is intended to bring out only important aspects of statistics—important in the sense that they are important in network capacity planning.

To that end we begin with a review of two very fundamental concepts in statistics: the average and the variation. Network data often follows some very well known statistical properties and we review these distributions both mathematically and by example. We often deal with combinations of data with different statistical properties and we go over the math for this too. It's practice time as we validate response time figures and we even analyze output from the `ping` command.

What about predicting performance from existing operational data, which is just a sequence of statistical samples? The answer is trend analysis and we have some examples lined up.

6.1 BASIC MEASUREMENTS: AVERAGE AND VARIATION

Measurements of network performance are not exact or repeatable because the nature of network traffic, with few exceptions, is neither deterministic (it cannot be predicted with certainty) nor stationary (time independent). Network administrators are forced to live in a statistical world and speak in terms of average response time and about how this response time varies about this average value.

Averages (or mean or expected) values are normally calculated by simply adding up all the samples and dividing this by how many samples we have. The mean value conceptually is a measure of central tendency and is taken as the most likely value about which samples cluster. The most straightforward mathematical notation representing the averaging process for N samples is

$$ave = \frac{x_1 + x_2 + x_3 + \ldots + x_N}{N}$$

where x_1 represents the first sample, x_2 represents the second sample and x_N represents the last sample.

Variation (the first moment about the mean) is calculated by subtracting each x value from the mean, squaring each of these differences, adding up these squared differences and dividing the sum by $N - 1$.

$$var = \frac{(ave - x_1)^2 + (ave - x_2)^2 + (ave - x_3)^2 + \ldots + (ave - x_N)^2}{N - 1}$$

The standard deviation is a related measurement and it is the square root of the variance:

$$dev = \sqrt{var}$$

The variance and standard deviation both calculate just how much variation the samples have about the mean value. Small deviations about the mean demonstrates a strong central tendency of the samples. Such samples have very little statistical randomness. Wide deviation about the mean demonstrates very little central tendency and shows very large statistical randomness. The samples {10.6, 10.4, 10.5} are clearly "good" samples with statistical high significance while the samples {11.7, 1.6, 18.2} are "bad" samples with little statistical significance. Both sets have the same average value, by the way (see also Figure 6-1).

$$x = \begin{array}{|c|c|} \hline & 1 \\ \hline 1 & 162 \\ \hline 2 & 83 \\ \hline 3 & 93 \\ \hline 4 & 6 \\ \hline 5 & 81 \\ \hline 6 & 21 \\ \hline 7 & 4 \\ \hline 8 & 4 \\ \hline 9 & 94 \\ \hline 10 & 28 \\ \hline \end{array}$$

$$ave: = \frac{\sum_{i=1}^{N} x_i}{N} \qquad ave = 57.6$$

$$var: = \frac{\sum_{i=1}^{N} (ave - x_i)^2}{N - 1} \qquad var = 2810.489$$

$$dev: = \sqrt{var} \qquad dev = 53.014$$

Figure 6-1 The average, variation, and deviation of $N = 10$ samples $x_1, x_2, x_3, \ldots, x_{10}$ are calculated here. The samples were synthesized using the exponential distribution with a mean value of 50, the only parameter this distribution has. Note the compact notation used for summation, the $\sum$ symbol. The average and deviation values calculated here are pleasingly close to the theoretical value of 50, considering that only 10 samples exist.

The motivation for averaging data samples is to get rid of the "noise" that's "obviously" present in them. When data samples show a lot of variation there is a tendency to collect even more of the samples and simply average them all together to "improve" the measurement. The belief is that the noise present is completely random and additive, has a zero mean value, and is uncorrelated with the actual data. Students performing experiments in physics are taught to take lots of readings at different points and to draw or calculate a "best fit" curve to the data. The truth is that it is better to have a few really good data points than a whole lot of bad (noisy) ones.

Situations come up when many of the data samples have the same value. Taking a series of response time measurements with a resolution of 0.1 seconds might result in this situation. The samples are usually ordered into groups and the frequency of each sample is counted. Sample x_1 occurs with a frequency of f_1 sample x_i occurs with frequency f_i and sample x_N occurs with frequency f_N. The formulas above are modified as follows

$$ave = \frac{\sum f_i \cdot x_i}{N} \quad \text{where } N = \sum f_i$$

$$var = \frac{\sum \left(f_i \cdot (ave - x_i)\right)^2}{N - 1}$$

$$dev = \sqrt{var}$$

6.2 USEFUL STATISTICS DISTRIBUTIONS: NORMAL, EXPONENTIAL, POISSON, UNIFORM, AND FIXED

Fundamental Properties—Discrete and Continuous Functions

A few very common statistical distributions will be introduced here. Each has a mathematical formula $f(x)$ describing its probability density function (PDF), which is equivalent to a histogram with all the frequencies of occurrence transformed into probabilities. The histogram in Figure 6-2 represents $\sum f_i = 50$ samples and dividing each frequency f_i by 50 gives p_i, the probability of occurrence of sample x_i. The probabilities always add up to exactly unity (one) and we write $\sum p_i = 1$. In other words, the area under the curve (of the histogram) is always 1.

For statistical distributions, the probability density function is called continuous because any numerical value is possible. Accordingly the integration notation is used instead of the summation notation and we have $\int p(x)\,dx = 1$. The formulas for average, variance, and standard deviation are rewritten thus

$$ave = \int x f(x)\,dx$$

$$var = \int (ave - x)^2 f(x)\,dx$$

$$dev = \sqrt{var}$$

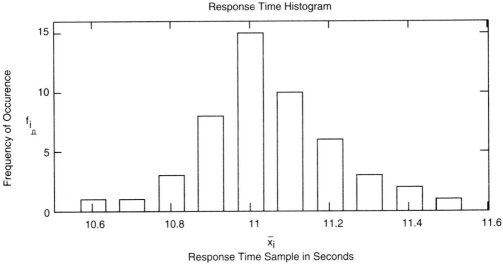

⊔ frequency of occurence

Figure 6-2 Histograms are often used to represent the frequency of statistical data. The response time (to transfer a file) is clearly clustered around 11.0 seconds. Applying the above formulas the average value is 11.046, the variance is 0.103 and the standard deviation is 0.321.

Graphical and Technical Information for Common Distributions

Table 6-1 shows the more common statistical distributions that will arise in the day-to-day work of network performance analysis. These distributions are illustrated and described in Figures 6-3 to 6-7.

TABLE 6-1 COMMON STATISTICAL PROBABILITY DENSITY FUNCTIONS

Distribution	Mean	Variance	Density function
Normal	μ	σ^2	$\dfrac{1}{\sigma\sqrt{2\pi}}e^{-\frac{(x-\mu)^2}{2\sigma^2}}$
Exponential	λ	λ	$f(x) = \dfrac{1}{\lambda}e^{-\frac{x}{\lambda}}$
Poisson	λ	λ	$p(x) = \dfrac{e^{-\lambda}\lambda^x}{x!}$
Uniform	$\dfrac{a+b}{2}$	$\dfrac{(b-a)^2}{12}$	$\dfrac{1}{b-a}$
Fixed	a	0	$\delta(x-a)$

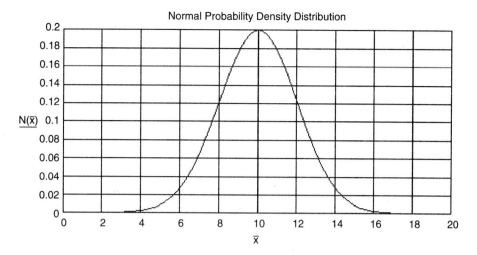

Figure 6-3 The normal distribution is also known as the bell curve due to its symmetry about the mean value. This one has a mean of 10.0 and a standard deviation of 2.0. As the mean increases the curve shifts to the right. As the standard deviation increases the curve widens out and the peak flattens. The tails of the normal distribution go to plus and minus infinity. In practice the lower limit is zero. The normal distribution purportedly describes student scores.

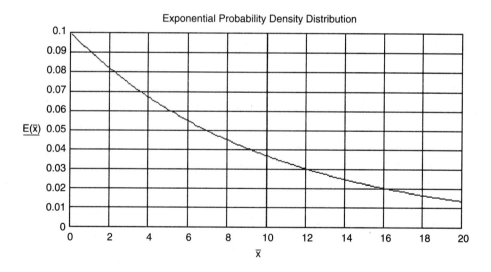

Figure 6-4 The exponential distribution is usually a negative exponential with its maximum at zero and a tail that goes to infinity. This one has a mean of 10.0, its only parameter, because the standard deviation is the same as its mean. This distribution is a favorite among the queuing theory and simulation practitioners and is often used to set the interarrival time between transactions.

Sec. 6.2   Useful Statistics Distributions   111

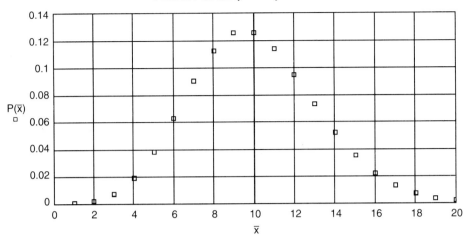

Figure 6-5 The Poisson distribution takes only integers as its argument and so it is shown as such here instead of a continuous curve. This one has a mean of 10.0, its only parameter. The interpretation is that if transactions arrive independently with a negative exponential interarrival time of 0.1 seconds, then the expected number of arrivals in a one second interval is 10.0. The probability of four arrivals in one second is 0.02 as seen above. The Poisson distribution describes the number of customers per hour visiting a cash machine.

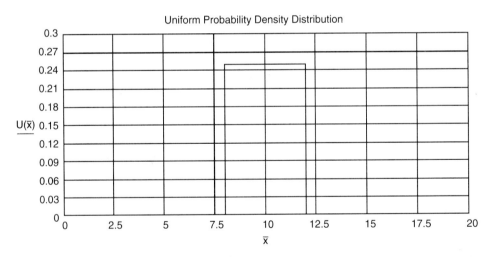

Figure 6-6 The uniform distribution has a constant value over a range of x values. The two parameters are a and b, with a low represented by a and a high represented by b. Here $a = 8$ and $b = 12$. The height is $1/(b-a)$ which keeps the area bounded by the curve exactly 1.0. A fair die is an example of a mechanism for generating discrete uniformly distributed random numbers between $a = 1$ and $b = 6$ with a probability of 1/6. Note that for integer-valued ranges, the correct formula for the probability density is $1/(b-a+1)$.

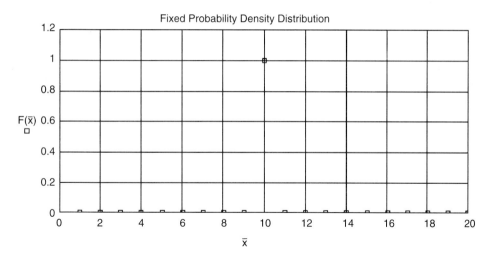

Figure 6-7 The fixed distribution has all of its probability fixed at one $\bar{x}$-value, 10.0 in this case. It is used in cases where arrivals occur at repetitive intervals.

In practice these ideal distributions are only approximated. A series of response time measurements will usually be almost normally distributed or almost exponentially distributed. To determine the statistics it's common to calculate the mean and variance of the data and to plot the density function. If it looks like one of the common distributions and fits the parameters then we know what it is. There are goodness of fit tests that can be conducted; these can be looked up in statistics textbooks.

Generating Random Numbers

A random process can be simulated using the standard uniform random number generator function commonly known as *rnd(x)*, which generates a pseudo-random floating point number between zero and x. Table 6-2 lists common methods to generate other distributions (see also Figures 6-8 to 6-10).

TABLE 6-2 GENERATING SPECIFIC RANDOM NUMBER DISTRIBUTIONS

Distributions	Formula	Comment
uniform between 0 and x	$rnd(x)$	standard library function
uniform between a and b	$a + rnd(b-a)$	uses *rnd* from the standard library
exponential with mean λ	$-\lambda \cdot \ln(rnd(1))$	ln is the standard natural logarithm
normal with mean μ and deviation σ	$\mu + \sigma \cdot \sqrt{-2 \cdot \ln(rnd(1))} \cdot \cos(2 \cdot \pi \cdot rnd(1))$	Box-Muller method

Sec. 6.2   Useful Statistics Distribtuions

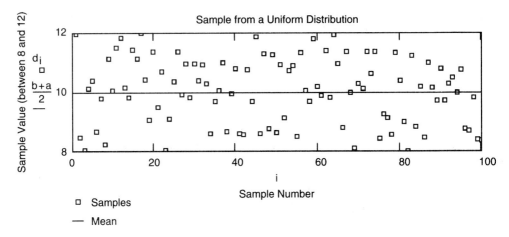

Figure 6-8 One hundred samples from the uniform distribution density function generated using the second formula in Table 6-2. Viewed on edge it is seen that all the samples are spread fairly evenly between $a = 8$ and $b = 12$. But viewed straight-on, the eye picks up patterns in the data, despite the pseudo-randomness.

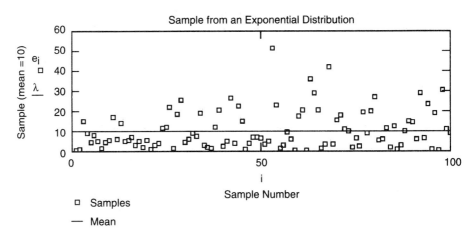

Figure 6-9 One hundred samples generated from the third formula in Table 6-2 show a tendency to cluster near zero. There are a few samples well in excess of the mean as well. The mean is $\lambda = 10$.

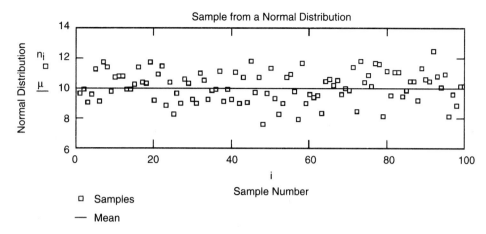

Figure 6-10 One hundred samples from the normal distribution generated using the fourth formula in Table 6-2. The samples tend to cluster about the mean value and most of the values lie within $\pm 3\sigma$ of the mean. Parameters for these samples are $\mu = 10$, $\sigma = 1$.

6.3 EXAMPLES OF STATISTICS DISTRIBUTION IN NETWORKING

Transactions usually arrive with exponential interarrival times. So do keystrokes, file accesses, Email messages at a user mailbox, name lookup requests, Mosaic HyperText lookups, and X-window protocol exchanges.

Fixed interval time network phenomena includes batch mail arrivals (often at 30-minute intervals for UNIX `sendmail`), backups (often at 24-hour intervals), routing protocol updates (every 30 seconds for RIP and every 10 seconds for AppleTalk Routing Table Maintenance Protocol (RTMP), and daily Domain Name System (DNS) zone transfers. Multimedia video and audio traffic over networks consists of steady isochronous packet rates.

Bimodal and multimodal distributions don't fit into the neat categories introduced so far. Bimodal means two common values are favored (there are two peaks in the probability density function). Multimodal means several peaks occur in the density function. Telnet traffic is multimodal because it consists of a great many 64-byte packets consisting of single-character transmissions and ACK packets plus occasional application responses that may vary from short to very long.

6.4 COMBINING STATISTICAL VALUES

Sampling

Samples are often taken from a large population that has a given probability density distribution (see Figure 6-11). In practice this may mean making a certain number of measurements and averaging them out to arrive at a "good" estimate of this distribution.

Now suppose that instead of just one population with uniform statistics there are several from which samples are drawn. The average and standard deviations calculated from these samples will be a composite of the populations samples and they will depend on the

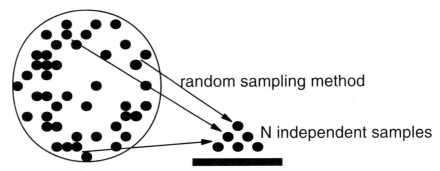

Figure 6-11 To estimate the statistics of the large population it is necessary to take samples that are uncorrelated. Any correlation among the samples will bias the estimates of the mean and standard deviation. If the probability density function is known in advance, then the mean and variance are estimates for the entire population. More samples improve these estimates.

proportions of each population that comprise the samples. The sampling may be done without knowledge that the populations have distinct statistics.

From a network performance point of view, the large population might represent all the transaction response times that could have been measured, and the N independent samples are those that were measured.

Combining Samples

Suppose that $N = 100$ response time measurements are taken and that the transactions are actually a mix of three distinct transactions, t_1, t_2 and t_3, each with its own statistical properties. There are n_1, n_2, and n_3 samples for a total of 100. If the response times can be separated as belonging to one of the three transaction types then the individual transaction statistics can be calculated easily enough. The group samples means are denoted as μ_1, μ_2, and μ_3. To estimate the average response time for each of the three transaction types

$$\mu_1 = \frac{1}{n_1}\sum t_1, \; \mu_2 = \frac{1}{n_2}\sum t_2, \; \mu_3 = \frac{1}{n_3}\sum t_3.$$

Applying the formula for the variance gives us

$$\sigma_1^2 = \frac{1}{n_1 - 1}\sum(\mu_1 - s_1)^2, \; \sigma_2^2 = \frac{1}{n_2 - 1}\sum(\mu_2 - s_2)^2, \; \sigma_3^2 = \frac{1}{n_3 - 1}\sum(\mu_3 - s_3)^2.$$

If the distinctions among the transaction types are unknown or we don't even know that there is a mixture of different transactions in our 100 samples, then a composite statistic can be calculated using all 100 samples

$$\mu = \frac{1}{N}\sum t, \; \sigma^2 = \frac{1}{N-1}\sum(\mu - t)^2$$

which follows the standard definition for mean and variance.

If the transaction means and variances need to be combined afterwards into a composite mean and variance the following method can be used to calculate the mean

$$\mu = \frac{1}{N}(n_1\mu_1 + n_2\mu_2 + n_3\mu_3).$$

In general, whenever independent random variables with distinct statistics are added together, the mean of the sum is the sum of the means. The variance of the sum is the sum of the variances. Taking the above example a step further, consider the sum of three samples $s = s_1 + s_2 + s_3$ taken from three distinct distributions with means μ_1, μ_2, μ_3 and variances $\sigma_1^2, \sigma_2^2, \sigma_3^2$. Accordingly the sum s has a mean value of $\mu_s = \mu_1 + \mu_2 + \mu_3$ and a variance of $\sigma_s^2 = \sigma_1^2 + \sigma_2^2 + \sigma_3^2$. If random variables are subtracted instead of added, the means are likewise subtracted, but the variances are still added.

Now suppose that a linear combination of the three random variables is needed. The new sum is now written as $s + as_1 + bs_2 + cs_3$, where the notation as_1 means to multiply a by s_1. The mean for the new sum is $\mu_s = a\mu_1 + b\mu_2 + c\mu_3$ and the variance is $\sigma_s^2 = a^2\sigma_1^2 + b^2\sigma_2^2 + c^2\sigma_3^2$. The multipliers a, b, and c can be any positive or negative value.

Special Cases

The probability density function of sums, differences, and linear combinations of random samples are generally not the same as the original populations, but there are several special cases worth noting here

- If the samples are taken from a normal distribution, then the resulting sums, differences, and linear combinations are also normally distributed, with the mean and variance given by the formulas above.
- If the samples represent a coming together (or a composite) of independent event streams with Poisson distributions, then the resulting stream of events is also Poisson with a mean equal to sum of the individual means. The resulting interarrival times are still exponential. Note that this procedure is not the same as adding up numbers from a Poisson distribution.
- If a stream of Poisson-distributed events is intercepted such that an event is directed to one stream with probability p and directed to a second stream with probability $1 - p$, then the resulting streams are still Poisson. The first stream's mean is reduced by factor p and the second stream's mean is reduced by factor $1 - p$.
- If enough samples from one or more distributions are averaged, the resulting average is normally distributed. This is the central limit theorem. Note that it does **not** say: *If you take enough samples from a population then its statistics are normally distributed.*

6.5 SPECIFYING THAT 99% OF RESPONSE TIMES ARE LESS THAN 5 SECONDS

Probability Density Functions for Response Time

Speaking statistically, it is not reasonable to insist that the response time for a certain transaction be less than five seconds all of the time. Response time depends on quite a few independent and not so independent components and the probability density function will likely have a long tail. This means that specifying that 99.9% of responses be less that five seconds is a great deal more severe than specifying that 99.0% of responses be less than five seconds.

To see this, consider the plot of the cumulative distribution function for the normal distribution (see Figure 6-12). It's formed by integrating the probability density function (which means adding up the area of the curve as we move to the left and plotting the cumulative area as we go).

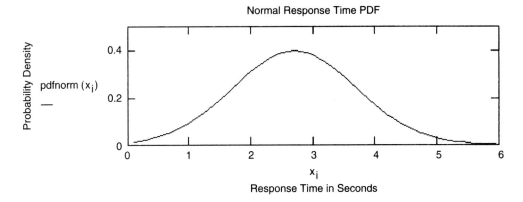

Figure 6-12 Suppose that the response time being measured is normally distributed with a mean $\mu = 2.7$ and standard deviation $\sigma = 1.0$. The probability density function is the familiar bell-shaped curve. There is some probability that the response time exceeds 5.0 seconds because the curve does not touch down at zero at this point. To find the probability that the response time is between 2 and 4 seconds the area under the curve between $x = 2.0$ and $x = 4.0$ is added up.

Tail of the Cumulative Density Function

The plots in Figures 6-13 to 6-15 show close-ups of the tail of the normal probability density function. The tails represent the extreme cases for response time and as such are of great interest to network managers.

The response time probability density function isn't generally known with any degree of confidence. The tail of the distribution has to be accurately known if response time probabilities are calculated from it. Otherwise response time has to be characterized by taking many thousands of independent samples to verify that 99.9% of them are below 5.0 seconds. For example, suppose that 1,000 samples are taken and only one exceeds the 5.0 second threshold. Is that solid evidence the network design meets its objectives? Suppose 10,000 samples are taken and 10 exceed the 5.0 second limit. This is more comforting but if the average value is 1.9 seconds then the trial takes 19,000 seconds (5.3 hours).

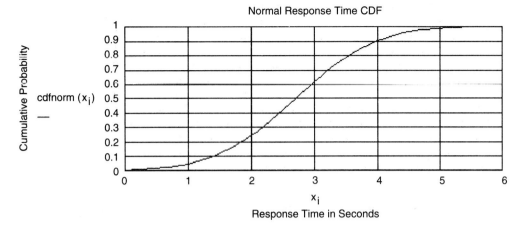

Figure 6-13 The cumulative probability function gives the probability that the response time is less than or equal to the x-value. The probability that the response time is less than 2.7 seconds (the mean) is precisely 0.5, and the probability the response time is less than 4.0 seconds is 0.9.

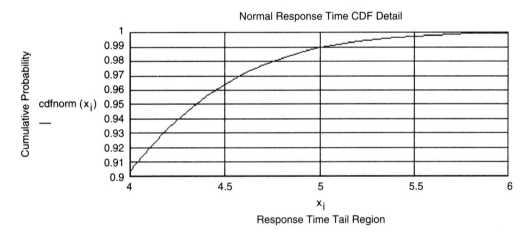

Figure 6-14 A close-up of the cumulative probability function near the tail of the distribution reveals that the response time will be under 5.0 seconds 99% of the time.

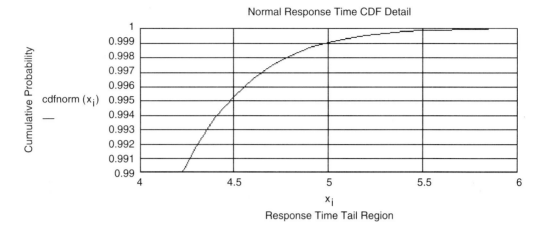

Figure 6-15 Suppose that specifications require the response time be less than 5.0 seconds 99.9% of the time. This plot is for the tail of a normal distribution with $\mu = 1.9$, $\sigma = 1.0$. It will be necessary to make adjustments to our network, client, and server to reduce the average response time below the original 2.7 seconds in order to meet this more severe specification. It is necessary to know the probability distribution of the response time statistics to confidently plot out the tail area.

6.6 USING ping OUTPUT STATISTICS TO CHARACTERIZE NETWORK PERFORMANCE

The `ping` command measures the network round-trip time of a loopback packet between the transmitter node and a remote node (see Figure 6-16). Recall that the UNIX `ping` command returns the following information

- total number of packets sent
- number of packets dropped
- minimum round-trip time
- average round-trip time
- the round-trip time of each packet
- maximum round-trip time
- which packets were dropped
- size of the echo packet

Here's how to create a response time plot with Lotus 1-2-3. First, recall that the output of the `ping` command looks like this

```
64 bytes from 15.4.2.1: icmp_seq =0. time = 169. ms
```

Next, separate the sequence numbers and the round-trip time. The following UNIX command will do

```
awk -F = '{print $3}' < pingtime.txt | sed 's/[a-z]//g' > pingcsv.txt
```

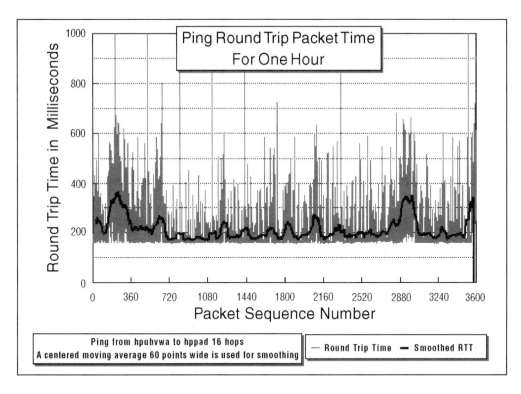

Figure 6-16 This is a real 3,600-second sample from the `ping` command on HP's network going between Bellevue, Washington, and Waterloo, Ontario, nine hops in all. Note that the 60-second moving average calculated from the data shows a distinct tendency for the response time average value to shift slowly up and down during the hour. The hour-long average reported by `ping` is not very representative of network response time but the one-minute average is. The hour-long average value for the round-trip time is 216.869 seconds and the standard deviation is 106.203 seconds.

Packets dropped should be located in `ping`'s verbose output and correlated with large round-trip times. In an IP network the time to live (TTL) field in each packet (the maximum is 255 seconds) is reduced by at least one by every router that forwards it. If the field goes to zero the packet is discarded and the originator is sent an ICMP message to that effect. See RFC 791. Packets may also be dropped by routers due to congestion. The distribution of the `ping` response times in the previous example is very informative (see Figures 6-17 and 6-18).

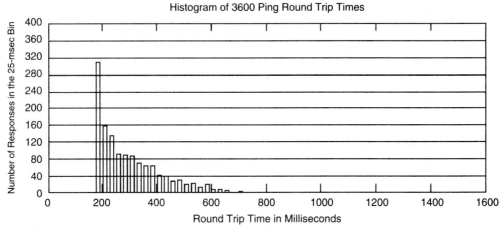

Figure 6-17 The same 3,600 `ping` round-trip times are shown sorted into 25-millisecond wide-bins to form a probability density histogram. The smallest round-trip time is 158 milliseconds and the largest is 1,438 milliseconds. The histogram clearly shows that most round-trip times are less than 700 milliseconds.

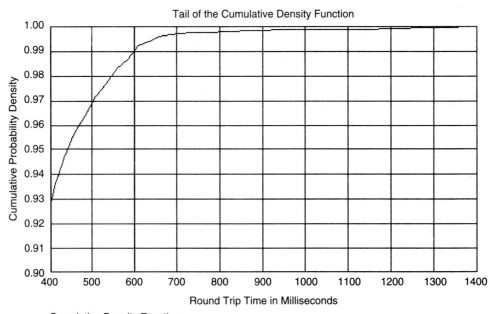

Figure 6-18 The same 3,600 round-trip time cumulative probability density function showing the details at the tail of the distribution. The 99th percentile is at 600 milliseconds.

122 Network Statistics 101: The Essentials Chap. 6

6.7 TREND ANALYSIS: PREDICTING FUTURE PERFORMANCE FROM PAST MEASUREMENTS

Linear Regression of Peak Performance Data

The most time-honored forecasting method is to plot the existing data, lay a straight-edge on it, draw a line through the points and extrapolate upwards and to the right. Since the data may be noisy, regression analysis is often used to find the best line through the points. This line minimizes the sum of the squared errors between the measured data and the line. The method can be extended to fit parabolas and other functions to the data in an effort to improve the goodness of the fit (see Figures 6-19 and 6-20).

High Water Mark Trending

Now consider a few month's worth of hourly line utilization data (synthesized) and a traffic forecast is required. Another predictive approach is outlined in these steps

- Plot the hourly line utilization data, which often looks cyclic or periodic.
- Trace the high-water mark from left to right, creating a monotonically increasing line.
- Fit a line to this monotone using regression analysis.
- Project this line out to predict future peak line utilization.

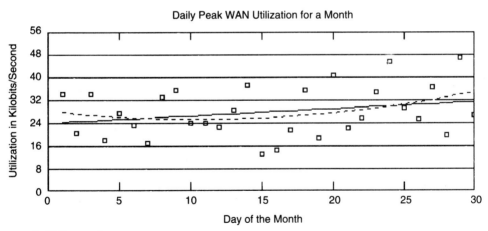

Figure 6-19 Predicting the trend in this one-month sample of WAN utilization data using a straight line and a parabola. As expected the linear fit is upwards and to the right—slightly. The parabolic fit suggests that the traffic actually dips slightly near the middle of the month. Frankly this data is too variable to predict its future trends. The actual data is synthesized using the formula $y = 0.5x + 5 + rnd(30)$ where y is the utilization in kilobits per second, x is the day of the month and $rnd(30)$ is noise.

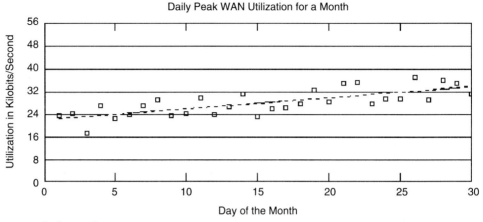

Figure 6-20 The same curve-fitting algorithm used on data generated by the formula $y = 0.5x + 15 + rnd(10)$. The positive trend in the underlying data is the same (0.5 kilobits per second per day increase in traffic) but the reduced noise allows a far better forecast. The parabolic fit is so close to the linear fit as to be indistinguishable in the graph. The data and the calculations to generate the above figures were done in Mathcad from Mathsoft.

To calculate the best line through a set of points, set up the following sequence of calculations

$(x_1, y_1), (x_2, y_2), ..., (x_n, y_n)$ the set of sample points to be trended

$\mu_x = \frac{1}{n} \sum x_i$ average of the x-values

$\mu_y = \frac{1}{n} \sum y_i$ average of the y-values

$\sigma^2 = \frac{1}{n-1} \sum (y_i - \mu_y)^2$ variance of the y-values

$b = \frac{\sum (x_i - \mu_x)(y_i - \mu_y)}{\sum (x_i - \mu_x)^2}$ y-axis intercept of the regression line

$a = \mu_y - b\mu_x$ slope of the regression line

$y = ax + b$ equation of the regression line

$\sigma_y^2 = \sigma^2 \left[\frac{1}{n} + \frac{(x - \mu_x)^2}{\sum (x_i - \mu_x)^2} \right]$ variance of y given x in the regression formula

The extrapolated line is subject to uncertainty, as shown in Figure 6-21.

In Figures 6-22 to 6-24, Mathcad Algebra was used to simulate line utilization data and make a six-month forecast.

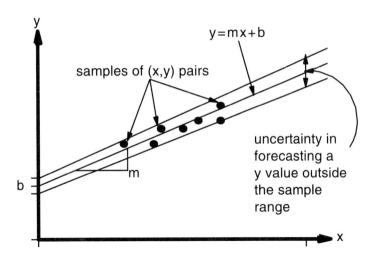

Figure 6-21 Plugging the (x, y) pairs into the regression formulas and superimposing the resulting regression line puts the quality of this method as a forecasting tool into perspective. Since the slope *m* and the intercept *b* are subject to statistical uncertainty, the resulting regression line can vary as shown here. The further to the right the extrapolation is done the greater the uncertainty in the estimate.

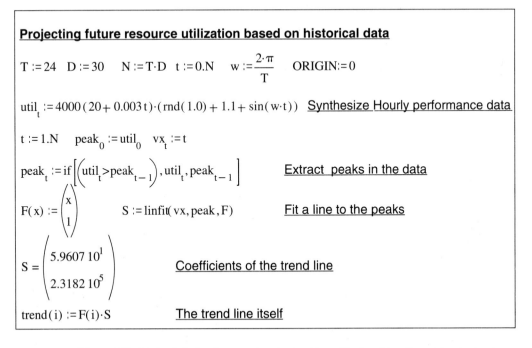

Figure 6-22 Mathcad algebra for generating simulated line utilization data with predetermined periodicity, amplitude growth rate, and random noise. Data generated by this method is reviewed Figures 6-23 and 6-24 from a forecasting perspective.

Sec. 6.7   Trend Analysis: Predicting Future Performance   125

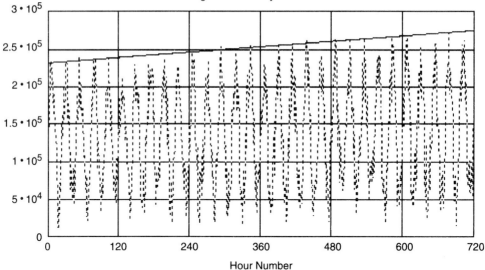

Figure 6-23 Artificially generated line utilization data consists of uniformly distributed random noise added to a slightly increasing sinusoidal signal with a 24-hour period, as seen in the dashed-line data. The line above the data depicts the best line to the envelope of the peaks.

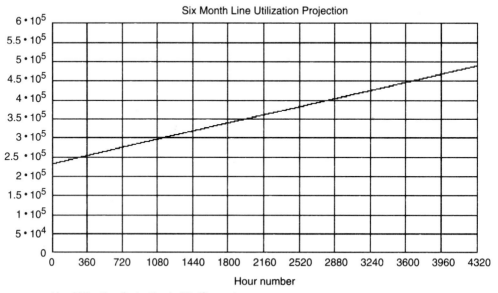

Figure 6-24 This is the same trend line as in Figure 6-23 but projected out six months. The future need to accommodate 512,000 bits per second peaks is now apparent.

Forecasting by Tracking PDFs and Weekly Averages

Another way to forecast network loading is to collect several weeks worth of (say) hourly utilization data and average the 24-hour data for each of the seven days of the week. Plotting this data reveals a more consistent daily traffic pattern. Repeating this method every few months allows more accurate trending because the daily trends are smoothed (see Figures 6-25 to 6-27).

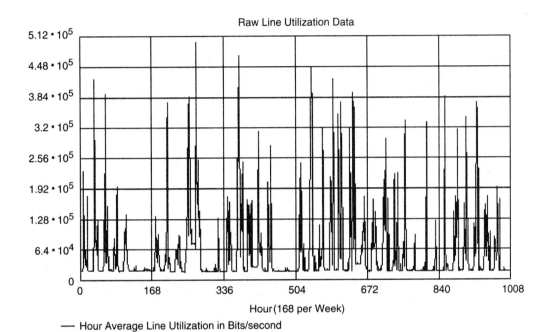

— Hour Average Line Utilization in Bits/second

Figure 6-25 Hourly line utilization data for a six-week period. Note this format makes it hard to see any specific pattern in the daily or weekly trend and attempting to draw a regression line through such data isn't going to result in an accurate forecast.

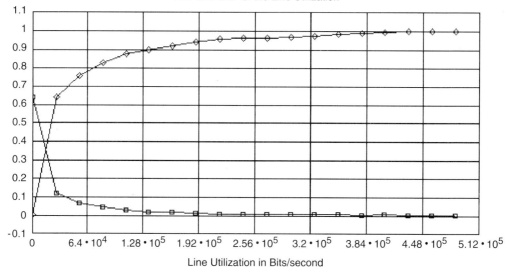

Figure 6-26 The same daily utilization data viewed as probability density functions. Note that 90% of the time the circuit utilization is 128,000 bits per second or less. By taking this same snapshot in another six weeks the network administrator can compare 90% points to see if line usage has increased significantly.

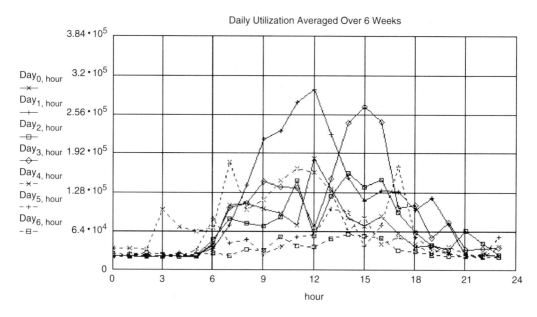

Figure 6-27 The same line utilization data viewed as daily hourly averages. We see that day 1 and day 3 are the highest use days. Repeating the graphing process at six-week intervals will reveal daily trends.

7

Predicting Average Values for Response Time and Throughput

7.0 INTRODUCTION

We can predict network response time and throughput based on first principles instead of depending on live measurements from a benchmark or live network. We calculate the time taken to copy a document through a frame relay network, the response time for telnet users over a WAN, and the impact of multiple WAN hops on response time. Predicting performance from first principles and getting good results requires an understanding of the underlying protocols. Finally we untangle the relationship between response time and throughput.

7.1 DOCUMENT RETRIEVAL OVER A FRAME RELAY NETWORK

Suppose that an 800-Kbyte file has to be copied from a file server at the hub site to a workstation at a spoke site, across a frame relay network as shown in Figure 7-1. An initial stab at sizing the links has the hub site port speed at 1.544 Kbps and the spoke site port speed at 56 Kbps. Will the document be available quickly enough? Let's vary the hub port speed to determine how it impacts response time.

The spreadsheet in Table 7-1 (graphically represented in Figure 7-2) calculates how much user data is transmitted per frame and how long it takes for the data frame to reach the client and for the acknowledgment frame to reach the server. This per-frame delay is multiplied by the number of such exchanges it will take to send the entire document.

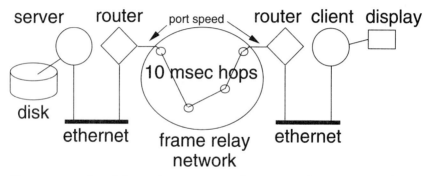

Document retrieval across a frame relay network

Figure 7-1 This is the network topology used to calculate the average document retrieval time. The network delays at the Ethernets, the frame relay access ports, and the internal frame relay cloud hops are used to calculate the time delays for data and acknowledgment packets. The client and server delays are budgeted for as well.

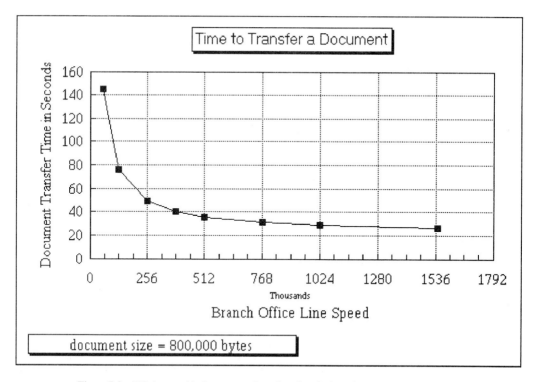

Figure 7-2 This is a graphical representation taken directly from the spreadsheet above. It shows that document transfer time drops rapidly as the port speed at the spoke office increases. If it is a requirement that the document be transferred in less than one minute, then a port speed of 256 Kbps is called for. Port speeds over 512 Kbps don't provide much improvement.

TABLE 7-1 DETAILED CALCULATION FOR DOCUMENT RETRIEVAL TIMES

User data	1,460	1,460	1,460	1,460	1,460	1,460	1,460	1,460
TCP/IP header	40	40	40	40	40	40	40	40
Datagram	1,500	1,500	1,500	1,500	1,500	1,500	1,500	1,500
MAC header	18	18	18	18	18	18	18	18
HDLC header	6	6	6	6	6	6	6	6
Ethernet frame	1,518	1,518	1,518	1,518	1,518	1,518	1,518	1,518
WAN frame	1,506	1,506	1,506	1,506	1,506	1,506	1,506	1,506
TCP ACK	40	40	40	40	40	40	40	40
TCP ACK on Ethernet	58	58	58	58	58	58	58	58
TCP ACK on WAN	46	46	46	46	46	46	46	46
Frame relay network delay	0.01	0.01	0.01	0.01	0.01	0.01	0.01	0.01
Ethernet speed	10,000,000	10,000,000	10,000,000	10,000,000	10,000,000	10,000,000	10,000,000	10,000,000
Spoke office line speed	56,000	128,000	256,000	384,000	512,000	768,000	1,024,000	1,544,000
Hub office line speed	1,544,000	1,544,000	1,544,000	1,544,000	1,544,000	1,544,000	1,544,000	1,544,000
Time budget								
Spoke office LAN	0.001214	0.001214	0.001214	0.001214	0.001214	0.001214	0.001214	0.001214
Spoke DS0 line	0.216857	0.094875	0.047438	0.031625	0.023719	0.015813	0.011859	0.007865
Network delay	0.01	0.01	0.01	0.01	0.01	0.01	0.01	0.01
Hub T-1 delay	0.007803	0.007803	0.007803	0.007803	0.007803	0.007803	0.007803	0.007803
Hub Ethernet	0.001214	0.001214	0.001214	0.001214	0.001214	0.001214	0.001214	0.001214
Server response time	0.01	0.01	0.01	0.01	0.01	0.01	0.01	0.01
ACK on Ethernet	0.000046	0.000046	0.000046	0.000046	0.000046	0.000046	0.000046	0.000046
ACK on Hub T-1	0.000238	0.000238	0.000238	0.000238	0.000238	0.000238	0.000238	0.000238
Network delay	0.01	0.01	0.01	0.01	0.01	0.01	0.01	0.01
ACK on DS0 line	0.006571	0.0002875	0.001438	0.000958	0.000719	0.000479	0.000359	0.000238
ACK on branch LAN	0.000046	0.000046	0.000046	0.000046	0.000046	0.000046	0.000046	0.000046
Total delay per packet =	0.263992	0.138313	0.089438	0.073146	0.065001	0.056855	0.052782	0.048667
Total data bytes to send	800,000	800,000	800,000	800,000	800,000	800,000	800,000	800,000
Time to send data (sec)	144.652944	75.787973	49.007151	40.08021	35.61674	31.15327	28.921535	26.666673
Spoke office line speed	56,000	128,000	256,000	384,000	512,000	768,000	1,024,000	1,544,000

The frame relay delay is fixed at 0.01 seconds, corresponding to one average hop. This is an assumption. If the frame relay service provider is able to indicate the number of hops, the line speed for each hop, the switching latency at each hop, and a degrading factor to allow for other traffic, then a better estimate can be placed in the spreadsheet. CIR, burst rate, and packet loss issues are ignored in this analysis. Simulation methods are suited for this level of detail.

The calculation assumes that the client TCP window size is 1,460 bytes. This prevents streaming and it's done to conserve precious low-memory RAM in PC architectures limited to 640/1,024 Kbytes of base memory.

7.2 RESPONSE TIME FOR TELNET USERS ON A 56 KBPS WAN

To calculate the response time of a telnet connection over a WAN link one begins with a review of the basic character-by-character protocol. Every time the user strikes a key, the character is wrapped in a TCP/IP frame and sent to the remote application. The application echoes the character at once, and the packet usually contains the TCP ACK for the original packet. The client receives the echo and sends a final TCP ACK to complete the handshake (which the user does not notice and which does not contribute to the response time calculation).

The packet sizes have to be calculated. The one-character payload is accompanied by a 40-byte TCP/IP header for a 41-byte total. When sent on the Ethernet the frame will be padded to its minimum of 64 bytes. On the wide area network, the HDLC encapsulation will add 6 bytes for a 47-byte frame. The potential increase in frame size due to bit stuffing (the process that inserts bits into the data to prevent it from being interpreted as a flag character) is ignored. Estimates for router latency and client/server side delays are included in the calculation in Table 7-2.

TABLE 7-2 RESPONSE TIME OF A TELNET CONNECTION ON A WAN

Forward direction	Client side			
	Description	Frame size	Media speed	Delay
	Ethernet	64	10,000,000	0.000051
	HDLC	47	56,000	0.006714
	Router latency			0.00001
	Client delay			0.0001
Reverse direction	Server side			
	Description	Frame size	Media speed	Delay
	Ethernet	64	10,000,000	0.000051
	HDLC	47	56,000	0.006714
	Router latency			0.00001
	Application delay			0.0001
Round-trip total			End-to-End Delay =	0.013751

The response time calculation above shows that a 56 Kbps link can provide excellent response time (0.013751 seconds) provided no other traffic is using the line. Note that after hitting the ENTER key, the application normally executes some code, performs some disk I/O, and returns several lines of output carried in a single packet.

To estimate throughput, suppose that a typist enters ten keystrokes per second. This is about the same rate as an auto-repeating key held down by the user, say the space bar. The line utilization is $\frac{10 \cdot 47 \cdot 8}{56,000} \cdot 100 = 6.7\%$ in both forward and reverse directions on the WAN circuit.

For situations employing other serial line types, such as frame relay, X.25, or PPP/SLIP, the appropriate frame header overhead and line speeds should be substituted in the calculation.

7.3 THE EFFECT OF MULTIPLE WAN HOPS ON RESPONSE TIME

Calculating response time for multiple WAN hops follows the same method as used in the previous section, repeating the delay calculation for each hop independently and adding up all the forward and reverse hop delays to get the end-to-end delay. The spreadsheet gets longer but the basic arithmetic is repeated for each hop. Obviously the more hops the longer the delay will be, and one of the hops may cause the dominant delay if the line speed is relatively small.

If a transaction involves the exchange of several packet pairs, then the response time calculation should be repeated for each such pair and the results added together.

To improve accuracy, the calculation should take into account any protocol header overhead and network layer fragmentation. If the application presents 8,192 bytes of data, the transport and network layers will add headers and the network layer will fragment the data to accommodate the physical layer. The result will more bytes of data than 8,192 and several packets will follow each other back-to-back between the source and destination systems.

7.4 RESPONSE TIME VS. THROUGHPUT ISSUES: THE NETWORK ROUND-TRIP TIME

Keeping the Network Pipe Full

Response time is the interval between the start of the client request (like a user hitting the ENTER key) and the end of the server reply. The network round trip time is like the response time for a single packet exchange. The bigger the packets the more data that can be moved. Hence the formula

$$throughput \sim \frac{data\_segment\_size}{network\_roundtrip\_time}.$$

Network protocols that have small packet sizes will generally deliver less throughput than protocols with large packet sizes. Thus one would expect that the AppleTalk Filing Protocol would not perform as well as the Network File System (NFS).

Streaming-capable transports like TCP can be tuned to "fill the pipe," meaning that they can continue to send data into the network before an ACK is returned. This is usually accomplished by providing a transport window wide enough to accommodate this much data. This is especially important when the network round-trip time is very long, such as that offered by a satellite in geosynchronous orbit (22,300 miles up). Data from very small aperture terminal (VSAT) endures two hops to get to the end system and any response endures two hops to get back. Four hops of 22,300 miles each at 186,000 miles per second represents a round-trip time of 480 milliseconds. Even a common terrestrial cross-country WAN circuit of 3,000 miles suffers a 32 millisecond round-trip time based on the speed of light. This is an optimistic estimate because the velocity factor of data transmission cable is perhaps 0.66 and the service provider's channel banks probably add more delays as they multiplex and demultiplex channels of data.

Note that streaming protocols suffer performance degradation when they have to restart after recovering from a time-out due to a lost packet. The network "pipe" drains during the time-out interval and it has to be refilled. Good transports like TCP will execute a "slow-start" algorithm when retransmitting dropped data. This means it will send just one packet at first, wait for the ACK, then send two, wait for the ACK, and so on until full streaming into the receiver's window is achieved.

NFS Response Time and Throughput

Benchmark data is often measured in transactions per second and specmanship by vendors is alive and well in the absence of industry standards. For example, the performance of an NFS server can be measured using the Laddis benchmark, which specifies a mixture of NFS I/O operations (NFS IOPS). The throughput of the NFS server increases with the workload as expected, and when the average response time equals 50 milliseconds, the throughput is considered the Laddis performance metric for that server (see Figure 7-3). The file server can doubtless be pressed to deliver more NFS IOPS, but response time would increase above 50 milliseconds.

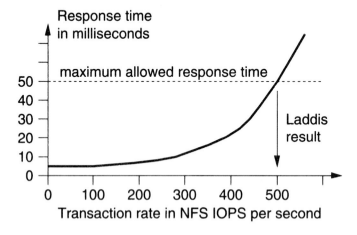

Figure 7-3 The Laddis NFS benchmark attempts to standardize NFS server performance transaction rates by referencing a maximum response time of 50 milliseconds. In general, response time increases as the transaction rate increases in any system. It is appropriate to determine some maximum acceptable response time for a system and measure its transaction throughput at this point.

8

Worst-Case Analysis

8.0 INTRODUCTION

After studying the statistics chapter the inescapable conclusion is that the average response time and throughput of a network don't tell the whole story. Because of the normal variability in the applied traffic we can't just design the network for the average case. Depending on the statistical distribution, perhaps half of the response times exceed the average, implying that fully half of our users get unacceptable response time. To get a better design point, let's consider methods for obtaining a worst-case design.

Applying measurement data from the network's busy hour instead of the average hour works well. So does taking data at especially busy times of the year, such as the end of the financial quarter. Knowing where fully utilized resources might impact performance is a plus. So does estimating the maximum number of concurrent users sensibly, as opposed to the average number of users. It is not usually sensible to assume that all users are active at one time. An interesting scenario worth looking at is when all users request service at the same time. A sanity check is to compare the worst case with the best case to see how much they differ.

Since a worst-case design may effect the choice of the LAN medium, we have a quick look at an Ethernet versus FDDI solution to a small server farm, waxing philosophically about routers-based solutions in the process.

8.1 ANALYZING THE BUSY HOUR

Collecting the Necessary Performance Data

Performance analysis requires us to make conservative traffic estimates, so busy hour measurements should be taken to characterize traffic so that the subsequent network design will operate under all required conditions. The more busy hour measurements that are available, the better the traffic estimates will be. Here is a list of some traffic operational performance metrics

- maximum packet rate
- peak media utilization
- maximum number of users
- average packet size
- packet size distribution
- number of concurrent transport connections
- number of transactions
- number of packets per transaction

These performance data should be cast into three core parameters used in later analysis

- λ, the average arrival rate of transactions submitted by one user
- μ, the average processing rate of transactions by the system/network
- N, the average number of active users

Analyzing a Closed System

The absolute worst case analysis begins with the assumption that the total number of active users is fixed in the system. A user thinks for some average interval $1/\lambda$ and submits a transaction, which enters a queue. There may be up to $N - 1$ transaction requests ahead of this user's request, and since the average transaction takes $1/\mu$ seconds, our user may have to wait an average of N/μ seconds for a response. This model also assumes that the user will patiently wait for a response, enter a thinking period averaging $1/\lambda$ seconds, and then submit another transaction. We ignore the possibility that user will abandon a transaction or balk at waiting for a response.

Worst-case analysis is performed to ensure that the network design is able to provide connectivity services under all anticipated traffic conditions. A design point has to be determined to which the network will be built. The network is mission critical for most organizations.

While lives and employee safety may not depend on its correct operation, perhaps the network should be designed with the same philosophy as the design of bridges, buildings, and spacecraft. Bridges are designed to operate when it's very windy, the earth is quaking, and traffic is parked in all lanes in both directions. Buildings too have to sustain winds, earthquakes, furniture, equipment, supplies, staff, and visitors. U.S. spacecraft are also designed with high safety margins.

Let's review the worst-case approach (Figures 8-1 to 8-3).

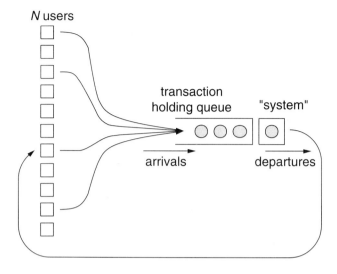

Figure 8-1 Topology for the worst-case analysis of a closed system. It consists of exactly N active users generating transactions and patiently waiting for a response, thinking a while, and submitting another transaction.

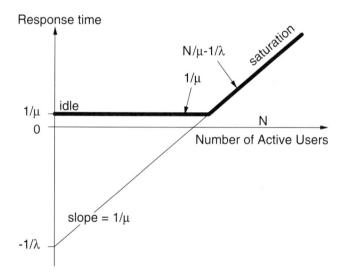

Figure 8-2 Basic graphical analysis for a closed system's response time. Construct a line with a y-axis intercept of $-1/\lambda$ and a slope of $1/\mu$. Also construct a horizontal line at a height of $1/\mu$. As seen here, the area above these two lines contains the possible response time solution. Experience shows that the worst-case response time follows these two lines or remains just above it, and for high transaction rates, response time lies in the saturation region shown.

The behavior of a closed system differs markedly from an open system. In a closed system, there are a fixed number of users. They wait for a response before submitting another transaction and this slows them down. The closed system most closely resembles reality because real users are indeed in fixed supply. For an N-user network, the queue needs to hold only N transactions.

Sec. 8.1 Analyzing the Busy Hour

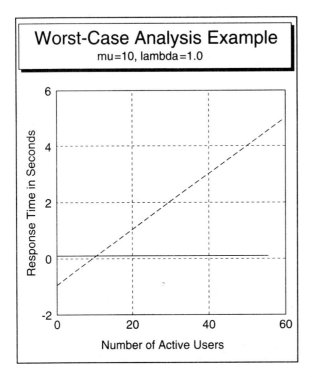

Figure 8-3 This is a numerical example created using Lotus 1-2-3 and it's very helpful for visualizing solutions for a worst-case analysis. Here is network capable of handling $\mu = 10$ transactions per second with users thinking on average $1/\lambda = 1.0$ seconds. The graphics constructions lines have been left in place for clarity. This is a classic curve that applies to computer systems and networks alike. Any closed resource system in saturation shows a linear increase in response time.

Analysis of an Open System

In an open system, the transaction arrivals are independent of the state of the system. Transactions arrive regardless of the number of outstanding transactions, as if the number of users is infinite. Under such conditions the transaction holding queue has to be quite large, and in practice this queue will overflow if the average arrival rate of transactions exceeds the average processing rate of the network. The open system behaves like a simple queuing system.

For single-server queues with a transaction arrival rate of λ and a service rate of μ the average wait time in the queue is given by $1/(\mu - \lambda)$ and it is clear from this formula that the network becomes unstable when the arrival rate exceeds the service rate. When the transaction arrival rate approaches the service rate, the delays can become very long. If the network more closely resembles an open system (an infinite user base) then busy hour statistics may be applied to an open queuing model. See Chapter 9 on queuing theory for details about this method.

8.2 NETWORK BEHAVIOR ON THE LAST DAY OF THE BUSINESS FINANCIAL QUARTER

A needs analysis is done to determine the traffic loading on a network. It has to account for that special time when businesses close out a fiscal period, such a calendar quarter. Here is a list of changes that occur during this time period, which may last perhaps a week:

- The type of workload changes:
  - More users are active.
  - Occasional users are now continuously active.
  - Transaction mixtures change.
  - New transactions are run.

- More happens:
  - Management reports are generated daily instead of weekly.
  - Customer orders increase in number and size.
  - Number of product quotations increases.
  - Commission checks are larger.
  - Network printing increases.
  - Email correspondence rises.
  - Factory-to-field correspondence goes way up.

8.3 BEHAVIOR OF FULLY UTILIZED RESOURCES

Earlier, the behavior of open and closed systems was discussed in terms of how response time depends on the offered transaction rate. In practice, the size of the transaction queue is limited so that arriving transactions are turned away and discarded. Indeed, for open systems such as routers, it behooves the network manager to limit the size of outbound packet queues on low-speed lines to prevent excessive end-to-end delays.

Resources in Tandem

As long as the network is well behaved, saturation conditions do not result in breakdowns and disconnects. The average response time simply increases linearly with the demand. Real networks always have more than a single resource that transactions utilize. Data usually traverses LANs, routers, WANs, and servers; each is a resource and each may be subject to saturation (see Figures 8-4 and 8-5 and Table 8-1).

Detecting Overloads Operationally

Excess demand is the amount of traffic that pushes the response time up the linear portion of the curve. Queues form under these conditions and queues are easy to measure

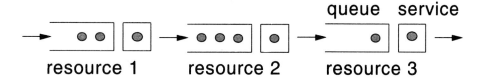

Figure 8-4 An example of three tandem resources that packets must pass through. Here, resource 2 will saturate first, then resource 1, and finally resource 3. Note that resource queue capacities may be limited and overflow packets may be discarded. If a resource queue is full, it may actually prevent the previous resource from functioning as well.

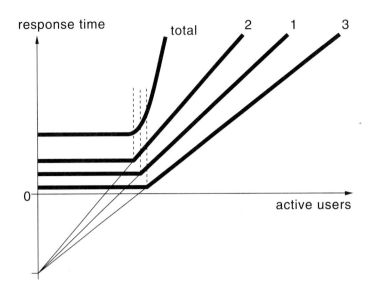

Figure 8-5 The relationship between three tandem resources forming a closed system, and the impact on response time. The individual response time curves are shown superimposed. The total response time of a transaction passing through these three resources is the sum of the individual response times. In a steady-state tandem system the transaction rate through each resource is identical, hence the three curves intersect at the y-axis. The important point of this graphic is how the slope of the response time increases each time a new bottleneck saturates. Note that simply summing up the response time curves is *not* an accurate solution to a tandem queue problem. The actual response time will lie above the curve.

TABLE 8-1 SOME NETWORK RESOURCES AND HOW THEY BEHAVE UNDER SATURATION

Resource	Behavior under congestion
Router, bridge, switch	Drops packets using some algorithm; may send a source quench packet.
Application server RAM	Program data spaces are swapped in/out of disk.
LAN adapter RAM	Driver returns an error to the network layer, forcing buffering in RAM.
Diskless node RAM	Applications spawning stops or swapping to a network disk begins.
Ethernet	Collisions force devices to reduce the offered traffic rate.
TCP receive buffer	The flow control sliding window closes, forcing the transmitter to wait.
Disk I/O rate	RAM queues form behind the disk driver, forcing some apps to wait.

operationally using SNMP. In subsequent sections we see how techniques based on queuing theory and simulation methods can be adopted to correlate real-time SNMP data with actual response time.

Response times achieved when resources are fully utilized often increase markedly if transport timers expire. Timers may expire if packets are discarded or if response times become excessive. The above analysis does not apply when transport data recovery algorithms kick in.

8.4 MAXIMUM OF NUMBER OF CONCURRENT USERS

One problem network managers face is how to characterize users. Some are active, some are logged on but drinking coffee, and the rest are inactive. Of those active, some are heads-down in-a-hurry types, others poke a few keys every few minutes and still others engage in bursts of high activity followed by periods of inactivity. The truncated exponential distribution applies to these users. How many concurrent users can the network support, then, given this mix?

Defining User Characteristics

See Figure 8-6.

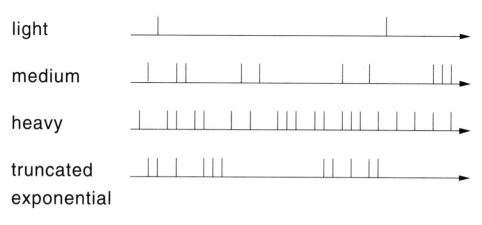

Figure 8-6 Categories for different user types based on volume of traffic they generate seems most convenient. Light users count as 1/10 of a user, medium users count as 1/2 a user, and heavy users are 9/10 of a user. The truncated exponential distribution allows a user to be active some of the time and take a coffee break the rest of the time. The duty factor is the fraction of time they're active. The baseline traffic the standard user generates is determined by benchmarking a mad user performing work as fast as humanly possible.

Figuring Maximum Active User Counts Statistically

Dealing with the duty factor of users who fit the truncated exponential distribution is an exercise in statistics. How many active users do we figure on when the duty factor of 5 users is 1/3? A worst-case analysis requires we assume all 5 users are active at once, not such an awful overestimate over 5/3 = 2 users an average analysis suggests. What about 100 such users? A worst case analysis supposes that all 100 users have coincident work periods. An average analysis presumes that 100 users times the 1/3 duty factor is 33 effective users. The analysis, predicated on the assumption that all users' work habits are independent and uncorrelated, is shown mathematically in Figure 8-7 and graphically in Figures 8-8 and 8-9.

$$p := \frac{1}{3}$$

Duty factor (probability the user is active)

$$q := 1 - p$$

Probability the user is idle

$$N := 100$$

Total number of such users being considered

$$C(n, N) := \frac{N!}{n! \cdot (N - n)!}$$

Number of combinations of n active users and (N-n) inactive users

$$P(n) := C(n, N) \cdot p^n \cdot q^{N-n}$$

Probability that exactly n users are active out of N

$$CDF(n) := \sum_{i=0}^{n} P(i)$$

Probability that less than or equal to n users are active at one time, also called the cumulative density function

$$n := 0 .. N$$

Iterated variable used for plotting purposes

Figure 8-7 The above formulas are more meaningful when viewed graphically. The intent is to figure out a reasonable worst-case user count, one that can be justified statistically based on the PDF for active users. The key here is that the user population is big enough that the statistics of large numbers favors us. The probability density function is almost normal for large user counts.

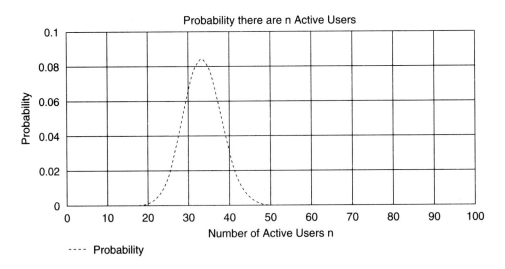

Figure 8-8 For 100 independent users that are active one-third of the time, this is the probability density function, with the expected maximum at 33 users. From this graph we see that there is virtually no probability that less than 20 users or more than 50 users are actually on line at the same time, so 50 seems an excellent worst-case design point.

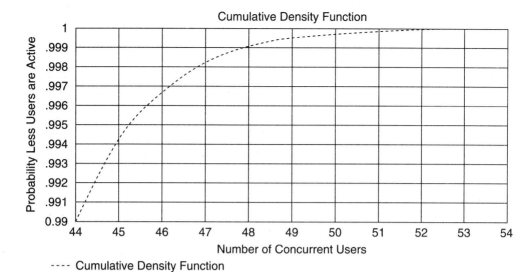

Figure 8-9 The cumulative probability density function showing the chance that less than or equal to n users out of 100 are active at one time when they are habitually on-line 1/3 of the time. This close-up view of the CDF shows that 99% of the time not more than 44 users are active, 99.9% of the time not more than 48 users are active, and about 99.99% of the time not more than 52 users are active. This supports the network planner in designing the network for 52 active users.

Effective Active User Count via Spreadsheet Method

For users who are on-line all the time, less mathematics is necessary. Given data about user counts and categories, it is simple to construct a spreadsheet to compute the total number of effective users (see Table 8-2).

TABLE 8-2 CALCULATING THE NUMBER OF EFFECTIVE USERS

User count	Traffic factor	Effective users	Comments
100	0	0	Inactive users
100	0.1	10	Occasional users
50	0.5	25	Medium users
20	0.9	18	Heads-down users
270			Total user population
		53	**Total effective active users**

8.5 When Everybody Hits the ENTER Key at Once: Multiple Concurrent Requests

When every user submits a request concurrently, all queues are suddenly filled at the maximum possible rate. For multiuser application servers, each user I/O request will be satisfied as fast as the operating system I/O processor can do so (subject to the speed of the CPU), often in a round robin fashion. A high-intensity brief pedestal in the CPU usage will be observed. Next, a rush of packets will be sent out on the network. For a token ring, the target token rotation timer (TTRT) and the existing traffic load will determine the delay before the packet rush can be transmitted. For Ethernet, the usual CSMA/CD rules will allow rapid transmission of the packet rush. Once at the wide area network, the packets will queue in the router buffer area waiting their turn for the thin wire (see Figure 8-10).

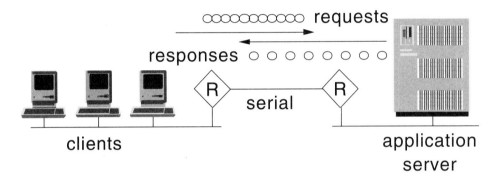

Figure 8-10 When a large number of concurrent client requests are generated, the LAN, WAN, and server briefly enter a fully utilized state. The responses are returned as fast as possible but they will be spread apart in time as shown here.

Given that the networks and systems spread out the request packets in time, users will receive their responses in a pseudo-random order. Suppose that 100 users are waiting for a response, that no packets are lost, and that each response averages 1/10 second. After hitting ENTER, a user's response might be the first to come back, the last to come back, or anywhere in between with equal probability. The response time will be uniformly distributed between 1/10 and 10 seconds, averaging nearly 5 seconds.

8.6 COMPARING THE WORST CASE WITH THE BEST CASE

Benchmarking a networked application might be done with just one user or with a great many users at once. The single-user case should result in superb response time and does not stress the network at all. There are few collisions on the Ethernet, the token rotates quickly on the token ring, there are no queue delays and transients, no congestion or retransmissions. The multiuser case will generate queues and transients, cause congestion, and probably encourage retransmissions.

Results Based on Stress Testing

For purposes of stress testing a networked application, it is generally appropriate to increase the number of active users in steps and record the response times of all transactions. The numbers can then be plotted along with the percentiles of interest, such as 90% and 99%. The effort required to collect this data is great. The network configuration, the server size, the user terminals, and the users themselves have to be provisioned and tied up for days while sufficient transactions are generated to collect meaningful results. If 99th percentile points are desired, then at least 500 transactions must be generated to produce statistically meaningful results. This approach is essential if firm evidence is the only acceptable proof of performance.

Traffic traces made under these conditions are self-contaminated. Packets from other concurrent transactions alter the timing of the one being measured on the LAN, the WAN, and the server. It is no easy matter to correct for these timing changes, especially for variable queuing delays and additional transport retransmissions. Stress testing does give good worst-case results against which a mathematical performance analysis can be checked.

This makes a case for benchmarking with a single user on a quiet LAN, WAN, and server. Statistics derived from such a pure packet trace can be used directly in statistical and in simulation methods for predicting performance for whatever configuration of LAN, WAN, and server size desired. Single user testing gives the best-case performance results.

Results Derived from a Promiscuous Packet Capture Session

In some situations there is no opportunity to set up a benchmark at all and the only data available is that taken from the existing network. Suppose that about 100 users are active at any time and that you have no way to identify a particular user. There is the choice of capturing the traffic from some randomly chosen user for about 17 hours or of capturing all user conversations over a ten-minute interval. Either will accumulate about 20 megabytes of 64-byte packet headers on the LAN analyzer hard drive.

Selecting one user at random means collecting 17 hours of data. But most users work in a bursty manner rather than in a continuous manner. They also tend to work 8-hour days. The user chosen here may not work very hard during the capture period and not be representative. The user may be bound to a low-end server for the day.

Taking a promiscuous ten-minute snapshot will require some postprocessing to sift through the data, identify client-server conversations, and calculate their performance characteristics. The number of bytes per second transmitted over the ten-minute period can be used to sort the conversations. The top talker can be taken as the worst-case user and the conversational properties can be used to design a network for X-many such users. Such a design is clearly conservative.

A best-case approach is to take the same ten-minute snapshot and calculate the average data rate per user by dividing total bytes transmitted by the total number of users captured. Table 8-3 is a short version of the exercise.

TABLE 8-3 SORTED CONVERSATIONS FOUND IN A TEN-MINUTE SNAPSHOT

User	Data rate (bits/sec)	Category
1	200,000	Worst-case user
2	100,000	
3	50,000	
4	40,000	About-average user
5	10,000	
6	2,000	
7	1,000	
8	300	
9	100	
10	100	Lowest traffic user
Total =	403,500	
Avg. =	**40,350**	Best-case (average) user

Here a worst-case design provisions 200,000 bits per second per user while the best-case design provisions only 40,350 bits per second per user.

Packet Size Extremes

Another best-case worst-case scenario is the small-packet versus large-packet application. Consider 64-byte applications such as `telnet` with 1,518-byte applications such as `ftp`. The telnet client sends 1 data byte in the packet while the ftp application sends 1,460 data bytes. The telnet client is considered inefficient compared to the ftp client. However, telnet is not intended to move volumes of data. It is supposed to let users work interactive character-mode applications across the network, and the small packets make it through very quickly compared to the large ftp data packets. The opposing needs for response time and throughput have never been more clear.

Performance can be controlled by the application program. Applications using the Berkeley sockets API can choose the size of the transmit and receive buffers. Their sizes should match for best performance for any buffer size. As buffer size increases, fewer calls to the API are needed, overhead is reduced, and performance increases. This is especially true in Asynchronous Transfer Mode (ATM) LANs where 1-K byte buffers may provide only 20-megabits-per-second throughput while 64-K byte buffers provide 120-megabits-per-second on a 155-megabits-per-second ATM switch. The ratio between worst-case and best-case is about 6:1 here.

Using `ping` to Explore Response Time Extremes

To predict the performance of a live network for various packet sizes, the UNIX `ping` command can be used to measure the round-trip time. Recall that `ping` builds an ICMP loopback request packet and sends it to the destination IP address. The network forwards the IP datagram along to the destination, which constructs an ICMP loopback reply and returns it to the source. When `ping` detects the response it calculates the round-trip time and prints out an one-line summary (see Figure 8-11).

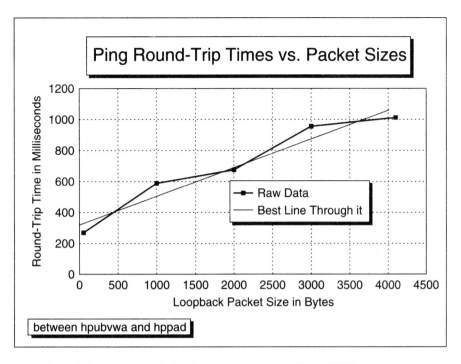

Figure 8-11 Real round-trip data for packet sizes between 64 and 4,000 bytes for a nine-hop network. Unknown background traffic levels were present during the testing. Note that small packets can be returned in about 300 milliseconds while 4,000-byte packets take over 1 second. Most importantly, note that the round-trip time does not approach zero as the packet size goes to zero. The best case network response time is about 300 milliseconds average and the worst case is nearly 1,100 milliseconds.

8.7 PRICING A NETWORK DESIGNED FOR THE WORST-CASE TRAFFIC

The consequences of a worst-case design may be higher-priced hardware and a change in topology being specified. We review the cost and add in a check to verify that the active user count and uptime statistics are consistent with the design.

Pricing the Worst-Case Design

Consider a situation where five servers support five work groups with a total of 300 users among them. Each user generates a worst case load of 1% Ethernet loading directed towards a server, and a user may only connect to any one server at time. Simulation results show that the servers should not be placed on the client subnets but on their own dedicated FDDI ring. The costs are shown in Table 8-4 and the indicated topology in Figure 8-12.

Given that prices vary, the prices shown here should be replaced with current prices. The purpose of the table is to provide a methodology for doing the cost estimate, not to provide current pricing.

TABLE 8-4 PRICING COMPARISON BETWEEN FDDI AND ETHERNET SOLUTIONS

FDDI solution		Ethernet solution	
Item	Cost	Item	Cost
router FDDI adapter	1,000	router Ethernet port	0
5-server FDDI adapters	5,000	5-server Ethernet adapters	1,500
FDDI concentrator	3,000	Ethernet hub	0
FDDI cables	1,000	UTP cable	500
Total Cost =	10,000	Total Cost =	2,000

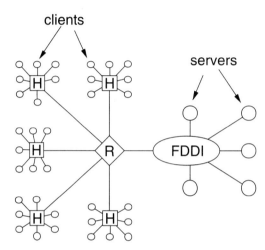

Figure 8-12 This topology satisfies a worst-case traffic load scenario. There was capacity for traffic growth on the client-side Ethernet hubs (H), which support a total community of 300 clients. Router (R) provides a high-speed backbone, and the FDDI subnet provides excess bandwidth for the five servers. The alternative solution places each server on a work group hub, which excessively loads the client LANs, per the network simulation.

This router-based network design has several advantages over alternative approaches

- The router high-speed backplane provides for concurrent forwarding of packets among the work group subnets and the FDDI subnet.
- The router also provides plenty of RAM buffering to store packets that cannot be immediately delivered to the target subnet due to congestion there. Should the buffers fill to capacity, the router can send a standard ICMP source-quench message to the senders.
- FDDI provides true 100 Mbps performance and can operate at near peak capacity without throughput degradation, due to the effectiveness of token passing technology.
- The servers operate more efficiently because the FDDI maximum transmit unit (MTU) is 4,500 bytes, three times that of Ethernet. The router provides standard IP fragmentation and reassembly to accommodate the MTU difference between Ethernet and FDDI.
- Placing the servers on their own FDDI subnet makes them immune to configuration problems on the client work groups. This increases the reliability of the network immensely.

- Placing clients in their own work group subnets makes the work groups immune to configuration problems on the other subnets.
- Using six subnets localizes broadcast and multicast traffic to each subnet.
- IP configuration is relatively simple, since each node simply points its default route to the local router interface.

Validating That the Design Satisfies the Worst-Case Requirements

Characterizing the worst-case traffic is important to ensure that the network capacity is not overspecified by an extremely large margin. In the needs analysis preceding the design the interviewer should ask questions such as: "Is it acceptable to let the network melt down $X\%$ of the time?" and if so, "What should X be?"

Suppose the answer is $X = 0.01\%$, which translates to three seconds in an eight-hour day. Suppose that out of 300 users an average of 150 will be active. A network management tool can measure the number of active users over time even better. Using the binomial formula used earlier will result in numerical overflows due to the large factorials involved, so the excellent approximation of the normal distribution for large numbers will be used instead. First we set up the basic formulas (see Figure 8-13).

$p := \dfrac{1}{2}$ Fraction of users that are active

$n := 300$ Total number of such users being considered

$\mu := n \cdot p$ Mean of the normal distribution

$\sigma := \sqrt{n \cdot p \cdot (1-p)}$ Variance of the normal distribution

$\text{pdf}(x) := \dfrac{1}{\sigma \cdot \sqrt{2 \pi}} \cdot e^{-\frac{1}{2} \left(\frac{x-\mu}{\sigma}\right)^2}$ The normal distribution, the probability that exactly x users are active out of n

$\text{cdf}(n) := \sum_{x=0}^{n} \text{pdf}(x)$ Probability that less than or equal to n users are active at one time, also called the cumulative density function

$x := 0..n$ A handy range variable

Figure 8-13 This computation lets us determine for certain how many of 300 total users we expect to be active as a worst-case check on the FDDI design.

We want to visualize the probability density and cumulative density functions as before. The PDF is plotted in Figure 8-14.

However, since the specifications allow for a meltdown $X = 0.0001$ of the time, the cumulative density function graph will be hard to work with, so a simple printout of the numbers will be used instead (see Figure 8-15).

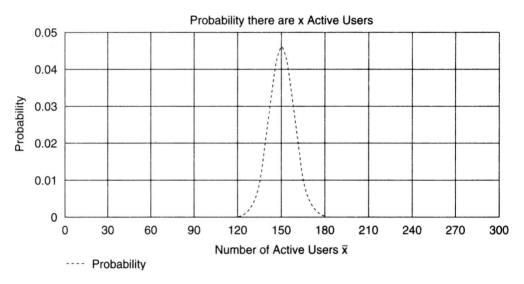

Figure 8-14 The normal approximation to the binomial distribution when half of 300 total users are active at a time, working independently of each other. Note that there is very little area under the tails of the distribution, with most of the probability centered between 120 and 180 users.

n	cdf (n)
176	0.998899
177	0.999236
178	0.999504
179	0.999673
180	0.999787
181	0.999863
182	0.999913
183	0.999946
184	0.999966
185	0.999979
186	0.999988
187	0.999993

Figure 8-15 The chance of 182 users being active is seen to be 0.999913, so the chance that more than 182 users being active is 0.000087, which satisfies the network meltdown criterion if we design the network to not melt at 182 users. The cost of the FDDI-based server subnet is thus justified because the simulation verified that response time for 182 active users is acceptable.

9

Applied Queuing Theory

9.0 INTRODUCTION

This chapter is intended as a practical introduction to using queuing theory in solving network performance problems. Entire books are devoted to in-depth queuing theory and an electronic book for Mathcad is available for the reader interested in pursuing this.

We begin with a look at the basic assumptions and properties of interarrival and service time statistics, examine the special results when they are exponentially distributed, and review the Kendall notation common to all queuing theory.

Next we calculate the average length of a simple M/M/1 queue and the waiting time distribution, and generalize for the M/G/1 queue, which generalizes the service time distribution. A pause is taken to reflect on those situations where queuing theory gives good and bad results, followed by methods to validate the results of queuing theory to real-world systems like UNIX systems, routers, and switches.

Because the simple queue isn't adequate for analyzing many networks, we go through a detailed Mathcad document analyzing the single queue, multiserver open queuing system. Undaunted, we check out a single queue multiuser closed system, again using Mathcad documents. Gaining our second wind, we analyze a single-queue open system with limited queue space.

A great deal of the analysis requires us to evaluate complex sums, so a few helpful tables are included to simplify the computation efforts for those without the benefit of a math scratchpad. Tables for Erlang's formula, total wait time for an M/M/1 queue, and the probability table for all servers busy in a multiserver system are given.

Next we review situations where queues are in tandem. Then we look a queuing example for a spooled network printer, consider how to decide between upgrading and replicating using queuing theory, and deal with packet loss calculations.

9.1 TRANSACTIONS AND SERVICE

Queuing theory can be applied to network capacity planning. We take transactions (or just packets) and move them along the various network elements such as routers, WAN links, and servers. Each of these network elements takes some amount of time to process the transaction and this is called the service time. The reciprocal of the service time is the service rate and it's usually measured in transactions per second. The transactions themselves have an interarrival interval and the actual arrival rate is also measured in transactions per second.

Two types of network models present themselves: open and closed systems. The open system accepts external transactions, processes them internally, and emits them. The number of transactions contained inside the system is variable. A closed system holds a fixed number of circulating transactions—there are no new ones admitted and none are lost.

To apply queuing theory correctly is to understand the basic assumptions that go into the mathematics

- Transaction interarrival times are statistically independent of each other. This means that there is no way to improve the accuracy of a prediction of the arrival time of the next transaction based on any known arrival history of previous packets.
- Service times are statistically independent of each other. This means that there is no information about the service time for previous transactions that can be used to more accurately predict the service time of the next transaction.
- Transaction arrival rates and service times are also independent of each other. This means the service does not change its behavior under various loading conditions.
- The statistics of the interarrival times and service times are time-invariant. This means they don't change with time.
- Transaction and arrival rates are independent of the size of the queues that may form at the server. In the real world, human users typically balk at waiting too long and "leave the system." Transport protocols tend to time out and retransmit packets that are not ACKed in time. Both are examples that violate the independence assumption.
- The size of the queue is unlimited. In practice, this is never true and in some analysis the queue depth is limited.
- The system is in a steady state. This means any startup transients have subsided and that the average behavior at the present time will be the same at some future time. How long does it take to reach the steady state? A rule of thumb is ten times the greatest of
  - the average interarrival time
  - the average service time
  - the average queue delay

The simplest possible queuing system is diagrammed in Figure 9-1.

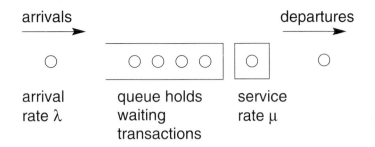

Figure 9-1 The simplest possible queuing system shown here consists of a single stream of transactions with identical statistical properties that may wait in a simple first-in first-out (FIFO) holding queue of infinite capacity before being processed by the server. The service time for each transaction is independent of the history of the system. The system is stable so long as the average arrival rate does not exceed the average service rate.

9.2 EXPONENTIAL SERVICE TIME AND INTERARRIVAL TIME

When both the transaction interarrival time and the service time are exponentially distributed, the simple queuing system lends itself to some easy analytical solutions based on some relatively simple formulas. The benefit of exponential interarrival times is that they exhibit bursty behavior (see Figure 9-2). A wide range of numbers are generated by the exponential distribution. This then is a model that fits a wide range of real network traffic patterns but not all traffic patterns. The exponential distribution has only one statistic—the mean. The standard deviation is the same as the mean.

To apply queuing theory to real-world networking problems it's necessary to estimate the actual interarrival time. One method is to use a stopwatch of some sort. Decide how long to count arriving transactions and start the stopwatch at a random point in time. Don't start the stopwatch when the first transaction arrives because this biases the measurement. Count transaction arrivals until the measurement interval expires. Don't halt the stopwatch when the last arrival occurs because this too biases the measurement. Calculate the average arrival rate by simple division

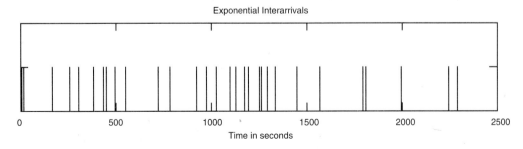

Figure 9-2 Every vertical line represents an arrival. The series is generated from the exponential distribution with a mean of 10 seconds. The formula to generate this series is $Expon(t) = -t \cdot \ln(rnd(1.0))$. Every call to the *Expon* function with the argument 10.0 returns the interarrival time of the next transaction. Notice that the arrivals come in clusters with gaps between them.

$$\lambda = \frac{transactions}{time}$$

The more transactions included in the arithmetic the more accurate the results are. At least 100 transactions will give acceptable accuracy (within a few percent).

Determining the average transaction service time is a little more involved because each individual transaction service time has to be measured and recorded. Assuming that $N = 100$ transactions have been measured and that the transaction times measured are $t_1, t_2, \ldots, t_{100}$, the average service rate is given by

$$\mu = \frac{N}{t_1 + t_2 + \ldots + t_N}$$

To check the assumption that the interarrival and service times are exponential, calculate their standard deviations and compare them to their respective means. If they're close (within 40%), call it a day. To be more certain, construct a cumulative distribution function of the data and superimpose the CDF of the exponential distribution with the sample mean over it. The fit at the tail won't be very good, but the rest of the fit should be close. Statistical purists will note that a Colgomoroff-Smirnoff test can be used to formally validate that the measured data is exponential.

9.3 OTHER STATISTICAL DISTRIBUTIONS

To accommodate a variety of queuing systems, the standard Kendall notation is used to describe the various properties in a compact universal method. The statistical distributions of the interarrival times and service times are specified. The number of servers, the system capacity, and the system population are indicated, and the queuing discipline is shown. Table 9-1 goes into the details.

TABLE 9-1 EXPLANATION OF THE KENDALL NOTATION M/G/m/ K/M/ HOL USED TO DESCRIBE QUEUING SYSTEMS

M		G		m	K	M	HOL	
Interarrival time statistics		Service time statistics		Number of servers	System capacity	Population in the system	Service discipline	
D	Deterministic fixed value			The number of servers may vary from 1 to infinity.	The maximum number of customers, packets, items, or transactions the system can hold. For open systems K is infinite.	The actual number of customers or transactions in the system.	FIFO	first-in first-out
E_r	Erlangian with r stages						FILO	first-in last-out
G	General (any) distribution						HOL	head of line
GI	General & independent statistics						FIRO	first-in random-out
H_R	R-stage Hyperexponential							
M	Memoryless exponential							
U	Uniform distribution							

The simple system described in the last section has exponential arrivals and service times and one server. It can accommodate any number of transactions and it uses the FIFO queuing discipline. The full notation for this system is M/M/1/∞/∞/FIFO, which is normally shortened to M/M/1 by dropping the defaults ∞/∞/FIFO.

9.4 CALCULATING THE AVERAGE LENGTH OF THE QUEUE

The average length of the queue is of great interest. The larger the average queue size, the longer a transaction has to wait before obtaining service. Taking an IP router into consideration, the more packets waiting for a serial line to become free, the longer the packets wait for transmission. If the average packet size can be estimated, then the average buffer size can be computed. Network administrators tuning the queue sizes on routers supporting priority queues need to calculate these numbers.

The simple queuing system has to be stable for the average queue length to be defined, implying the usual requirement that the average service rate exceeds the average arrival rate. Assuming exponential independent distributions for arrivals and service (M/M/1) the average length of the queue is given by

$$L_q = \lambda^2 / (\mu(\mu - \lambda)).$$

The average number of transactions in the system is given by

$$L = \lambda / (\mu - \lambda).$$

Now the average queue length does not tell the whole story. The number of transactions in the queue clearly varies all over the acreage as transactions arrive in bunches. The formula for the statistical distribution of the number of items in the system is

$$P_n = (1 - \lambda/\mu)(\lambda/\mu)^n, n = 0, 1, \ldots \infty.$$

Figures 9-3 and 9-4 graph a probability curve and cumulative density function derived from these equations.

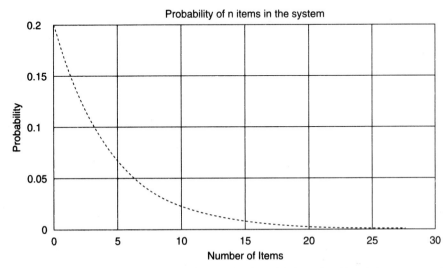

Figure 9-3 Plotting out the probability curve for $\lambda = 0.9$ and $\mu = 1.0$ shows that although the average number of transactions in the system is $L = \lambda/(\mu - \lambda) = 9$, there is some probability that up to 25 transactions may be in it.

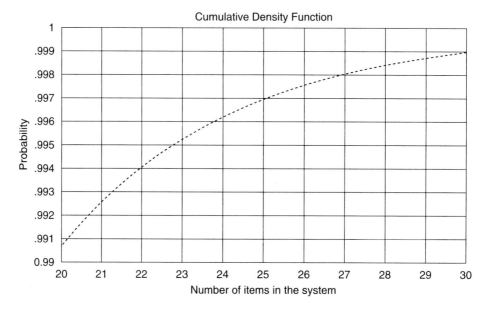

Figure 9-4 The cumulative probability density function shows there is a 0.999 probability that there will be less than or equal to 30 items in the system. If it is acceptable to drop items from the queue with probability of 0.001, then 30 can be the design point. Given an arrival rate of 0.9 items per second, a transaction will be dropped from the queue on average once every 1,111 seconds (18.5 minutes).

9.5 AVERAGE WAIT TIME IN THE SYSTEM

An important, yet very simple relationship exists between the average wait time spent in the queuing system W and the average number of items in the system L:

$$L = \lambda \cdot W \quad \text{Little's Law}$$

The wonderfully simple relationship applies to any M/G/m/K/M/HOL queuing system. Using it to calculate the average time in the M/M/1 system results in the formula

$$W = 1/(\mu - \lambda)$$

and plugging in the numbers $\lambda = 0.9$ and $\mu = 1.0$ gives an average wait time of $W = 10$ seconds in the system. Since averages don't tell the whole story, here is the probability density function of the wait time. Note that it's exponential

$$p(t) = (\mu - \lambda) e^{(\mu - \lambda)t}$$

Instead of plotting this directly, the more useful cumulative density function should be calculated (see Figure 9-5). Wait time is a continuous quantity rather than a discrete one, which means that instead of summing up the probabilities, an integration must be done. Consulting a table of standard integrals gives the cumulative density function

$$cdf(t) = 1 - e^{-(\mu - \lambda)t}$$

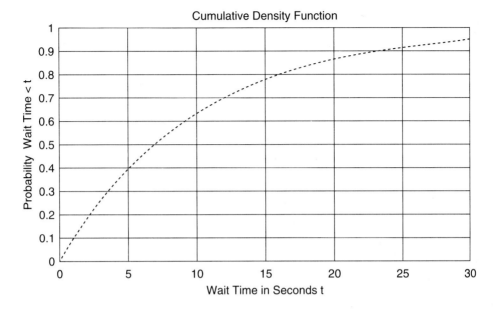

Figure 9-5 Wait time cumulative probability density function for the single-server queuing system example. While the average wait time is 10 seconds, the graph reveals that the probability the wait time is less than or equal to 10 seconds is 69.3%. There is a 5% chance the wait time is greater than or equal to 30 seconds.

Calculating the wait time distribution for data communications systems can give insight into transport layer time-outs because if we know that there is a one-second time-out then we can compute the chances that the packet has to wait longer than this. This is the probability of a transport time-out occurring, seemingly at random.

When the interarrival times are exponentially distributed but the service time is general, we have the M/G/1 queuing system. The formulas for this situation are as follows

M/G/1 QUEUING FORMULAS

- arrival rate (Poisson) mean $\quad \lambda$
- service rate (general) mean $\quad \mu$
- service rate standard deviation $\quad \sigma_s$
- server utilization $\quad \rho = \lambda / \mu$
- Pollaczek-Khinchin formula: average number in the system
$$N = \frac{2 \cdot \rho - \rho^2 + \lambda^2 \cdot \sigma_s^2}{2 \cdot (t - \rho)}$$
- average time in the system $\quad T = N / \lambda$
- average queue waiting time $\quad W = T - \frac{1}{\mu}$
- average queue length $\quad N_q = \lambda \cdot W$

This means we can relax the usual exponential service time assumption, but we lose a general formula for the wait time distribution.

Sec. 9.5 Average Wait Time in the System

Summary of Formulas for a Simple M/M/1 Queuing System

Transactions enter the queue at rate λ with exponential distribution. The single server processes transactions at rate μ, also exponential. $\lambda < \mu$ in order to assure stability, or else the queue grows linearly in time, without bound.

1. Probability of n items in the system $\quad P_n = (1 - \lambda/\mu)(\lambda/\mu)^n, n = 0, 1, \ldots$
2. Average number of items in the system $\quad L = \lambda/(\mu - \lambda)$
3. Average number in the queue $\quad L_q = \lambda^2/(\mu(\mu-\lambda))$
4. Average number in nonempty queues $\quad \hat{L}_q = \mu/(\mu - \lambda)$
5. Distribution of waiting times (excluding service) $\quad P\{w = 0\} = 1 - (\lambda/\mu)$
   $\psi(\omega) = (1 - \lambda/\mu) e^{-(\mu - \lambda)\omega}, \omega > 0$
6. Average waiting time excluding service $\quad P_q = \lambda/(\mu(\mu - \lambda))$
7. Average waiting time given an item has to wait $\quad \hat{W}_q = 1/(\mu - \lambda)$
8. Distribution of total time (including service) $\quad \phi(v) = (\mu - \lambda) e^{-(\mu-\lambda)v}$
9. Average total time including service $\quad W = 1/(\mu - \lambda)$
10. Utilization factor $\quad p = \lambda/\mu$
11. Little's Law $\quad L = \lambda W, L_q = \lambda W_q$

9.6 WHEN QUEUING THEORY GIVES GOOD RESULTS

Good predictive results are obtained when the assumptions behind the queuing theory are more or less met by the physical network being analyzed. In addition to the list of mathematical assumptions listed earlier, additional practical matters are involved.

Real network applications usually have to wait for a response before submitting the next query. Transport protocols such as TCP support a sliding window algorithm capable of transmitting up to (say) 8 Kbytes worth of data before being forced to wait for some of the data to be ACKed by the receiver. This means that a small population of transaction sources may not satisfy the necessary assumptions. A large population of transaction generators each of which generates a small transaction rate together can satisfy the necessary assumptions (see Figure 9-6).

The independent service time assumptions in networks are usually valid, but the exponential service time assumption can only be satisfied if the packet sizes are distributed widely enough. On a WAN circuit, the service time is the time to transmit the packet, which is directly proportional to the number of bits it contains. If the packet size distribution is approximately exponential, then the service times will be also. A segment monitor such as a LAN Analyzer, an HP LanProbe III, or an HP EASE Traffic Probe can collect packet size statistics to check.

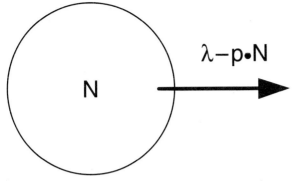

Large independent population

Figure 9-6 When a large population of N independent transaction generators each generates a transaction at a much smaller rate p, the aggregate transaction rate is $\lambda = p \cdot N$ and their statistics satisfy the independence assumption. So long as the number of transactions in the queuing system $\lambda/(\mu - \lambda)$ remains much smaller than N most of the time, the assumption remains true. "Much smaller" means 1/10 and "most of the time" means 95%.

9.7 VALIDATING QUEUING THEORY RESULTS

Comparing the results of a queuing analysis with real network measurements can increase confidence in the method, validate the methodology, and fine-tune the parameters used. Real systems always have finite queues and looking at their performance characteristics using whatever tools are available is the basis for validation. Real systems we'll look at here include UNIX systems, LAN adapters, and ATM/Ethernet switches.

The basic validation method is that we predict the packet loss rate from queuing theory and measure it in the field. We need to measure packet loss in the network.

Transport layer time-outs occur when packets are lost due to buffer overflows (and other reasons which should be accounted for or eliminated). The average packet loss probability should be in the same ball park as that calculated by queue overflows. Since packet loss is supposed to be a fairly rare event, a long data collection interval should used to ensure enough packets are dropped to give a statistically significant estimate of the mean loss percentage. Note that the type of transport mechanism impacts the retransmission algorithm. For Van Jacobson TCP, the retransmission time-out value is dynamically calculated to reflect the current round-trip time. This timer is typically configured to vary between a minimum of 1 second and a maximum value of 60 seconds. Other transports have fixed timers. Fixed timers make it easy to calculate the probability that a packet will spend longer than this value in the system. The UNIX command `netstat -s` gives information about transport activity.

LAN adapters have a fixed amount of RAM, in the neighborhood of 32–64 Kbytes. This resource may be shared by incoming and outgoing packets or it may be partitioned for incoming and outgoing packets. The UNIX command `landiag` gives statistics about packets not delivered or transmitted due to a lack of resources. Some computer systems (the HP 3000) allocate additional inbound buffers in system memory for the LAN adapter to overcome this problem.

Ethernet and ATM switches also provide buffers that may overflow on occasion. Presumably the vendors provide access to the switch performance statistics via the on-board SNMP agent or via an RS-232 port.

Validation also requires that the basic queuing theory assumptions are intact. This requires a check that the average transaction/packet/customer/item arrival rate is constant over the observation interval. Transactions should not be related to each other and impact each other's service time. And the system being analyzed should represent a queuing system where transactions do not occupy multiple queues concurrently; that is, they should not hold multiple resources at one time.

9.8 SINGLE-SERVER QUEUES AND MULTI-SERVER QUEUES

Real networks often provide more then one server (in the queuing sense)

- multiple network paths to the same destination
- extra compute engines
- several network printers
- multiple file servers
- several mail hubs

There are two ways to regulate access the these services. One method simply allows the users to queue up for the service they want, much like they choose a checkout at the supermarket. The other method provides a single queue and the person at the head of the queue gets the next available server, much like better bookstores. The single queue method provides the best service.

A full computational method for analyzing such queues is given here. The math is best done using a math scratch pad such as MathPad, Mathcad, Mathematica, or MATLAB. What you are about to experience is a Mathcad document consisting of formulas, results, graphs, and explanatory text (see Figures 9-7a and 9-7b).

The calculations assume identical servers. The important results are the average wait time and the wait time distribution. If the predicted network wait times exceed your requirements, it is a simple matter to change the average service rate μ and the number of servers cc until a suitable design is obtained.

When the open system assumption is not valid, a closed queuing analysis is needed, such as a single server and a finite number of active identical users. Each user thinks for a period of time, generates a transaction request, waits as long as necessary for the response, and starts the cycle over again. The analysis proceeds as shown in Figure 9-8.

When the network really is better modeled as an open system and we wish to consider the impact of the finite buffer capacity of the hardware, a multistep approach is necessary. We begin by initializing the variables (see Figure 9-9).

With packets/jobs/transactions/items arriving at 0.9 per second and being serviced at the rate of 1.0 per second, the simple network is roughly 90% utilized. Instead of jobs queuing up without bound, excess jobs are discarded. This means that if a job can get a position in the queue, the wait time will be more reasonable. The jobs turned away are assumed to be lost (see Figure 9-10).

The next step is to plug in various values for K to determine the overall impact on response time. To control the response time it is possible to lower the allowable queue depth K. This technique is essential when the number of actual users that might physically use a service would overwhelm it. For example, an Internet service provider with 1,000 customers might provide 100 incoming modem ports. Customer 101 gets a busy signal and gives up this attempt to crawl the Web.

Multiserver Single Queue System

$cc := 7 \quad \lambda := 6.0 \quad \mu := 1.0 \quad a := \dfrac{\lambda}{\mu} \quad \rho := \dfrac{a}{cc}$

$C(c, a) := \dfrac{\dfrac{a^{cc}}{cc!}}{(1-\rho) \cdot \sum_{n=0}^{c-1} \dfrac{a^n}{n!} + \dfrac{a^{cc}}{cc!}}$ Function used later

$Lq := \dfrac{\rho \cdot C(cc, a)}{1 - \rho}$ Queue length $Lq = 3.683$

$Wq := \dfrac{Lq}{\lambda}$ Wait time in queue $Wq = 0.614$

$Ws := \dfrac{\rho \cdot cc}{\lambda}$ Average service time $Ws = 1$

$W := Wq + Ws$ Average time in the system $W = 1.614$

$L := \lambda \cdot W$ Average users in system $L = 9.683$

$p_0 := \left[\sum_{n=0}^{cc-1} \dfrac{a^n}{n!} + \dfrac{a^{cc}}{cc! \cdot (1-\rho)} \right]^{-1}$ Probability the system is empty $p_0 = 0.002$

$Wq(t) := 1 - C(cc, a) \cdot \exp(-\mu \cdot t \cdot (cc - a))$

$T := 6 \quad t := 0, 0.1 .. T$

Legend

- cc number of servers
- λ rate of arrivals into the system
- μ rate of service at each server
- C probability all servers are busy
- a ratio λ/μ
- ρ entire facility utilization
- Lq average queue length
- L average users in system
- Wq average time in queue
- Ws average time in service
- W average total time in system
- p0 probability of 0 items in system
- Wq(t) queue waiting time distribution
- W(t) total waiting time distribution of having to wait <= t seconds

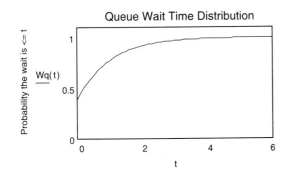

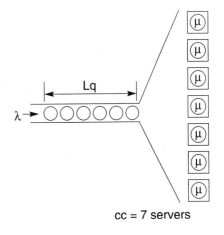

cc = 7 servers

Figure 9-7a This Mathcad document lays out the basic calculations for solving the multiserver single queue. The queue wait cumulative distribution function is plotted. The notation here is used later in other queuing examples.

$$W(t) := \text{if}\Big[\, a = (cc - 1),\, 1 - (1 + C(cc, a) \cdot \mu \cdot t) \cdot \exp(-\mu \cdot t),$$

$$1 - \frac{a - cc + Wq(0)}{(a + 1 - cc)} \cdot \exp(-\mu \cdot t) - \frac{C(cc, a)}{(a + 1 - cc)} \cdot \exp(-cc \cdot \mu \cdot t \cdot (1 - \rho))\Big]$$

T := 6   t := 0, 0.1 .. T

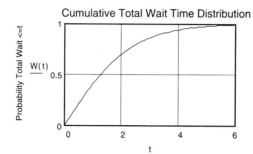

Formulas are adapted to Mathcad from the book
<u>Probability, Statistics and Queuing Theory</u>,
chapter 5, pp. 274-278

Figure 9-7b Total waiting time for the multiserver single queue system, continued from Figure 9-7a.

The value of *K* is varied from 1 to 1,000 and the results are, of course, very interesting (see Figure 9-11).

A final queuing example analyses of what admittedly is more computer-system centric problem is the Jackson Analysis method. The system is closed, has multiple servers, and one common resource, the CPU (see Figure 9-12).

The transition probabilities and service demands have to be determined be measurement, by an interview process or by educated guesswork. The next step is to iterate the analysis over *n*, number of jobs circulating in the system (see Figure 9-13).

Finally, we print the results (see Figure 9-14).

Erlang's formula $\quad B(N,z) := \left[\sum_{k=0}^{N} \frac{N!}{(N-k)!} \cdot \left(\frac{1}{z}\right)^k \right]^{-1}$

Terminal think time $\quad T := 20$

Service time $\quad Ws := 2.0$

Number of terminals $\quad N := 20$

Formulas to compute response time vs number of users

$z := \dfrac{T}{Ws} \quad p_0 := B(N,z) \quad r := 1 - p_0 \quad W := \dfrac{N \cdot Ws}{\rho} - T$

$i := 1..20 \quad wait(N) := \left(\dfrac{N}{1 - B(N,z)} - z \right) \cdot Ws$

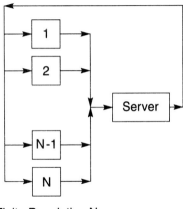

Finite Population N

Reference:
Probability, Statistics and Queueing Theory
pp. 381-385

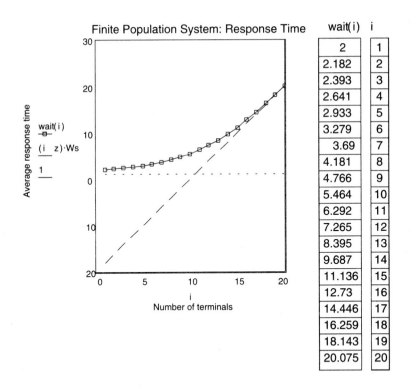

wait(i)	i
2	1
2.182	2
2.393	3
2.641	4
2.933	5
3.279	6
3.69	7
4.181	8
4.766	9
5.464	10
6.292	11
7.265	12
8.395	13
9.687	14
11.136	15
12.73	16
14.446	17
16.259	18
18.143	19
20.075	20

Figure 9-8 Mathhcad analysis for a closed queuing system—a simple network with a few active users. The think times and service times are the usual exponentials. Notice the familiar asymptotic behavior of the response time curve. The maximum size of the queue is fixed at N, the number of users, so it cannot overflow. The closed system behaves in a stable manner at saturation and wait times do not go to infinity.

Queuing Analysis with Limited Buffer Space

In practice, network devices do not have unlimited buffer space to accomodate the waiting queue. A LAN adaptor might hold 64 Kbytes, a disk controller might have 1 Mbyte buffer and an IP router may have 4 Mbytes for store and forward.

In this section we allow for K-1 jobs (or packets) in the queue and one in the server for a total of K jobs in the system.

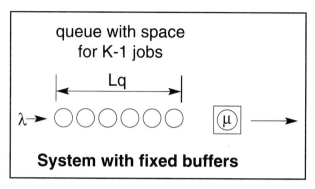

Reference:
Probability, Statistics and Queueing Theory, pp. 269-274

Step 0: Initialize the variables

ORIGIN=0	Sets Mathcad's array origin at 0
K := 40	Total Jobs in the system
n := 0..K	Range variable for jobs
$\lambda\lambda$:= 0.9	Arrival rate of jobs
λ_n := if(n≥K,0,$\lambda\lambda$)	Set the arrival rate to zero if the buffer is full
$\mu\mu$:= 1.0	Service rate of a job
μ_n := if(n>K,0,$\mu\mu$)	Set the service rate to zero for rejected transactions
a := $\frac{\lambda\lambda}{\mu\mu}$	

Figure 9-9 The first step in analyzing the performance of a limited-size queue system is to initialize all the variables. As with previous examples, it is very important to make a note of every math variable and assumption before plunging ahead. Here we have a system with room for 30 jobs in the queue and one in the server. Arrivals get service unless the queue is full, in which case the service rate is zero.

Step 1: Calculate the system statistics

$$p_n := \text{if}\left[\lambda\lambda = \mu\mu, \frac{1}{K+1}, \frac{(1-a)\cdot a^n}{1-a^{K+1}}\right]$$ Probability of n jobs being in the system

$$L := \text{if}\left[\lambda\lambda = \mu\mu, \frac{K}{2}, \frac{a}{1-a} - \frac{(K+1)\cdot a^{K+1}}{1-a^{K+1}}\right]$$ Average number of jobs in the system $\quad L = 8.447$

$Lq := L - (1 - p_0)$ Average jobs in the queue $Lq = 7.549$

$\lambda a := \lambda\lambda \cdot (1 - p_K)$ Rate jobs enter the queue $\lambda a = 0.899$

$\lambda e := \lambda\lambda - \lambda a$ Rate jobs are dismissed $\lambda e = 0.001$

$W := \dfrac{L}{\lambda a}$ Average time spent in the system $W = 9.4$

$Wq := \dfrac{Lq}{\lambda a}$ Average time spent in the queue $Wq = 8.4$

$\rho := (1 - p_K) \cdot a$ Average server utilization $\rho = 0.899$

Figure 9-10 Calculating the system statistics reveals that with room for $K = 40$ jobs, the chance of dismissing a job is only 0.1%. The queue depth is effectively infinite! Still, if the time scale is changed, this percentage drop rate translates to 1 packet per second being dropped at 1,000 packets per second throughput.

Step 2: Execute the formulas above for a range of buffers K and place the wait time manually into the array called Wait and put the corresponding number of buffers into the array called Index. Then plot the two arrays on a log-x axis. Note that a large value of K is essentially the equivalent of an unlimited queue. λ=1.0 and μ=0.9.

i := 1..15 Range variable for the number of points to be plotted

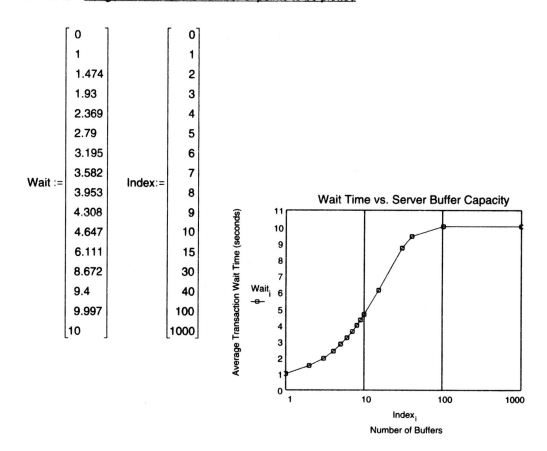

$$\text{Wait} := \begin{bmatrix} 0 \\ 1 \\ 1.474 \\ 1.93 \\ 2.369 \\ 2.79 \\ 3.195 \\ 3.582 \\ 3.953 \\ 4.308 \\ 4.647 \\ 6.111 \\ 8.672 \\ 9.4 \\ 9.997 \\ 10 \end{bmatrix} \quad \text{Index} := \begin{bmatrix} 0 \\ 1 \\ 2 \\ 3 \\ 4 \\ 5 \\ 6 \\ 7 \\ 8 \\ 9 \\ 10 \\ 15 \\ 30 \\ 40 \\ 100 \\ 1000 \end{bmatrix}$$

Figure 9-11 Recall that the average wait time for an M/M/1 system is $1/(\mu - \lambda)$, which evaluates to a maximum average wait time of ten seconds. This is the graph's asymptote, which is a nice check on the method. If we want to keep the average wait time below five seconds it is necessary to limit the queue depth to ten buffers.

Jackson Queueing Analysis of a Closed System

Reference: Probability, Statistics and Queueing Theory, pp. 389-396

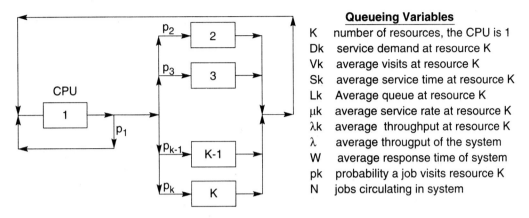

Queueing Variables

K	number of resources, the CPU is 1
Dk	service demand at resource K
Vk	average visits at resource K
Sk	average service time at resource K
Lk	Average queue at resource K
μk	average service rate at resource K
λk	average throughput at resource K
λ	average througput of the system
W	average response time of system
pk	probability a job visits resource K
N	jobs circulating in system

Step 0, define parameters $K := 3 \quad k := 1..K \quad N := 10 \quad n := 1..N$

Define transition probabilities for the cpu (pcpu) and the other resources (pother)   Probabilities must add up to 1

$pcpu := 0.1 \quad pother := \dfrac{0.9}{K-1} \quad p_1 := pcpu \quad i := 2..K \quad p_i := pother$

Define service times for the CPU (Scpu) and the other resources (Sother)

$Scpu := 0.01 \quad Sother := 0.2 \quad S_1 := Scpu \quad S_i := Sother$

$$\sum_{k=1}^{K} p_k - 1 = 0$$

$$p = \begin{bmatrix} 0 \\ 0.1 \\ 0.45 \\ 0.45 \end{bmatrix} \quad S = \begin{bmatrix} 0 \\ 0.01 \\ 0.2 \\ 0.2 \end{bmatrix}$$

Calculate the service demand at each resource using the transition probabilities and the service times at each server.

$V_1 := \dfrac{1}{p_1} \quad i := 2..K \quad V_i := p_i \cdot V_1 \quad D_k := V_k \cdot S_k \quad$ Display service demands --> $D = \begin{bmatrix} 0 \\ 0.1 \\ 0.9 \\ 0.9 \end{bmatrix}$

Figure 9-12 The Jackson method lets us analyze a closed system with a CPU and multiple servers. The servers in the analysis can be different because the service demands can be varied—a pleasant change over other analysis methods. This allows the network administrator to toss in an additional server resource to check the impact on response time. Here we begin by defining the basic parameters, noting that the CPU is server 1.

Step 1, Initialize for k=1,2,...,K $L_{k,0} = 0$

Step 2, Iterate for n=1,2,...,N

$n := 1 \quad W_{k,n} := D_k \cdot (1 + L_{k,n-1}) \quad WW_n := \sum_{k=1}^{K} W_{k,n} \quad \lambda_n := \frac{n}{WW_n} \quad L_{k,n} := \lambda_n \cdot W_{k,n}$

$n := 2 \quad W_{k,n} := D_k \cdot (1 + L_{k,n-1}) \quad WW_n := \sum_{k=1}^{K} W_{k,n} \quad \lambda_n := \frac{n}{WW_n} \quad L_{k,n} := \lambda_n \cdot W_{k,n}$

$n := 3 \quad W_{k,n} := D_k \cdot (1 + L_{k,n-1}) \quad WW_n := \sum_{k=1}^{K} W_{k,n} \quad \lambda_n := \frac{n}{WW_n} \quad L_{k,n} := \lambda_n \cdot W_{k,n}$

$n := 4 \quad W_{k,n} := D_k \cdot (1 + L_{k,n-1}) \quad WW_n := \sum_{k=1}^{K} W_{k,n} \quad \lambda_n := \frac{n}{WW_n} \quad L_{k,n} := \lambda_n \cdot W_{k,n}$

$n := 5 \quad W_{k,n} := D_k \cdot (1 + L_{k,n-1}) \quad WW_n := \sum_{k=1}^{K} W_{k,n} \quad \lambda_n := \frac{n}{WW_n} \quad L_{k,n} := \lambda_n \cdot W_{k,n}$

$n := 6 \quad W_{k,n} := D_k \cdot (1 + L_{k,n-1}) \quad WW_n := \sum_{k=1}^{K} W_{k,n} \quad \lambda_n := \frac{n}{WW_n} \quad L_{k,n} := \lambda_n \cdot W_{k,n}$

$n := 7 \quad W_{k,n} := D_k \cdot (1 + L_{k,n-1}) \quad WW_n := \sum_{k=1}^{K} W_{k,n} \quad \lambda_n := \frac{n}{WW_n} \quad L_{k,n} := \lambda_n \cdot W_{k,n}$

$n := 8 \quad W_{k,n} := D_k \cdot (1 + L_{k,n-1}) \quad WW_n := \sum_{k=1}^{K} W_{k,n} \quad \lambda_n := \frac{n}{WW_n} \quad L_{k,n} := \lambda_n \cdot W_{k,n}$

$n := 9 \quad W_{k,n} := D_k \cdot (1 + L_{k,n-1}) \quad WW_n := \sum_{k=1}^{K} W_{k,n} \quad \lambda_n := \frac{n}{WW_n} \quad L_{k,n} := \lambda_n \cdot W_{k,n}$

$n := 10 \quad W_{k,n} := D_k \cdot (1 + L_{k,n-1}) \quad WW_n := \sum_{k=1}^{K} W_{k,n} \quad \lambda_n := \frac{n}{WW_n} \quad L_{k,n} := \lambda_n \cdot W_{k,n}$

Figure 9-13 These steps iteratively calculate the average wait times, job rate, and queue depth at each server. The method looks tedious, but is very straightforward because each line is the same, except for the value of *n*. Some easy cut-and-paste work is the bulk of the effort.

Step 3. Print the results

number of circulating jobs   N = 10

number of resources   K = 3

Average wait time $WWW := WW_N$ $WWW = 9.911$

Average jobs/second $\lambda\lambda := \lambda_N$ $\lambda\lambda = 1.009$

$$\rho_k := \lambda\lambda \cdot D_k$$

Utilization of each resource
1 is the CPU (0 is a place saver)
2,...,K are the other resources

$$\rho = \begin{bmatrix} 0 \\ 0.101 \\ 0.908 \\ 0.908 \end{bmatrix} \quad L^{<N>} = \begin{bmatrix} 0 \\ 0.112 \\ 4.944 \\ 4.944 \end{bmatrix}$$

Average queue at each resource
1 is the CPU
2,...,K are the remaining resources

How does response time depend on the number of Servers?

The closed Jackson model is the most complex algorithm implemented here using Mathcad. To plot the behavior of the closed model, we collected the following data from the above calculations with a fixed value N = 10 circulating programs and with a varying number of servers K.

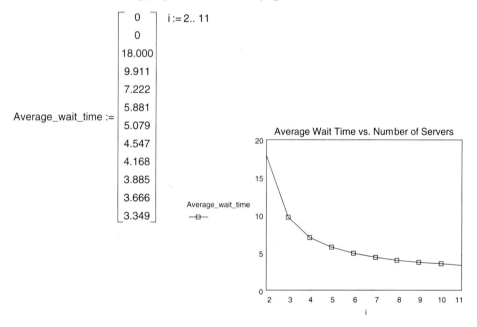

$$\text{Average\_wait\_time} := \begin{bmatrix} 0 \\ 0 \\ 18.000 \\ 9.911 \\ 7.222 \\ 5.881 \\ 5.079 \\ 4.547 \\ 4.168 \\ 3.885 \\ 3.666 \\ 3.349 \end{bmatrix} \quad i := 2..11$$

Figure 9-14 For $N = 10$ circulating programs, the response time drops rapidly as the number of servers increases past two. After about eight servers, the response time decreases less rapidly.

9.9 HELPFUL TABLES IN QUEUING THEORY ANALYSIS

To avoid the time-consuming error-prone summations that must be done in queuing problem analysis, the Tables 9-2 to 9-4 may be consulted to speed up the arithmetic, reduce mistakes and put the fun back into network performance analysis.

TABLE 9-2 VALUES FOR ERLANG'S FORMULA, $B(N,z)$, WHERE N IS THE NUMBER OF CUSTOMERS AND z IS THINK TIME DIVIDED BY SERVICE TIME

											z									
N	1	2	3	4	5	6	7	8	9	10	11	12	13	14	15	16	17	18	19	20
1	0.5	0.6667	0.75	0.8	0.8333	0.8571	0.875	0.8889	0.9	0.9091	0.9167	0.9231	0.9286	0.9333	0.9375	0.9412	0.9444	0.9474	0.95	0.9524
2	0.2	0.4	0.5294	0.6154	8.6757	0.72	0.7538	0.7805	0.802	0.8197	0.8345	0.8471	0.8579	0.8673	0.8755	0.8828	0.8892	0.8892	0.9002	0.905
3	0.0625	0.2105	0.3462	0.4507	0.5297	0.5902	0.6375	0.6755	0.7064	0.7321	0.7537	0.7721	0.788	0.8019	0.814	0.8248	0.8344	0.8344	0.8508	0.8578
4	0.0154	0.0952	0.2061	0.3107	0.3983	0.4696	0.53	0.5746	0.6138	0.6467	0.6745	0.6985	0.7192	0.7373	0.7532	0.7674	0.78	0.78	0.8016	0.8109
5	0.0031	0.0367	0.1101	0.1991	0.2849	0.3604	0.4247	0.479	0.5249	0.564	0.5974	0.626	0.6516	0.6737	0.6932	0.7106	0.7262	0.7262	0.7529	0.7644
6	0.0005	0.0121	0.0522	0.1172	0.1918	0.2649	0.3313	0.3898	0.4405	0.4845	0.5227	0.5561	0.5854	0.6112	0.6341	0.6546	0.6729	0.6729	0.7045	0.7181
7	0.0001	0.0034	0.0219	0.0628	0.1205	0.1851	0.2489	0.3082	0.3616	0.409	0.451	0.488	0.5209	0.55	0.5761	0.5994	0.6204	0.6204	0.6566	0.6723
8	0	0.0009	0.0081	0.0304	0.0701	0.1219	0.1788	0.2356	0.2892	0.3383	0.3828	0.4227	0.4584	0.4905	0.5193	0.5452	0.5687	0.5687	0.6093	0.627
9	0	0.0002	0.0027	0.0133	0.0375	0.0751	0.1221	0.1731	0.2243	0.2732	0.3187	0.3604	0.3984	0.4328	0.4639	0.4922	0.5179	0.5179	0.5626	0.5822
10	0	0	0.0008	0.0053	0.0184	0.0431	0.0787	0.1217	0.168	0.2146	0.2596	0.3019	0.3412	0.3773	0.4103	0.4406	0.4682	0.4682	0.5167	0.538
11	0	0	0.0002	0.0019	0.0083	0.023	0.0477	0.0813	0.1208	0.1632	0.2061	0.2478	0.2874	0.3244	0.3588	0.3905	0.4198	0.4198	0.4716	0.4945
12	0	0	0.0001	0.0006	0.0034	0.0114	0.0271	0.0514	0.0831	0.1197	0.1589	0.1986	0.2374	0.2746	0.3096	0.3424	0.3729	0.3729	0.4275	0.4518
13	0	0	0	0.0002	0.0013	0.0052	0.0144	0.0307	0.0544	0.0843	0.1185	0.1549	0.1919	0.2282	0.2632	0.2965	0.3278	0.3278	0.3845	0.4101
14	0	0	0	0.0001	0.0005	0.0022	0.0071	0.0172	0.0338	0.0568	0.0852	0.1172	0.1512	0.1858	0.22	0.2531	0.2847	0.2847	0.3429	0.3694
15	0	0	0	0	0.0002	0.0009	0.0033	0.0091	0.0199	0.0365	0.0588	0.0857	0.1159	0.1478	0.1803	0.2126	0.244	0.244	0.3028	0.33
16	0	0	0	0	0	0.0003	0.0015	0.0045	0.0111	0.0223	0.0389	0.0604	0.086	0.1145	0.1446	0.1753	0.2059	0.2059	0.2645	0.292
17	0	0	0	0	0	0.0001	0.0006	0.0021	0.0058	0.013	0.0245	0.0409	0.0617	0.0862	0.1132	0.1416	0.1707	0.1707	0.2282	0.2557
18	0	0	0	0	0	0	0.0002	0.0009	0.0029	0.0071	0.0148	0.0265	0.0427	0.0628	0.0862	0.1118	0.1388	0.1388	0.1941	0.2213
19	0	0	0	0	0	0	0.0001	0.0004	0.0014	0.0037	0.0085	0.0165	0.0284	0.0442	0.0637	0.0861	0.1105	0.1105	0.1625	0.1889
20	0	0	0	0	0	0	0	0.0002	0.0006	0.0019	0.0046	0.0090	0.0181	0.03	0.0456	0.0644	0.0859	0.0859	0.1338	0.1589

TABLE 9-3 TOTAL AVERAGE WAIT TIME FOR A SINGLE-SERVER SINGLE-QUEUE NETWORK

Ratio of Arrival Rate to Service Rate	Wait Time
0.0	1
0.05	1.0526
0.10	1.1111
0.15	1.1765
0.20	1.25
0.25	1.3333
0.30	1.4286
0.35	1.5385
0.40	1.6667
0.45	1.8182
0.50	2
0.55	2.2222
0.60	2.5
0.65	2.8571
0.70	3.3333
0.75	4
0.80	5
0.85	6.6667
0.90	10
0.95	20

TABLE 9-4 PROBABILITY THAT ALL SERVERS ARE BUSY IN A MULTISERVER SINGLE-QUEUE NETWORK

Number of servers	Arrival Rate/Service Rate									
	1	2	3	4	5	6	7	8	9	10
1	1									
2	0.333	1								
3	0.0909	0.444	1							
4	0.0204	0.1739	0.5094	1						
5	0.0038	0.0597	0.2362	0.5541	1					
6	0.0006	0.018	0.0991	0.2848	0.5875	1				
7	0.0001	0.0048	0.0377	0.1351	0.3241	0.6138	1			
8	0	0.0011	0.013	0.059	0.1673	0.357	0.6353	1		
9	0	0.0002	0.0041	0.0238	0.0805	0.196	0.3849	0.6533	1	
10	0	0	0.0012	0.0088	0.0361	0.1013	0.2217	0.4092	0.6687	1
11	0	0	0.0003	0.003	0.0151	0.0492	0.1211	0.245	0.4305	06821
12	0	0	0.0001	0.001	0.0059	0.0225	0.0626	0.1398	0.266	0.4494
13	0	0	0	0.0003	0.0021	0.0096	0.0306	0.076	0.1575	0.2853
14	0	0	0	0.0001	0.0007	0.0039	0.0142	0.0393	0.0892	0.1741
15	0	0	0	0	0.0002	0.0015	0.0062	0.0193	0.0482	0.102
16	0	0	0	0	0.0001	0.0005	0.0026	0.009	0.0249	0.0573
17	0	0	0	0	0	0.0002	0.001	0.004	0.0123	0.0309
18	0	0	0	0	0	0.0001	0.0004	0.0017	0.0058	0.0159
19	0	0	0	0	0	0	0.0001	0.0007	0.0026	0.0079
20	0	0	0	0	0	0	0	0.0003	0.0011	0.0037

9.10 TRANSACTION MOVING SERIALLY THROUGH MULTIPLE SERVERS

Real networks often contain multiple queues that must be traversed by data packets. The analysis of this situation is reasonably straightforward, and two forms of the problem will be discussed.

The first tandem-queue network provides a single queue for packets/items/customers/transactions (the author was tempted to invent the acronym PICT but thought better of it). A transaction conceptually waits in this queue as each service stage in turn processes it (see Figure 9-15). The service time is the sum of the service times for each stage. Assuming the service times are independent, the variance of the total service time is the sum of the individual variances.

When the N stages are identical and the individual service rate $N \cdot \mu$ is exponentially distributed, the following nice results fall out

- total service time average value $\quad \dfrac{1}{\mu}$
- total service time variance $\quad \dfrac{1}{N \cdot \mu^2}$
- total service time distribution $\quad \dfrac{N \cdot \mu \cdot (N \cdot \mu \cdot t)^{N-1} \cdot e^{-N \cdot \mu \cdot t}}{(N-1)!}$

The total service time distribution is Erlangian. Figure 9-16 plots the distribution for 1, 3, and 20 stages.

Another more likely scenario in networking has packets traversing multiple network hops with a queue at each point. Unlike the stages example below, each packet now moves from service to service, entering a queue at that service if necessary (see Figure 9-17). Each such service center is independent of the others. With the usual assumptions of independent exponential service and interarrival times, each service can be dealt with independently. The total delay is the sum of the individual delays and we already know that the individual waiting times are exponentially distributed—ergo the total waiting time is Erlangian if the services are identical.

Assuming different service rates at the service centers $\mu_1, \mu_2, \ldots, \mu_N$ and an arrival rate of λ, the average total service time is:

$$\frac{1}{\mu_1 - \lambda} + \frac{1}{\mu_2 - \lambda} + \ldots + \frac{1}{\mu_N - \lambda}$$

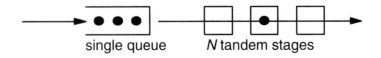

single queue   N tandem stages

Figure 9-15 The single-queue multiple-stages system forces arriving transactions to wait in the queue until the active transaction has visited each of the N stages. There is no storage at these stages to hold waiting transactions. With independent identical stages the average service time is N times that of each stage and the distribution is Erlangian.

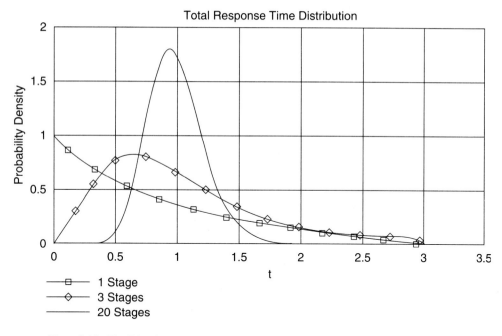

Figure 9-16 The Erlangian distribution for 1, 3, and 20 stages tend from the exponential (1 stage) to the normal (20 stages). The 3-stage example has stages 1/3 as fast as the 1-stage example and the 20-stage example has stages 1/20 as fast as the 1-stage example. The Erlangian formula is useful for combining several values that are exponentially distributed and have the same mean value.

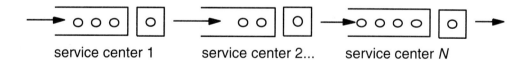

Figure 9-17 Tandem queues are presumed independent of each other, an assumption that might not hold true in real networks. The mean arrival rate is constant throughout the tandem queues because transactions are neither created nor destroyed. It is essential that the average service rate at each service center exceeds the mean arrival rate because we want the network to be stable. Otherwise packets will accumulate in the queue, eventually overflowing it, which reduces the arrival rate to the downstream queues. The average wait times for each service center can be added up to get the total wait time.

9.11 QUEUING THEORY APPLIED TO A SPOOLED NETWORK PRINTER

Networked users often take advantage of a print server to avoid waiting for the printer to free up and to avoid tying up their application waiting for the printout to complete. The user typically runs a network operating such as Banyan Vines, Novell Netware, LANTastic, LAN Manager, or UNIX that redirects the print output to the print server via the LAN (see Figure 9-18). This inspooling operation takes relatively little time with the high-speed Ethernet LAN and modern server disk drives in use today.

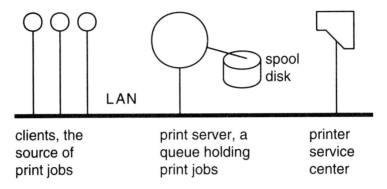

Figure 9-18 Print jobs arrive from a population of clients and inspool to the print server disk, which acts like a queue. The printer itself is considered a server in the queuing sense. The flow of print jobs can be analyzed in terms of simple queuing theory.

To analyze the performance of this printing environment we need to take our performance parameters and translate them into queuing theory parameters. The number of print jobs per hour is the transaction arrival rate λ. This number can be obtained either by interviewing the users, checking the print server log file, or watching the printer for a few hours and counting print jobs directly. The average print rate is the service rate μ (print jobs per hour) and this number can be obtained as before. It may be easier to estimate average number of pages per print job, assume it's exponential, and use the printer rating to figure the average job print rate.

Some simplifying assumptions will be made

- Printer "warm-up" time is negligible.
- Outspool time is negligible.
- LAN utilization is negligible.
- Server utilization does not impact outspooling.
- Print jobs are exponential.
- Printer RAM is not an issue.

Let's work a numerical example. The user demand is 30 print jobs per hour ($\lambda = 0.5$ jobs per minute) with an average of 20 pages each. The printer is rated at 17 pages per minute so the jobs are printed at the rate of 17 per 20 giving $\mu = 0.85$ jobs per minute. Notice that all quantities should be converted to the same units of measure, which is why pages were converted to jobs and hours were converted to minutes. The calculations are shown in Table 9-5.

TABLE 9-5 SPOOLER PERFORMANCE VALUES

Parameter	Formula	Value
job arrival rate	λ	0.5 jobs/minute
job service rate	μ	0.85 jobs/minute
print jobs in system	$L = \lambda/(\mu - \lambda)$	1.43 jobs
total wait time	$W = L/\lambda$	2.46 minutes

The average wait time for a print job to complete is only 2.46 minutes, not unreasonable.

9.12 DECIDING WHETHER TO UPGRADE OR REPLICATE

This section is devoted to studying what happens to network response time as we trade off the service rate and the number of servers. In this study we fix the arrival rate at $\lambda = 20$ and vary the number of servers and their service rates. This is an M/M/m analysis with exponential interarrival and service times and m- servers. The results are shown in Table 9-6 and graphed in Figure 9-19.

TABLE 9-6 RESPONSE TIME DEPENDENCY ON SERVICE RATE AND SERVER QUANTITY

Case number	Number of servers	Service rate per server in transactions per second	Average response time in seconds
1	1	32	0.083
2	2	16	0.103
3	4	8	0.156
4	8	4	0.264
5	16	2	0.501
6	32	1	1.001

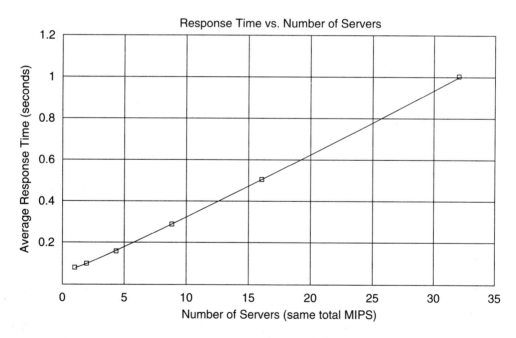

Figure 9-19 The transaction response time increases as we add progressively slower servers to the server farm, always keeping the same total service rate of 20 transactions per second. The average server utilization is always 62.5%. The lesson here is that it is always better to have one very fast service than a lot of slower ones. The raw data for this graph is Table 9-6.

The arithmetic used to generate this graph and table is given in Figure 9-20, with the numbers worked out for $cc = 32$ servers

$cc := 32 \quad \lambda := 20.0 \quad \mu := 1.0 \qquad cc \quad$ number of servers
$\qquad \qquad \qquad \qquad \qquad \qquad \qquad \lambda \quad$ rate of arrivals into the system
$a := \dfrac{\lambda}{\mu} \quad \rho := \dfrac{a}{cc} \quad \rho = 6.25 \cdot 10^{-1} \qquad \mu \quad$ rate of service at each serve:
$\qquad \qquad \qquad \qquad \qquad \qquad \qquad a \quad$ ratio λ / μ
$\qquad \qquad \qquad \qquad \qquad \qquad \qquad \rho \quad$ entire facility utilization

$$C(c, a) := \dfrac{\dfrac{a^{cc}}{cc!}}{(1 - \rho) \cdot \sum_{n=0}^{c-1} \dfrac{a^n}{n!} + \dfrac{a^{cc}}{cc!}} \qquad \text{Probability that a 1 servers are busy}$$

$Lq := \dfrac{\rho \cdot C(cc, a)}{1 - \rho} \qquad Lq = 1.494 \cdot 10^{-2} \qquad$ Queue length

$Wq := \dfrac{Lq}{\lambda} \qquad \qquad \quad Wq = 7.47 \cdot 10^{-4} \qquad$ Wait time in queue

$Ws := \dfrac{\rho \cdot cc}{\lambda} \qquad \qquad Ws = 1 \qquad \qquad \quad$ Average service time

$W := Wq + Ws \qquad \qquad W = 1.001 \qquad \qquad$ Average time in the system

Figure 9-20 This is the Mathcad document used to work out the numbers for this problem. You vary the number of servers (cc) and their performance (μ) so their product is constant and record the average time spent in the system at each step. The case for upgrading wins out over the case for replicating.

9.13 PREDICTING BUFFER OVERFLOW AND PACKET LOSS IN BRIDGES AND ROUTERS

Queuing analysis can be used to predict packet loss in bridges, routers, and other store-and-forward devices that depend on buffering to handle speed mismatches between input and output ports. The packet loss is typically the result of arrivals that encounter a full buffer.

The device buffer management scheme may provide a number of fixed-size buffers for small, medium, and large packet sizes. The device may simply provide so many megabytes of RAM, which will hold on the average so many packets of average size. In any case, the arithmetic to convert the buffer capacity to packets has to be done so the queue length calculations can be done. The probability that the queue length exceeds this capacity is one way to estimate the packet loss rate. Doing an M/M/1/k analysis (queue limited to k packets) is more accurate but more complex.

With the large amounts of buffer space installed in routers these days, the amount of time spent in the queue may be higher than the transport timers and trigger a retransmission. Queuing theory can address this too, by computing the wait time distribution to determine the chances that the wait time will exceed the transport retransmission timer.

The general approach, then, is to compute the queue length and wait time distributions and examine the tail of these distributions, either mathematically, numerically, or graphically. On a good day, we have a probability density function (PDF) available, instead of only the mean and variance of the distribution. With only the mean and variance at hand, there is not enough information to work with to determine queue overflow probabilities and wait time-outs.

Hopefully the PDF is easy to integrate to obtain the cumulative density function (CDF), using a calculus textbook with a table of integrals, resorting to first principles, or using a symbolic math scratchpad program such as Mathcad (which incorporates the Maple symbolic math processor from Waterloo). Table 9-7 provides a mercifully brief list of integrals as applied to PDFs and CDFs.

The CDF for the normal distribution is two-tailed and the formula includes the error function $erf(t)$. This is a standard mathematical function and it looks like the CDF for the normal distribution with a mean of zero and a variance of one (see Table 9-8 and Figures 9-21 and 9-22).

Otherwise the PDF can be integrated numerically by chopping it into thin slices along the x-axis and tabulating the increasing sum of the areas of these slices, starting at $x = 0$ and moving to the right. Equivalently, the area can be determined by plotting the PDF and manually estimating the area under the tail (a manual method of integration).

A few words of caution about the tails of density functions. Given that the numerical inputs to queuing analysis are not exact and that some of the simplifying assumptions are probably not fully valid, the resulting PDF will not be any more exact either. This means that the tail of the distribution and the area underneath it will be very sensitive to input variations and any practical interpretations should be stated with an appropriate degree of uncertainty.

An example to illustrate this is a simple queuing system with service rate of $\mu = 20.0$ and three values for the arrival rate $\lambda = 18.1, 18.3, 18.5$ (see Figure 9-23). Recall that the total waiting time probability density function is $\frac{1}{\mu - \lambda} \exp \frac{-t}{\mu - \lambda}$ and the cumulative density function (the PDF's integral) is $1 - \exp \frac{-t}{\mu - \lambda}$.

TABLE 9-7 INTEGRALS APPLIED TO PDFS AND CDFS

Description	Probability density	Cumulative density
Exponential	$\frac{1}{\mu} \exp\left(\frac{-t}{\mu}\right)$	$1 - \exp\left(\frac{-t}{\mu}\right)$
Normal	$\frac{1}{\sigma \cdot \sqrt{2 \cdot \pi}} \exp\left(-\frac{(t-\mu)^2}{2 \cdot \sigma^2}\right)$	$\frac{1}{2} \cdot \left(1 - erf\left(\frac{\sqrt{2}}{2} \cdot \frac{-t+\mu}{\sigma}\right)\right)$
Uniform	$1, a \leq t \leq b$	$\frac{t-a}{b-a}, a \leq t \leq b$
	$0, a > t > b$	$0, a > t$
		$1, t > b$

Note: Because statistics tends to use μ for the **mean** and σ for the **standard deviation,** so does the table above. Because queuing theory uses μ for the **average service rate** and λ for the **average arrival rate,** it is possible to be confused by this table.

TABLE 9-8 VALUES FOR THE ERROR FUNCTION

t	0	0.5	1	1.5	2	2.5	3	3.5
value	0.5	0.69146	0.84134	0.93319	0.97725	0.99379	0.99865	0.9998

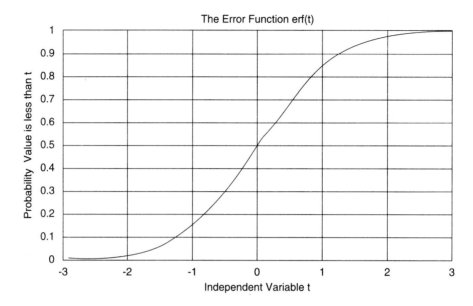

Figure 9-21 The error function *erf(t)* is the same as the normal distribution cumulative density function with zero mean and unity deviation. Each division of the *x*-axis is one standard deviation in this normalized version of the normal CDF. Note that both tails nearly vanish beyond 3 standard deviations from the mean.

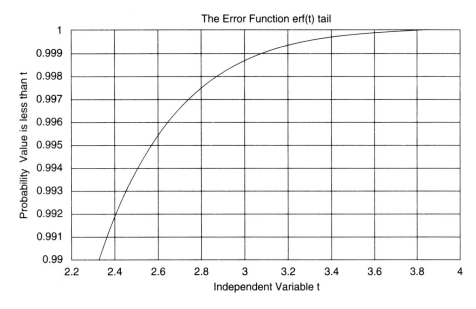

Figure 9-22 The upper tail of the error function approaches 1.0 rapidly between 3 and 4 standard deviations. Any small error in the mean can shift the curve left or right to give a significant probability difference.

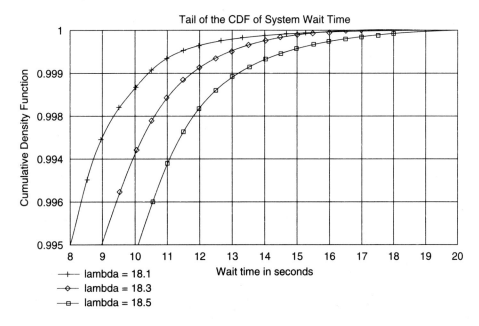

Figure 9-23 The cumulative density function for the system waiting time of a simple M/M/1 queue is sensitive to the precise value of the arrival rate, which is allowed to vary by plus and minus 0.2. Note that the probability the wait time is less than 8 seconds is 0.995—or is it the probability the wait time is less than 10 seconds, or 12?

10

Simulating Discrete Time Events

10.0 INTRODUCTION

Discrete event simulation is a valuable tool for predicting network performance. In this chapter we analyze a simple queue by developing the mechanics for generating events that arrive at specific times, join a queue, wait there for a time, obtain service, and finally depart. The methodology is laid out in columns for a manual solution. Then we redo the analysis as a Mathcad document to allow us to simulate thousands of events and evaluate the results of the simulation graphically.

Next we look at an example of the Monte Carlo statistical method, which depends on random number generation to solve performance problems. We finally enjoy a brief introduction into the world of C-language simulation libraries.

10.1 SIMULATING DISCRETE TIME EVENTS

The basic reason for simulation is to handle mathematically intractable (hard) problems. The advantage of simulation is that it can deal with fairly arbitrary events rather than just Poisson-distributed ones. An event is moved along from queue to service onto the next position until it reaches the termination point, whereupon a reply event may propagate back to the source. Events are scheduled and the simulation engine simply moves an event to its next position when that event's time is reached. Conceptually the simulation engine examines a linked list of events and advances the clock to the next one. This event usually creates a future event (such as the expiration of service time), the simulator keeps track of time spent in the particular queue, and then advances the clock to the next event scheduled. For a large simulation there may be hundreds or thousands of concurrent events to be managed. The simulator quits when the stop event occurs, which is typically when the simulated clock reaches a given value such as 60 seconds. The actual wall time it takes the simulator to perform a simulation may be much longer than that.

Simulator States

The simulator is generally in one of four states. In the *initialization state,* the system being simulated is empty of events and all traffic generators are set to generate their first event. The simulator clears all its counters at this time. Then follows a *startup transient state* during which events propagate through the system and start to fill queues and servers. The simulator should be configured not to collect any statistics during this startup period. The *steady state* is reached when the average statistics measured over some time period remain stable. Hopefully the simulation engine has reached the steady state and has spent most of time in that state when the last event occurs. The *ending transient state* may or may not occur, depending on the simulation engine. Events generally dissipate during this interval until the system is again empty. Events during this period are not generally of interest and statistics should not be collected during this state. The simulator writes the simulation statistics to disk when the simulation is over.

After the stop event occurs, a report generator summarizes the statistics generated by the simulation engine. Tables of delays, utilization, and throughput may be printed out or exported to a statistical graphing tool such as SPSS or to a spreadsheet program such as Lotus 1-2-3. The simulation tool may also provide built-in report generators.

Simulating a Simple Queue

To demonstrate a simple discrete event simulation, let's analyze the M/M/1 queue with its Poisson interarrival and service times. This example is fairly simple to construct and can be manually simulated. More complex systems are probably going to take too long to set up and debug, and it is more appropriate to purchase discrete event simulation tools such as PlanNet, COMNET III, or GPSS. The M/M/1 simulation proceeds as follows

1. We determine that we want to generate just six events numbered one through six and begin by numbering them accordingly in column 1. Make room for hypothetical event number zero. It's needed later on for initialization purposes. Leave room for eight columns and we'll be filling in the first six during the simulation.
2. Generate the interarrival times for each event using a Poisson random number generator (since we specified M/M/1 queuing). This simply generates a sequence of samples from the desired statistical distribution. We could use any statistical number generator we want here. Write these samples in column 2.
3. Starting the clock at $t = 0$, calculate when each event joins the queue (enters the head of the queue) by adding up all the interarrival times of the events prior to and including the current event. Since we already know when the previous event joins the queue, we calculate when the current event joins the queue by adding its interarrival time to the arrival time of the previous event. Write all these event arrival times down in column 3. Note that the first event is not forced to occur at $t = 0$, nor should it be.

4. For each event, use a Poisson random number generator (since we specified M/M/1 queuing) to figure the service time for each event. Again, any statistical distribution can be used here. We're not limited to Poisson's distribution. Write all the service times down in column 4.

5. In column 6 in the row for event zero, write in a zero. This column records the time an event leaves the server. Column 5 keeps track of the time at which each event gets service (after any queuing delays it may have encountered). Now things get interesting as we begin the actual simulation.

6. **For** each event from 1 to 6
   Do
   - **if** the previous event leaves the server before the current event joins the queue
     then the current event gets service when it joins the queue
     else the current even gets service when the previous event leaves the server
   - write down when the time the current event gets service in column 5
   - calculate when the current event leaves the server by adding its service time to the time the current event gets service and write it down in column 6
   Done

The simulator rules above can be written more compactly if we adopt a bit of clear, practical mathematical notation. This is important when implementing the discrete event simulator using a programming language, a spreadsheet, or a math scratchpad tool. We will then rewrite the psuedo-code above in terms of the new notation (see Table 10-1).

The discrete event simulation for the M/M/1 queue expressed in the new notation looks like this

```
LSAT(0)=0
FOR I = 1 TO 6
DO
    IF LSAT(I-1) < JQAT(I)
        THEN GSAT(I) = JQAT(I)
        ELSE GSAT(I) = LSAT(I-1)
    LSAT(I) = ST(I) + GSAT(I)
DONE
```

TABLE 10-1 MATHEMATICAL NOTATION FOR THE M/M/1 QUEUE DISCRETE EVENT SIMULATION

Symbol notation	Meaning of the symbol	Worksheet column
I	The event number, which goes from 0 to the last event number	1
IAT(I)	Inter-Arrival Time for event I	2
JQAT(I)	Join Queue At Time for event I	3
ST(I)	Service Time for event I	4
GSAT(I)	Get Service At Time for event I	5
LSAT(I)	Leave Server At Time for event I	6
TSIS(I)	Time Spent In System for event I	7
TSIQ(I)	Time Spent In Queue for event I	8

Simulation Using a Spreadsheet

Following the method, we manually perform the functions of the simulation engine and construct a worksheet (Table 10-2), which at this point will contain just the raw simulation results. Figure 10-1 examines the processing of event 3 on the worksheet.

TABLE 10-2 WORKSHEET FOR PERFORMING THE M/M/1 DISCRETE EVENT SIMULATION

1	2	3	4	5	6	7	8
Event I	Interarrival Time IAT	Join Queue At Time JQAT	Service Time ST	Get Service At Time GSAT	Leave Server At Time LSAT		
0		0			0		
1	0.2	0.2	0.2	0.2	0.4		
2	0.3	0.5	0.2	0.5	0.7		
3	0.1	0.6	0.1	0.7	0.8		
4	0.2	0.8	0.4	0.8	1.2		
5	0.3	1.1	0.2	1.2	1.4		
6	0.2	1.3	0.3	1.4	1.7		

Worksheet for Performing the M/M/1 Discete Event Simulation					
1	2	3	4	5	6
Event	Interarrival Time	Join Queue At Time	Service Time	Get Service At Time	Leave Server At Time
I	IAT	JQAT	ST	GSAT	LSAT
0		0			0
1	0.2	0.2	0.2	0.2	0.4
2	0.3	0.5	0.2	0.5	0.7
3	0.1	0.6	0.1 +	0.7 =	0.8
4	0.2	0.8	0.4	0.8	1.2
5	0.3	1.1	0.2	1.2	1.4
6	0.2	1.3	0.3	1.4	1.7

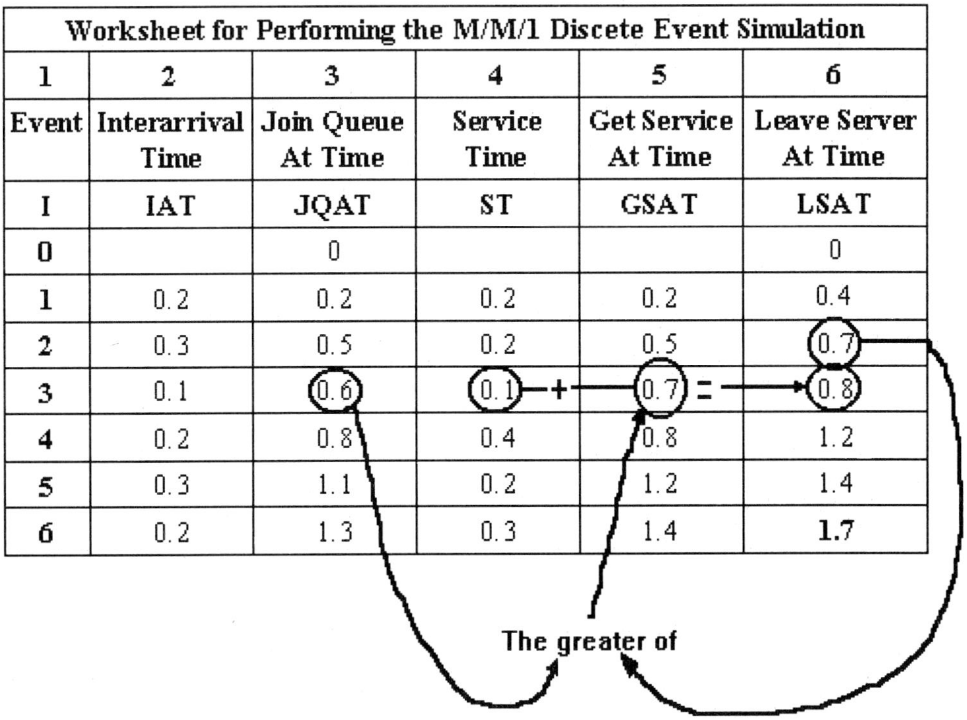

The greater of

Figure 10-1 An example of the arithmetic done to process event 3. Notice that the previous event 2 leaves the server at $t = 0.7$, forcing event 3 to wait in the queue from the time it joins it at $t = 0.6$ to the time event 2 leaves the server.

Sec. 10.1   Simulating Discrete Time Events

Now that the simulation engine is finished, it's time to extract the relevant statistics from the worksheet. The performance of this queuing system can be derived directly from the worksheet. First notice that the entire simulation covers 1.7 seconds. This is not known beforehand. The simulation implicitly waits for the last event to leave the system.

The actual average interarrival time and actual average service times can be computed just by averaging columns 2 and 4 individually. The actual time each event spends in the system is the difference between the time the event joins the queue and the time the event leaves the server. This lets us add a seventh column to the worksheet equal to the difference between LSAT and JQAT. The average value of column 7 is the average time spent in the system by the six events. Now on a roll, add an eighth column which shows the difference between columns 3 and 5. This is the time the event spent waiting in the queue itself. The augmented worksheet now looks like Table 10-3.

Little's Law states that the average number of events in the system is $N = \lambda \cdot T$, the product of the average arrival rate λ multiplied by the average time in the system T. Our results above show that $\lambda = 1 / 0.21667 = 4.6153846$ events per second and $T = 0.28333$ second per event. Thus $N = 4.6153 \cdot 0.28333 = 1.307692$ events are in the system on the average.

Applying Little's Law to the queue, we use the same $\lambda = 4.6153846$, let $T = 0.05$, and calculate that $N = 4.6153846 \cdot 0.05 = 0.23076923$ events are in the queue, on the average.

Accuracy of the Simulation

This is a nice example of how to do discrete event simulations, and it has been a mercifully short one, and fairly easy to follow as a result. But because this specific simulation covered only six events over 1.7 seconds, it has the following shortcomings (which can be remedied by running a much longer simulation with the aid of some automated tools)

- The values calculated for μ and λ are not very accurate, based on only six event samples. A few hundred to a few thousand events are preferred.

TABLE 10-3 WORKSHEET FOR PERFORMING THE M/M/1 DISCRETE EVENT SIMULATION

1 Event I	2 Interarrival Time IAT	3 Join Queue At Time JQAT	4 Service Time ST	5 Get Service At Time GSAT	6 Leave Server At Time LSAT	7 Time Spent In System TSIS	8 Time Spent In Queue TSIQ
0		0			0		
1	0.2	0.2	0.2	0.2	0.4	0.2	0
2	0.3	0.5	0.2	0.5	0.7	0.2	0
3	0.1	0.6	0.1	0.7	0.8	0.2	0.1
4	0.2	0.8	0.4	0.8	1.2	0.4	0
5	0.3	1.1	0.2	1.2	1.4	0.3	0.1
6	0.2	1.3	0.3	1.4	1.7	0.4	0.1
Averages:	0.21667		0.23333			0.28333	0.05

- The startup and ending transient states are included in the statistics. This can be overcome by excluding the first and last 10% of the events from the statistical analysis and by running the simulation about 25% longer to keep the same number of events.
- The steady state was never reached at all, since the simulation was so brief. A rule of thumb is to figure out the longest event duration in the system and multiply it by ten. The system should be in a steady state after this amount of time. In our example, the average time spent in the system is 0.28333 seconds, so the startup transient should have died out by $t = 2.8333$ seconds. The simulation should last at least ten times this long, or 28 seconds.
- The simulation elapsed time includes the time taken by the ending transient. If transient analysis is not of interest, exclude the last 10% of the events from the statistical analysis.
- The interarrival and service times have not been validated as Poisson. In truth the above example is too brief to prove any statistical distribution. A few hundred to a few thousand events are enough to allow a histogram analysis of the interarrival and service times.
- The average service time exceeds the average interarrival time. This is OK if the intent is to study an unstable system that does not reach a steady state. Since our example is so short, these average values are not accurate enough to make this assertion.
- Applying Little's Law to the server itself, or equivalently, subtracting the average time in the system from the average time in the queue, we find there are $1.307692 - 0.23076923 = 1.07692377$ events in the server on the average. Of course this is impossible, since the server can only hold exactly 1.0 events at a time. The reason for the slight discrepancy is that we don't have perfect estimates—only statistics, and frankly the error is surprisingly small. Also, remember that Little's Law applies to long-term averages, which we don't really have. Still, it's pleasantly surprising to find how well Little's Law holds up.

Simulating with Mathcad

Since few network managers are interested in performing long discrete event simulations by hand, so let's implement a Mathcad implementation of the M/M/1 discrete event simulation method (see Figures 10-2 to 10-8).

Section 10.1   Discrete Event Simulation   Part 1

Step 1   Initialiation

$\text{EXPON}(t) := -t \cdot \ln(\text{rnd}(1))$ Formula generates exponential events

$\lambda := 0.7$ Event arrival rate in events/second

$\mu := 1.0$ Service rate in events/second

$\text{LE} := 1000$ Last Event we plan to process

$i := 1..\text{LE}$ Index of event numbers

Step 2   Generate the interarrival times for each i

$\text{IAT}_i := \text{EXPON}\left(\dfrac{1}{\lambda}\right)$ Inter Arrival Time

Step 3   Generate the time the event arrive at the queue

$\text{JQAT}_0 := 0$ Join Queue At Time

$\text{JQAT}_i := \text{JQAT}_{i-1} + \text{IAT}_i$

Figure 10-2 The discrete event simulation begins by defining the statistical distributions and the arrival and service rates. Then an array is filled with the interarrival times, from which the actual queue arrival times are determined.

Step 4   Generate the service time for each event   Part 2

$\text{ST}_i := \text{EXPON}\left(\dfrac{1}{\mu}\right)$ Service Time

Step 5   Initialize the calculations

$\text{LSAT}_0 := 0$ Leave Server At Time

Step 6   Calculate when the events leave the server

$\text{LSAT}_i := \text{ST}_i + \text{if}(\text{LSAT}_{i-1} < \text{JQAT}_i, \text{JQAT}_i, \text{LSAT}_{i-1})$

Figure 10-3 After filling array ST with each transaction's service time, we perform the simulation in one line at step 6. The array LSAT contains the exact time each event leaves the server.

Step 7   Extract Queueing statistics from the arrays   Part 3

$TSIS_i := LSAT_i - JQAT_i$ Time Spent In System

$GSAT_i := LSAT_i - ST_i$ Get Service At Time

$TSIQ_i := TSIS_i - ST_i$ Time Spent In Queue

$ASR := \dfrac{LE}{JQAT_{LE}}$ Average Arrival Rate for this simulation

$ASR := \dfrac{LE}{\sum_{j=1}^{LE} ST_j}$ Average Service Rate for this simulation

$ATSIS := \dfrac{1}{LE} \cdot \sum_{j=1}^{LE} TSIS_j$ Average Time Spent In System for this simulation

$N := ATSIS \cdot AAR$ Average number of events in the system

Figure 10-4 The simulation is over. Next we calculate how long each transaction spent in the system, keeping this important statistic in array TSIS. Working backwards from this we can figure out (and save in array GSAT) exactly when each transaction got service, and thence how long it spent in the queue (array TSIQ). Finally we're able to compute the important performance metrics like the actual arrival rate the simulation achieved, the actual service rate, the average time spent in the system, and the average number of transactions in the system.

Summary of Simulation Results   Part 4

Statistic	**Simulation**	**M/M/1 prediction**
Number of events	$LE = 1 \cdot 10^3$	n/a
Simulation duration	$LSAT_{LE} = 1.477 \cdot 10^3$	$\dfrac{LE}{\lambda} = 1.429 \cdot 10^3$
Average Arrival Rate	AAR = 0.68	$\lambda = 0.7$
Average Service Rate	ASR = 0.978	$\mu = 1$
Average Time Spent In System	ATSIS = 3.176	$\dfrac{1}{\mu - \lambda} = 3.333$
Average Number In System	N = 2.158	$\dfrac{\lambda}{\mu - \lambda} = 2.333$

Figure 10-5 Comparing the discrete event simulation with the theoretical results, we see that they agree pretty well. Note that the statistical results included all events in the simulation. We can improve the accuracy of the results by first figuring when the simulation reaches the steady state. Then we can ignore events up to that point, as well as points at the end of the simulation, when transactions are draining from the system. Remaining events should comprise at least ten times the duration of the startup and ending transients.

Display the Time Spent In System statistics   **Part 5**

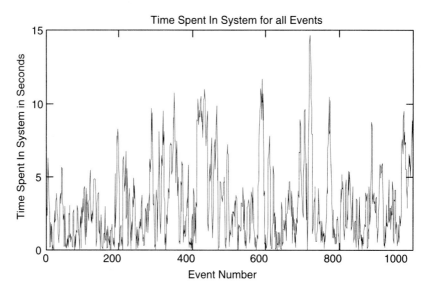

Figure 10-6 A distinct advantage of the discrete event simulation method is that the distribution of the statistics can be determined. For example, since we're always interested in the distribution of the total time transactions spend in the system, we plot all 1,000 of them here. Notice how the total system wait times for adjacent events are strongly correlated in time.

Calculate and display the histogram of waiting times   **Part 6**

$\text{NumSteps} := 10 \quad j := 0..\text{NumSteps} \quad \text{MAX} := \max(\text{TSIS}) \quad \text{Intervals}_j := \frac{\text{MAX}}{\text{NumSteps}} \cdot j$

$\text{PDF} := \text{hist}(\text{Intervals}, \text{TSIS}) \quad \text{PDF}_{\text{NumSteps}} := 0 \quad \text{PDF}_j := \frac{\text{PDF}_j}{\text{LE}}$

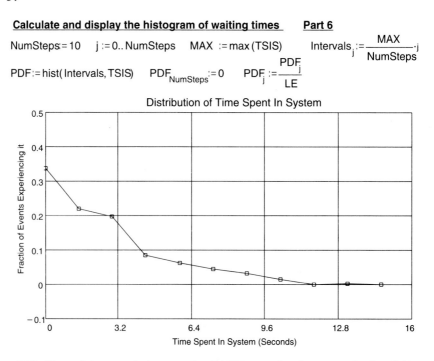

Figure 10-7 The total time spent in the system by all 1,000 transactions is now sorted and stuffed into a histogram. This gives us the wait time probability density distribution. As we expected, it closely resembles the exponential distribution as predicted from the M/M/1 theoretical model. This further validates the simulation.

Create an augmented matrix to display the worksheet   Part 7

W := augment(IAT, JQAT)   W := augment(W, ST)   W := augment(W, GSAT)
W := augment(W, LSAT)   W := augment(W, TSIS)   W := augment(W, TSIQ)

IAT   JQAT   SAT   GSAT   LSAT   TSIS   TSIQ

W =

	0	1	2	3	4	5	6
0	0	0	0	0	0	0	0
1	9.529	9.529	3.014	9.529	12.543	3.014	0
2	2.348	11.876	2.148	12.543	14.691	2.815	0.667
3	0.766	12.642	0.301	14.691	14.992	2.35	2.049
4	1.498	14.141	5.423	14.992	20.415	6.274	0.852
5	0.279	14.419	0.045	20.415	20.46	6.04	5.996
6	2.497	16.916	0.287	20.46	20.746	3.83	3.543
7	0.488	17.405	0.388	20.746	21.134	3.73	3.342
8	1.701	19.106	0.411	21.134	21.545	2.44	2.029
9	3.418	22.523	2.643	22.523	25.167	2.643	0
10	2.736	25.259	0.149	25.259	25.409	0.149	$1.416 \cdot 10^{-15}$
11	0.017	25.276	0.118	25.409	25.526	0.25	0.133
12	3.04	28.316	1.882	28.316	30.198	1.882	0

Figure 10-8 Mathcad can display the worksheet of results with a little array augmentation work. This lets us see each and every event's timetable. Only the first 12 transactions are shown.

10.2 STATISTICAL METHODS OF SIMULATION

The Monte Carlo method is a simple simulation technique that generates random numbers and compares the results with a hit-or-miss criterion, much like its namesake. To use it in network simulation work, consider the following example. A statistical analysis of an existing communication system finds that packets are lost when the packet size and congestion level lie above a certain curve (see Figure 10-9). To predict the packet loss rate of this network under a certain type of traffic, random number generators with the appropriate statistical distribution (Poisson, normal, uniform, etc.) are used to create pairs of random numbers representing the packet size and congestion levels. Each such point is plotted on the graph. If the point lies above the curve, then it counts as a lost packet, otherwise it counts as a transmitted packet. After generating a few thousand packets, the packet loss rate can be determined reasonably accurately.

Monte Carlo simulation methods have advantages over analytical solutions. They're much faster to implement in terms of people time, the results are excellent when enough events are generated, and the outcomes can be verified by simple graphical solutions and by repeated trials. Arbitrary statistical distributions can be used to generate events, overcoming the sometimes inappropriate Poisson distributions that are the favorite of analytic solutions. Analytical solutions are not generally available for many practical networks and the approximations and simplifying assumptions necessary to obtain an analytical solution may limit is applicability. Let's use Mathcad to implement a Monte Carlo simulation for the communication system shown above (see Figures 10-10 to 10-13).

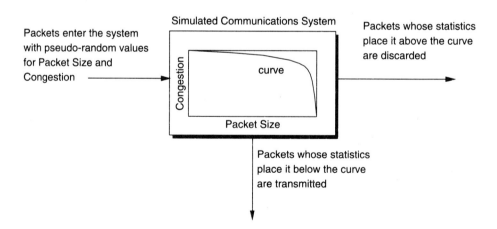

Figure 10-9 A Monte Carlo simulation example of a communications system characterized by a statistical understanding model of how packets are transmitted and discarded. One thousand packets with the anticipated statistical distributions may be generated and those whose points fall above the curve are considered lost packets. To halve the statistical uncertainty of the simulation results, 4,000 packets must be generated.

Section 10.2   Statistical Methods of Simulation—Monte Carlo

$$\text{Curve}(x, y) := \frac{y^2}{100^2} + \frac{x^2}{1518^2}$$

Curve above which packets are considered lost
x = packet size in bytes
y = congestions expressed as a percentage

$$Y(x) := 100\sqrt{1 - \frac{x^2}{1518^2}}$$

This is the same formula as the curve above rewritten as a function so we can plot it later on.

$$X := 0, 2 .. 1518$$

Range variable for plotting the curve.

$$N := 200 \quad i := 1..N$$

Number of packet events to generate.

$$\text{EXPON}(t) := -t \cdot \ln(\text{rnd}(1))$$

The exponential distribution with mean **t**.

$$\text{SIZE}(t) := \max\left[\left[\min\left(\begin{pmatrix}64\\ \text{EXPON}(t)\end{pmatrix}\right)\right]\right]$$

Packet size distribution is poisson with mean **t** and limited between 64 and 1518 bytes, the legal range of Ethernet frames.

$$\text{CONGESTION}(t) := \min\left(\begin{pmatrix}100\\ \text{rnd}(2 \cdot t)\end{pmatrix}\right)$$

Congestion distribution is uniform with mean **t** and limited between 0 and 100 percent.

PacketSizeMean := 576
CongestionMean := 50

Define the mean values for the packet size and congestion distribution functions.

$$\begin{pmatrix}x_i\\ y_i\end{pmatrix} := \begin{pmatrix}\text{SIZE}(\text{PacketSizeMean})\\ \text{CONGESTION}(\text{CongestionMean})\end{pmatrix}$$

Generate and save all samples.

$$\text{Lost} := \left[\sum_{j=1}^{N} \text{Curve}(x_j, x_j) > 1\right]$$

Sift through all the packet events and count only those packets that will be dropped because they lie above the curve.

Lost = 28

This is how many packets were dropped.

Figure 10-10 The Monte Carlo simulation implemented using Mathcad. The probability distribution function for congestion is uniformly distributed between zero and 100 with mean 50, and for packet size is exponentially distributed with mean 576 with a lower cutoff of 64 and upper cutoff of 1,518. The curve defined here is an ellipse centered on the origin with y-axis intercept of 100% and with x-axis intercept of 1,518 bytes. The simulation generates packet events, stores them in arrays, and counts events laying above the curve. Out of 200 events generated, 28 packets were lost.

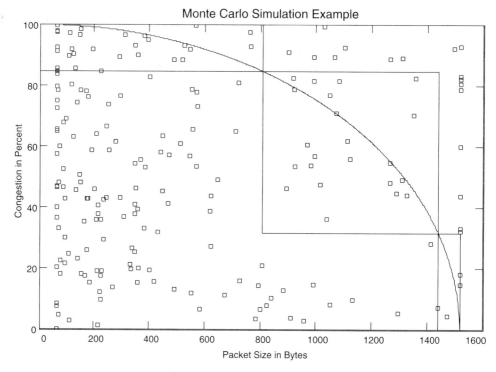

Figure 10-11 The Monte Carlo simulation results are best understood when the 200 packet events are plotted along with the decision curve. It's easily seen that 28 events lie above the curve where packet losses are known to occur for the communication system under study. The simulation wall time is only a few seconds, so various parameters can be changed to fully characterize the system performance. To improve the accuracy of the results, more events need to be generated. To double the accuracy, four times as many events are needed—800 events.

Trials =

	N	Lost	% Loss
	0	1	2
0	100	13	13
1	200	28	14
2	400	72	18
3	800	116	14.5
4	1600	257	16.0625
5	3200	486	15.1875
6	6400	1006	15.71875
7	12800	1973	15.414063
8	25600	3931	15.355469
9	51200	8032	15.6875
10	256000	39966	15.611719

$i := 0..10 \quad PercentLoss_i := \frac{Trials_{i,1}}{Trials_{i,0}} \cdot 100$

$Trials_{i,2} := PercentLoss_i$

The Monte Carlo simulation was run with various numbers of events and the results were put in an array called **Trials**, shown below. After converting these results to percentages, a plot is produced to demonstrate how the accuracy of the result improves with the number of trials.

Figure 10-12 Because the Monte Carlo simulation method is psuedo-random, the statistical accuracy increases as more and more samples are generated. Typically the accuracy doubles every time the number of samples quadruples—as one would expect from basic statistical principles. The results of several simulations are given in the array to demonstrate this.

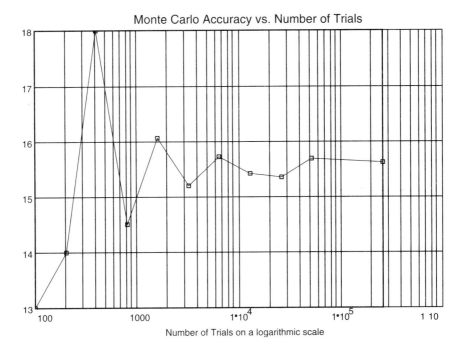

Figure 10-13 Graphical depiction of the results of the Monte Carlo simulations done above. Note that the *x*-axis is logarithmically scaled to improve the presentation. The results clearly converge to a stable result as the number of trials increase. We see that the average packet loss rate lies between 15% and 16% and this is useful information. It is not as important to find out if the loss is 15.5% or 15.6%. The advantage of plotting the results of successively longer trials is that you soon realize that the answer is in hand so you can stop analyzing and get back to work!

10.3 USING C-LANGUAGE MODELING LIBRARIES

Network performance simulations have historically been done using various programming languages, often in FORTRAN. The nineties programming language appears to be the original barefoot Kernighan & Ritchie (K&R) C, ANSI C (after the American National Standards Institute), C++, and now Visual C++. We won't do any programming in this section, anticipating that writing C-language programs is beyond the normal scope of reason for network managers pursuing performance management. This section is included for general information and completeness.

Information on accessing C-language simulation libraries is presented in Table 10-4. Simulation libraries generally include the following modules

- random number generators for the popular statistical distributions
- create and destroy events
- move events from point to point
- obtain and release resources
- queues with various disciplines
- service center

TABLE 10-4 C-LANGUAGE SIMULATION LIBRARIES REFERENCE INFORMATION

Name	Software Location
Discrete Event Simulation Library	$3\frac{1}{2}$ inch diskette supplied with the book *Discrete Event Simulation in C* by Kevin Watkins (McGraw-Hill, 1993)
REAL 3.0	`ftp://icsi-ftp.Berkeley.EDU:pub/tenet/REAL`

NEST	`ftp://columbia.edu/pub/nest-25-doc.tar`
	`ftp://columnest-25-doc2.tar`
	`ftp://columnest-25-src.tar`
	`ftp://columnest-25-disp.tar`

SIMPACK	`ftp://ftp.cis.ufl.edu/pub/simdigest/tools/` `simpack-2.22.tar.Z`

SIMULA	`ftp://rascal.ics.utexas.edu/mac/programming/simula/`
	`lund_simula_4pt07.sit_bin`
	`ftp://rascal.ics.utexas.edu/mac/programming/simula/`
	`simula_4pt07_reference_stack.sit_bin`
	`ftp://rascal.ics.utexas.edu/mac/programming/simula/`
	`sinterfaces.sit_bin`

GPSS	`ftp://NERVM. NERDC. UFL. EDU/DICKE.194/RUNENV. EXE`
SMPL	`ftp://bikini.cis.ufl.edu/tools/`
QSIM	`ftp://bikini.cis.ufl.edu`
Computer simulation digest and archive	`ftp://bikini.cis.ufl.edu/pub/simdigest` `ftp://bikini.cis.ufl.edu/pub/simdigest/tools`

The notation above is taken from the World Wide Web (WWW) notation for Universal Resource Locator (URL). For example, to get a copy of SIMPACK, the URL is `ftp://ftp.cis.ufl.edu/pub/simdigest/tools/simpack-2.22.tar.Z` per the above. Use the file transfer protocol (ftp) command, connect to the system called `ftp.cis.ufl.edu` (logging in as the user `anonymous` and entering your Email address for a password as a courtesy), and go to the directory `/pub/simdigest/tools/` and *get* the file called `simpack-2.22.tar.Z` (in binary mode since it's a UNIX compressed file per the `.Z` suffix).

- delay center
- central event measurement and statistics collector
- report generator for tables and histograms
- event scheduler
- dot-h files
- statistics generator (for mean and variance)
- confidence interval
- error handler
- code templates
- program examples
- documentation

The programmer is responsible for specifying, writing, and debugging the C main() program before the simulation results can be trusted.

A middle-of-the-road approach to using C-language code is exemplified by Mathcad 5.0 Plus. It allows you to invoke external C-language functions from within the math scratchpad and use the results returned.

11

Using Spreadsheets for Capacity Planning

11.0 INTRODUCTION

Spreadsheets are useful tools for the network capacity planning process. In this chapter we'll explore spreadsheet features and techniques that are particularly well suited to our task.

It's assumed that the reader has some basic understanding of how to use his or her spreadsheet of choice. The examples in this chapter are all based on Lotus 1-2-3 and readers are asked to make the necessary translations if they use another spreadsheet such as Excel, Quattro Pro, or ClarisWorks.

We begin by listing the rather rich set of mathematical functions supported by spreadsheets, including transcendental, hyperbolic, integer, trigonometric, and statistics functions. Then we digress a bit to review getting help about built-in functions, learn how to organize our work in multiple worksheets, review precision and accuracy issues, and introduce various data types supported by cut-and-paste.

Many performance problems include mathematical formulas and we go into methods for evaluating them over a range of values. Producing graphs and charts is covered in some detail because they are an important product of any analysis. A discrete event simulation example is also worked out in Lotus 1-2-3. A worst-case visualization follows.

Sometimes problems are solved graphically by plotting formulas and discovering where their curves intersect, peak, or cross the x-axis. Next we go into interactive methods and use the factorial and Fibonnaci number series as an example. The Lotus 1-2-3 macro feature is demonstrated as a programming feature that can save considerable manual labor.

In recognition of those who have to write network capacity plans, we go into all the details, tricks, and methods for creating documentation from their spreadsheets. Finally we list spreadsheets available in the marketplace.

11.1 FUNCTIONS AVAILABLE IN SPREADSHEETS

Spreadsheets provide a tremendous variety and richness of mathematical functions that take as their arguments a cell, a list of cells, a range of cells, or a combination of these. Ranges are often named for convenience. Tables 11-1 through 11-7 provide a partial list of Lotus 1-2-3 functions by category.

TABLE 11-1 TRANSCENDENTAL FUNCTIONS

Function Name	Description
@ABS	absolute value
@EXP	exponential
@EXP2	exponential($-x2$)
@FACT	factorial
@FACTLN	natural log of factorial
@INT	integer portion
@LARGE	finds nth largest value in a range
@LN	natural logarithm
@LOG	common logarithm
@MOD	remainder of a division
@QUOTIENT	integer portion of a division
@RAND	random number between 0 and 1
@SIGN	sign of a number
@SMALL	nth smallest value in a range
@SQRT	positive square root
@SQRTPI	square root of number times pi

TABLE 11-2 HYPERBOLIC INVERSE (ARC) FUNCTIONS

Function Name	Description
@ACOSH	arc hyperbolic cosine
@ACOTH	arc hyperbolic cotangent
@ACSCH	arc hyperbolic cosecant
@ESECH	arc hyperbolic secant
@ASINH	arc hyperbolic sin
@ATANH	arc hyperbolic tangent

TABLE 11-3 HYPERBOLIC FUNCTIONS

Function Name	Description
@COSH	hyperbolic cosine
@COTH	hyperbolic cotangent
@CSCH	hyperbolic cosecant
@SECH	hyperbolic secant
@SINH	hyperbolic sine
@TANH	hyperbolic tangent

TABLE 11-4 INTEGER-BASED FUNCTIONS

Function Name	Description
@EVEN	round upwards to next even integer
@ODD	round upwards to next odd integer
@ROUND	round to n decimal places

TABLE 11-5 TRIGONOMETRIC FUNCTIONS

Function Name	Description
@ACOS	arc cosine
@ACOT	arc cotangent
@ACSC	arc cosecant
@ASEC	arc secant
@ASIN	arc sine
@ATAN	arc tangent (first quadrant)
@ATAN2	arc tangent (four quadrants)
@COS	cosine
@COT	cotangent
@CSC	cosecant
@PI	pi
@SEC	secant
@SIN	sine
@TAN	tangent

TABLE 11-6 STATISTICS DISTRIBUTIONS

Function Name	Description
@BINOMIAL	binomial cumulative distribution
@CHIDIST	chi-squared distribution information
@COMBIN	binomial coefficient
@FDIST	F-function cumulative distribution
@NORMA	normal distribution
@PERMUT	permutations
@POISSON	Poisson distribution
@TDIST	T-distribution

Sec. 11.1   Functions Available in Spreadsheets

TABLE 11-7 STATISTICS CALCULATING FUNCTIONS

Function Name	Description
@REGRESSION	multiple linear regression
@AVEDEV	deviation
@AVE	average
@CORREL	correlation coefficient
@COUNT	counts the number of nonblank cells
@COV	covariance
@DEVSQ	sum of squared deviates
@GEOMEAN	geometric mean
@GRANDTOTAL	sum of subtotal formulas
@HARMEAN	harmonic mean
@KURTOSIS	kurtosis
@MAX	maximum value
@MEDIAN	median
@MIN	minimum
@PRODUCT	product
@SEMEAN	standard error of sample mean
@SKEWNESS	skew
@STD	population standard deviation
@STDS	sample standard deviation
@SUM	sum of all values
@SUMNEGATIVE	sum of negative values
@SUMPOSITIVE	sum of positive values
@SUMPRODUCT	sum of products
@SUMSQ	sum of squares
@SUMXMY2	sum of squared differences
@VAR	population variance
@VARS	sample variance
@WEIGHTAVG	weighted average

Lotus 1-2-3 also has statistical functions for regression and distribution functions under the **Range->Analyze** menu.

Learning More about Spreadsheet Functions

Each function has unique arguments and requirements that may be different if you're using another spreadsheet, so be prepared to look up a function using the help feature by pulling down the **Help** menu, choosing **Search** and entering the word **Function** in the dialog box (see Figure 11-1).

As an example of using a function, suppose we want to add up the numbers in column D from row 5 to 11 and put the result in cell D13. Enter into cell D13 the formula **@SUM(D5..D11)**.

Other Tips for Using Spreadsheets in Network Capacity Planning

To keep work organized it is usually desirable to use several worksheets within the same spreadsheet (see Figure 11-2).

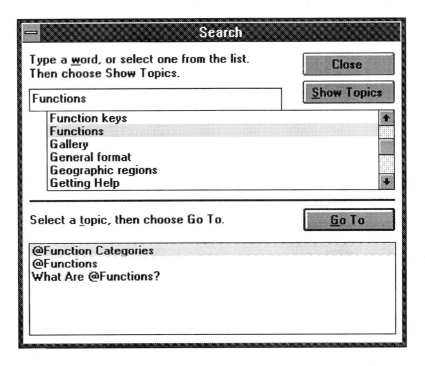

Figure 11-1 To get information about a Lotus 1-2-3 function, choose the function category of interest and read the description. Another way to get function help is to type @ and press F3 and scroll through the list of functions.

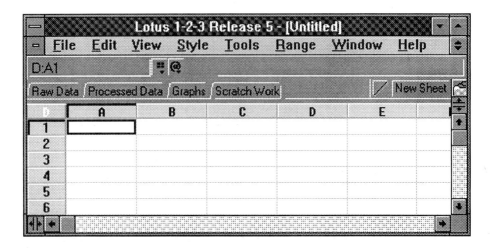

Figure 11-2 There are four worksheets contained in this spreadsheet, for Raw Data, Processed Data, Graphs, and Scratch Work. Organizing work in this fashion makes moving around the data much easier.

Sec. 11.1   Functions Available in Spreadsheets

A word about precision and accuracy is in order. Lotus 1-2-3 will display results in a variety of numeric formats and precision. However, keep in mind that numerical representations are rarely exact. For example, suppose we place 0.0 in cell A1, put the formula **+A1+0.1** in cell A2 and copy this formula into cells A3 to A21. The number 2.0 is displayed in cell A21, even when the displayed precision is set to 15 digits. Yet, if you put the formula **+A21−2.0** into cell B21, the result is **2.2E−19** instead of 0.0. This is because the number 0.1 is not exactly represented by the spreadsheet and the slight inaccuracy is carried around in the arithmetic. This phenomenon matters when the results of two lengthy calculations are numerically close and the difference between them is calculated.

Once results have been calculated it's not unusual to include them into a report. For this discussion assume we're in the world of MS Windows 3.1. This report will probably require copying a range of rows and columns into a word processing document so the user typically rubber-bands the desired cells and does an **Edit->Copy** (or a **Control-C**) or presses the appropriate smart icon. The spreadsheet places the contents onto the clipboard in as many formats as possible. It is now up to the user to switch to the word processing package and paste one of these formats into the document via an **EDIT->Paste Special** (see Figure 11-3).

Suppose we're using Ami Pro, then we get the results shown in Table 11-8 after pasting, depending on the clipboard data format chosen.

The Rich Text Format is preferred since it looks good and still allows us to edit the text. The Windows Metafile format is preferred for pasting in graphics, since it scales well

Figure 11-3 The **Paste Special** formats available in AmiPro.

TABLE 11-8 RESULTS OF CHOOSING VARIOUS SPECIAL PASTE FORMATS

Format	Result
Rich Text Format	A table with text retaining its formatting
Text	A table with text with formatting information removed
Windows Metafile	A frame with a nicely scaleable mostly accurate graphic
DIB (device independent bitmap)	A frame with an accurate bitmap which scales poorly
Windows Bitmap	A frame with an accurate bitmap which scales poorly

and looks good. In a pinch, you can take a screen shot of the spreadsheet window (**ALT-PrtSc**) if none of the formats meet your needs. This places a windows bitmap on the clipboard.

11.2 CONVERTING NETWORK PERFORMANCE FORMULAS TO COLUMNS AND ROWS OF VALUES

Network performance analysis often requires the use of functions evaluated over some range. Spreadsheets can make this very easy with just a little planning up front.

Begin by deciding the starting and ending values for the x-values and the number of points. For example, suppose we wish to evaluate the function $f(x) = 1/(1-x)$ between $x = 0$ and $x = 0.9$ at 11 points. Enter these values as shown below and then create the column of x-values by entering only the first and second values for x. The second value for x is the first value plus the incremental x-value. The rest of the x-values are computed by simply copying the formula from the second value in cell B11 into cells B12 to B20 (see Figure 11-4).

	A	B	C	D	E	F
1	Define the basic x-value ranges here					
2		Value	Formula			
3	Start value for x	0				
4	End value for x	0.9				
5	Number of points	11				
6	Stepsize	0.09	(B4-B3)/(B5-1)			
7						
8	Create a column of the x-values here			Evaluate the function here		
9		Value	Formula		Value	Formula
10	Start Value for x	0	+B3		1	1/(1-B10)
11	Second value for x	0.09	+B10+$B$6		1.098901	1/(1-B11)
12		0.18	+B11+$B$6		1.219512	1/(1-B12)
13		0.27	+B12+$B$6		1.369863	1/(1-B13)
14		0.36	+B13+$B$6		1.5625	1/(1-B14)
15		0.45	+B14+$B$6		1.818182	1/(1-B15)
16		0.54	+B15+$B$6		2.173913	1/(1-B16)
17		0.63	+B16+$B$6		2.702703	1/(1-B107
18		0.72	+B17+$B$6		3.571429	1/(1-B18)
19		0.81	+B18+$B$6		5.263158	1/(1-B109
20	Last value for x	0.9	+B19+$B$6		10	1/(1-B20)

Figure 11-4 Functions are evaluated over a range of x-values by first creating a column of x-values. These are usually equally spaced, but this need not be so. The function is then evaluated for each x-value in a separate column.

The easy part is to enter the formula $1/(1-x)$ into cell D10 as **1/(1−B10)** and then to copy the formula into cells D11 to D20. The function values are calculated and displayed at once.

Note that the formula for computing the *x*-values takes advantage of both relative and absolute addressing. When the formula **+B10+$B$6** is copied to the other cells, the reference to B10 is copied in a relative manner as B11, B12, etc. But the reference to cell B6 must remain absolute so it is written as **$B$6**.

The formula $f(x) = 1/(1-x)$ is the average wait time in a single server single (M/M/1) queue with an average service rate of 1 per second and an arrival rate of *x* per second.

11.3 Producing Charts and Graphs from Rows and Columns

Once the *x*-axis and function values have been computed, the next step is to represent the results graphically. Visualizing the data helps both to interpret what is happening and to present the information to others. Since the graphs reflect the tabular data, any changes you make in the numbers on the spreadsheet immediately reflect themselves in the graphs. This is a wonderful what-if analysis method. To create a simple $x - y$ graph of the data used in the previous section, proceed as follows

- Choose the **Tools->Chart** menu to get the **Chart Assistant** (see Figure 11-5).

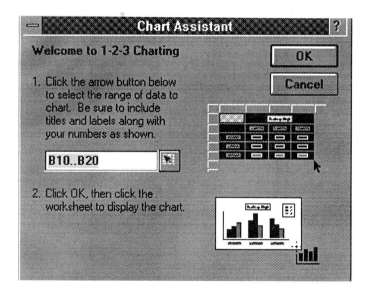

Figure 11-5

- Select the *x*-value range B10 to B20 after pressing the button in step 1 in the Assistant.
- Click OK and select a location in the worksheet for the graph to appear.
- Choose **Chart->Type** and make this an XY chart (the chart becomes blank—stay cool).

- Choose **Chart->Ranges,** select range **B10..B20** for the *x*-axis values and **E10..E20** for *y* (see Figure 11-6).

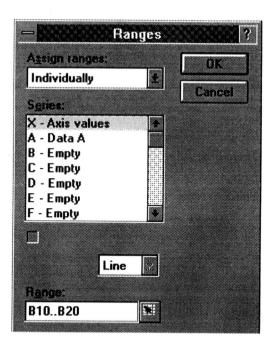

Figure 11-6

- The result is the very plain-looking graph in Figure 11-7.

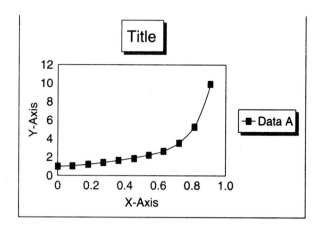

Figure 11-7

- Go through the **Chart** menus sequentially to spruce up the graphs appearance by adding labels and grid lines. The resulting graph (see Figure 11-8) is a little crowded.

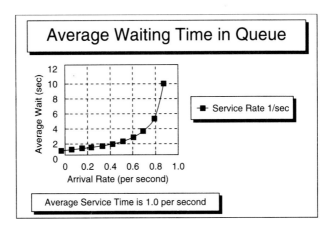

Figure 11-8

- Each of the graphs parts can be selected by clicking on it. Handles appear that can be stretched at will. The entire graph can also be stretched. Each part can also be dragged into position. Double-clicking on a part allows you to change it (see Figure 11-9).

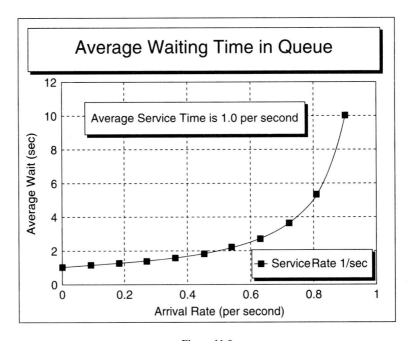

Figure 11-9

- Final improvements might be made by using various colors and shades (see Figure 11-10).

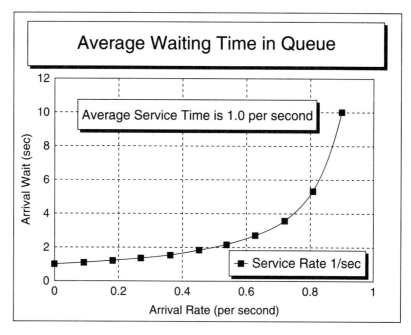

Figure 11-10

11.4 A QUEUING EXAMPLE WITH DISCRETE EVENT SIMULATION

In the last chapter we simulated a single-server single-queue system. Here we adopt the same methodology and implement the algorithm using Lotus 1-2-3. Figure 11-11 shows the contents of each cell (displayed using the Text number format). The effort to create this spreadsheet is quite small. The row corresponding to event 1 has to be filled in by hand of course. Then you copy the entire row to the clipboard and paste it across and down as many rows as you want. Each row down becomes another event.

To extend this example to generate hundreds of events, it is expedient to create a named range spanning across ten rows and downwards hundreds of columns. A formula to automatically generate the event number in column 1 is needed in that case.

The "recalculate spreadsheet" smart icon may be pressed to automatically produce another simulation. This is very handy in getting the results you want.

The spreadsheet should be configured such that the recalculation order is **By row** instead of **Natural** or **By column.** Select **Tools->User Setup** from the menu and press the **Recalculation** button to set this up (see Figure 11-12).

The numerical results are as shown in Figure 11-13.

Average Arrival Rate =0.7		Average Service Rate =1.0					
1	2	3	4	5	6	7	8
Event	Interarrival Time	Join Queue At Time	Service Time	Get Service At Time	Leave Server At Time	Time Spent In System	Time Spent In Queue
0		0			0		
1	@RAND	(-1/$B$1)·@LN(B6)	+D5+C6	@RAND	(-1/$E$1)·@LN(E6)	@MAX(H5,D6)	+F 6+G6	+H6-D6	+G6-D6
2	@RAND	(-1/$B$1)·@LN(B7)	+D6+C7	@RAND	(-1/$E$1)·@LN(E7)	@MAX(H6,D7)	+F 7+G7	+H7-D7	+G7-D7
3	@RAND	(-1/$B$1)·@LN(B8)	+D7+C8	@RAND	(-1/$E$1)·@LN(E8)	@MAX(H7,D8)	+F 8+G8	+H8-D8	+G8-D8
4	@RAND	(-1/$B$1)·@LN(B9)	+D8+C9	@RAND	(-1/$E$1)·@LN(E9)	@MAX(H8,D9)	+F 9+G9	+H9-D9	+G9-D9
5	@RAND	(-1/$B$1)·@LN(B10)	+D9+C10	@RAND	(-1/$E$1)·@LN(E10)	@MAX(H9,D10)	+F 10+G10	+H10-D10	+G10-D10
6	@RAND	(-1/$B$1)·@LN(B11)	+D10+C11	@RAND	(-1/$E$1)·@LN(E11)	@MAX(H10,D11)	+F 11+G11	+H11-D11	+G11-D11
7	@RAND	(-1/$B$1)·@LN(B12)	+D11+C12	@RAND	(-1/$E$1)·@LN(E12)	@MAX(H11,D12)	+F 12+G12	+H12-D12	+G12-D12
8	@RAND	(-1/$B$1)·@LN(B13)	+D12+C13	@RAND	(-1/$E$1)·@LN(E13)	@MAX(H12,D13)	+F 13+G13	+H13-D13	+G13-D13
9	@RAND	(-1/$B$1)·@LN(B14)	+D13+C14	@RAND	(-1/$E$1)·@LN(E14)	@MAX(H13,D14)	+F 14+G14	+H14-D14	+G14-D14
10	@RAND	(-1/$B$1)·@LN(B15)	+D14+C15	@RAND	(-1/$E$1)·@LN(E15)	@MAX(H14,D15)	+F 15+G15	+H15-D15	+G15-D15
Averages	@AVG(C6..C15)		@AVG(F6..F15)			@AVG(I6..I15)	@AVG(J6..J15)

Figure 11-11 This table shows the actual formulas in the spreadsheet cells that implement the first ten events arriving in our M/M/1 queue discrete event simulation. The @RAND function generates a uniformly distributed number between 0 and 1, and additional columns have to be included in the spreadsheet to calculate the Interarrival and Service times. The formula −1/$B$1·@LN(B6) generates an exponentially distributed sample from the value in the preceding column and from the average arrival rate value in cell B1. Likewise the formula −1/$E$1·@LN(E6) generates the exponentially distributed service time for each event. Columns have been labeled using the same numbers as in Chapter 10 for this method.

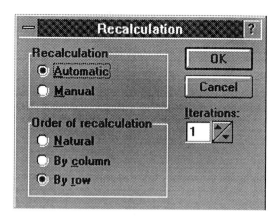

Figure 11-12 For the simulation to work correctly, it's critical that the spreadsheet be recalculated from left to right and from top to bottom. It is prudent to ensure this is the case.

	A	B	C	D	E	F	G	H	I	J
1	Average Arrival Rate =	0.7		Average Service Rate =	1.0					
2										
3	1		2	3		4	5	6	7	8
4	Event		Inter Arrival Time	Join Queue At Time		Service Time	Get Service At Time	Leave Server At Time	Time Spent In System	Time Spent In Queue
5	0			0				0		
6	1	0.403	1.299	1.299	0.637	0.452	1.299	1.751	0.452	0.000
7	2	0.841	0.247	1.546	0.870	0.140	1.751	1.890	0.344	0.205
8	3	0.388	1.354	2.900	0.998	0.002	2.900	2.902	0.002	0.000
9	4	0.751	0.409	3.309	0.124	2.088	3.309	5.396	2.088	0.000
10	5	0.624	0.673	3.982	0.207	1.577	5.396	6.974	2.992	1.414
11	6	0.746	0.418	4.400	0.980	0.020	6.974	6.994	2.594	2.574
12	7	0.436	1.187	5.587	0.284	1.260	6.994	8.254	2.667	1.407
13	8	0.498	0.996	6.583	0.620	0.478	8.254	8.732	2.149	1.672
14	9	0.719	0.472	7.055	0.334	1.096	8.732	9.828	2.774	1.677
15	10	0.686	0.538	7.593	0.720	0.329	9.828	10.157	2.565	2.236
16										
17	Averages		0.759			0.744			1.863	1.118

Figure 11-13 This is a screen shot for the Discrete Event Simulation method used in the last chapter. The M/M/1 queue uses a mean service rate of 1.0 events per second and a mean arrival rate of 0.7 events per second. The time each event occurs, and the time spent in various parts of the system are all calculated in the labeled columns. For such a short ten-event simulation the calculated averages are not that accurate—a matter easily remedied by simulating a few hundred events and excluding the first and last 5–10% of them.

11.5 VISUALIZING THE WORST CASE PERFORMANCE EXAMPLE

Recall that in a closed system, there is a simple formula for determining the lower limit of the worst case response time versus the number of transactions/packets/customers/events in the system. Two lines bound this limit. One line has the formula $f(n) = 1/\mu$, which is the minimum response time for just one user. The second line has the formula $f(n) = -1/\lambda + n/\mu$, which has a y-axis intercept at $-1/\lambda$ and a slope of $1/\mu$. Note that symbol μ may be written as Mu and λ may be written as Lambda.

Now suppose we know that the actual service rate is directly proportional to the line speed, s, of the system. The formula is $\mu = s/512$ where s is measured in bits per second, so a 512,000 bps line will pass 1,000 packets per second. To visualize the impact of various line speeds, let's use the formulas to create tables and graphs using Lotus 1-2-3 (see Figure 11-14).

The plot is very simple to produce. Rubber-band the cells containing the number of users and then drag the mouse to the right to encompass a total of four columns. Select the **Tools->Chart** menu and rubber-band a blank section of the spreadsheet to contain the graphic. Change the chart type to XY and fix up the labels meaningfully and—voila—you can see the effect of line speed on response time at a glance (see Figure 11-15).

Packet Arrival Rate =	30		
Line Speed =	128,000	256,000	512,000
Mu =	+B2/512	+C2/512	+D2/512
Number of Users	Response Time Maximum Value		
1	@MAX(1/$B$3,(-1/$B$1+A5/$B$3))	@MAX(1/$C$3,(-1/$B$1+A5/$C$3))	@MAX(1/$D$3,(-1/$B$1+A5/$D$3))
5	@MAX(1/$B$3,(-1/$B$1+A6/$B$3))	@MAX(1/$C$3,(-1/$B$1+A6/$C$3))	@MAX(1/$D$3,(-1/$B$1+A6/$D$3))
10	@MAX(1/$B$3,(-1/$B$1+A7/$B$3))	@MAX(1/$C$3,(-1/$B$1+A7/$C$3))	@MAX(1/$D$3,(-1/$B$1+A7/$D$3))
15	@MAX(1/$B$3,(-1/$B$1+A8/$B$3))	@MAX(1/$C$3,(-1/$B$1+A8/$C$3))	@MAX(1/$D$3,(-1/$B$1+A8/$D$3))
20	@MAX(1/$B$3,(-1/$B$1+A9/$B$3))	@MAX(1/$C$3,(-1/$B$1+A9/$C$3))	@MAX(1/$D$3,(-1/$B$1+A9/$D$3))
25	@MAX(1/$B$3,(-1/$B$1+A10/$B$3))	@MAX(1/$C$3,(-1/$B$1+A10/$C$3))	@MAX(1/$D$3,(-1/$B$1+A10/$D$3))
30	@MAX(1/$B$3,(-1/$B$1+A11/$B$3))	@MAX(1/$C$3,(-1/$B$1+A11/$C$3))	@MAX(1/$D$3,(-1/$B$1+A11/$D$3))
35	@MAX(1/$B$3,(-1/$B$1+A12/$B$3))	@MAX(1/$C$3,(-1/$B$1+A12/$C$3))	@MAX(1/$D$3,(-1/$B$1+A12/$D$3))
40	@MAX(1/$B$3,(-1/$B$1+A13/$B$3))	@MAX(1/$C$3,(-1/$B$1+A13/$C$3))	@MAX(1/$D$3,(-1/$B$1+A13/$D$3))
45	@MAX(1/$B$3,(-1/$B$1+A14/$B$3))	@MAX(1/$C$3,(-1/$B$1+A14/$C$3))	@MAX(1/$D$3,(-1/$B$1+A14/$D$3))

Figure 11-14 The table is created by first entering the formula into the cell B5. Paste this formula into cells C5 and D5 and editing them to correct the reference to column A and row 3. Finally paste the formula in cell B5 downwards, and then the one in cell C5 downwards and finally the one in cell D5 downwards. The final worksheet looks like the one above and the actual numbers are shown below.

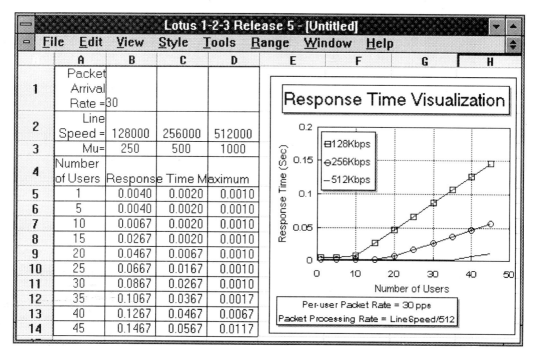

Figure 11-15 A spreadsheet screen shot (**ALT-PrtSc**) showing the numbers and graph for the visualization exercise. The packet arrival rate (per user) is λ and the service rate Mu is μ, which is calculated from the line speed. After the graph is produced it is useful to vary some of the parameters because they instantly affect the appearance of it. It is important to properly label the graph for maximum clarity.

11.6 GRAPHICAL SOLUTIONS WITH SPREADSHEETS

Suppose we work for a large dial-up service provider. Each line provisioned to support a group of users has an initial and a recurring cost. More lines improve response time and availability to the customer but the customer is charged more in order to recoup costs and maintain a profit margin. Our marketing and engineering departments provide the relevant data, which we graph as shown in Figure 11-16.

Another use for spreadsheet graphics is in finding peak values (or zero values) in functions that on the face of it are not apparent. An example is shown in Figures 11-17 and 11-18.

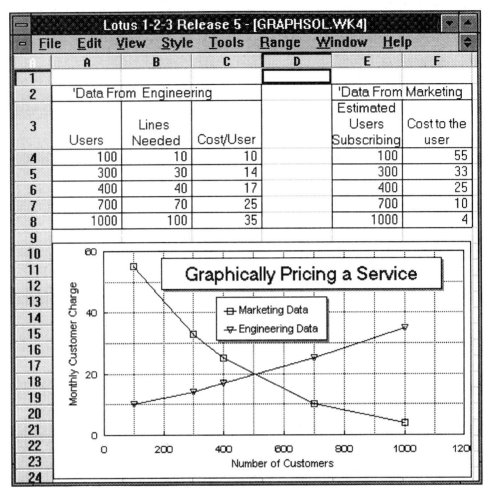

Figure 11-16 This screen shot shows how two tables of numbers can be plotted to determine in a repeatable documentable manner how to find a common solution. If tabular data is available, this method is quick to use. If formulas are provided instead, it is not that much more difficult to generate the numerical columns from them. Here we see that a $20.00 monthly charge will attract 500 dial-up customers based on marketing and engineering data.

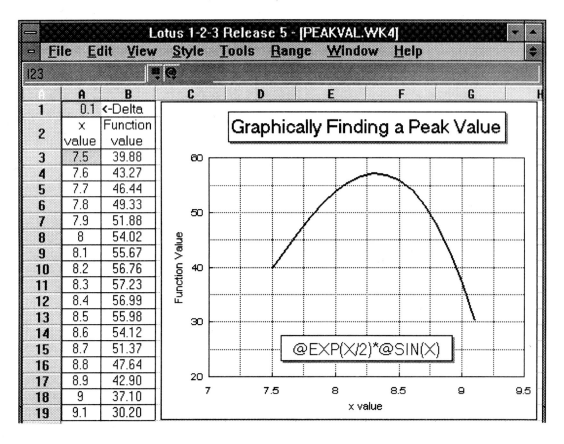

Figure 11-17 The function $\exp(x/2)\cdot\sin(x)$, a formula that has quite a few peaks by the way, can be manually inspected by varying the starting x-value in cell A3 and the increment value in cell A1 (these cells are highlighted). At first we don't know what the function looks like and the increment value will be as large as 1 or 10. Then we adjust the starting x-value to the left of an apparent peak and reduce the increment to see the peak detail. Here the peak value is about 57 at $x = 8.3$.

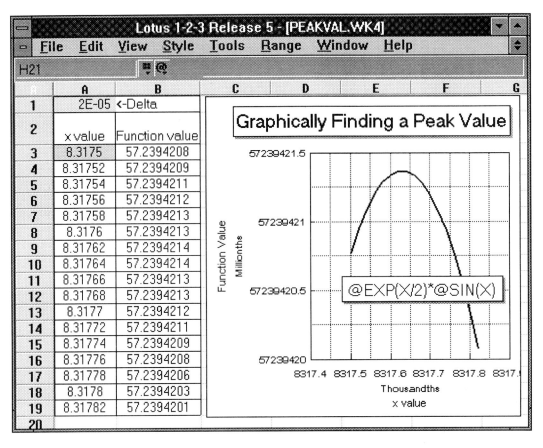

Figure 11-18 By manually tweaking the starting x-value and increment we've succeeded in homing in on the function peak value of 57.2394214 at $x = 8.31763$. This example shows the power of the method in resolving peaks.

11.7 ITERATIVE METHODS USING SPREADSHEETS

Iteration is a method of calculation that allows you to start with one or more initial values and apply a formula over and over (iterate) to come up with an answer. Each step in the iteration is usually governed by an index. In the absence of a neat closed-form solution, iterative methods can be used if a relationship between successive values is available.

Simple examples of iteration include calculating the factorial of a number and calculating the Fibonacci numbers. The factorial method begins by setting zero factorial equal to 1, that is to say that $0! = 1$. The relationship for factorials is that $n! = n \cdot (n-1)!$, which is to say that the next factorial $n!$ can be calculated from the previous factorial $(n-1)!$, which we have in hand, times n. To calculate $5!$ proceed as follows

Iterative Method for Calculating 5 Factorial

$$0! = 1$$
$$1! = 1 \cdot 0! = 1 \cdot 1 = 1$$
$$2! = 2 \cdot 1! = 2 \cdot 1 = 2$$
$$3! = 3 \cdot 2! = 3 \cdot 2 = 6$$
$$4! = 4 \cdot 3! = 4 \cdot 6 = 24$$
$$5! = 5 \cdot 4! = 5 \cdot 24 = 120$$

The Fibonacci numbers begin with the initial values $f_0 = 1$ and $f_1 = 1$ and the iterative formula $f_n = f_{n-1} f_{n-2}$ which we see depends on two previous values. The calculation for f_5 is given

Iterative Method for Calculating the 5th Fibonacci number

Iteration Step or Index i	Iteration
0	$f_0 = 1$
1	$f_1 = 1$
2	$f_2 = f_1 + f_2 = 1 + 1 = 2$
3	$f_3 = f_2 + f_1 = 2 + 1 = 3$
4	$f_4 = f_3 + f_2 = 3 + 2 = 5$
5	$f_5 = f_4 + f_3 = 5 + 3 = 8$

For short iterations the arithmetic seems trivial enough, especially with these integer-based examples. Automating the iterative process using a spreadsheet helps reduce mistakes, improves accuracy, and saves time.

Iteration methods should not be confused with the summation of series, which can be done using the Lotus 1-2-3 function **@SERIESSUM(x;n;n;coefficients)**, where **x** is the input value to the series, **n** is the value of the initial power, **m** is its increment, and **coefficients** is the range of cells that contain the numerical values for the coefficients.

Iteration is not to be confused with recursion. Recursion occurs when a function calls itself with a modified argument. For example, the psuedo-code to calculate a factorial might be

```
integer function factorial(n:integer)
  if n==1
    then return 1
    else return factorial(n-1)
  end
```

Sec. 11.1 Functions Available in Spreadsheets

In the case of the factorial, this is an expensive method simply to multiply together successive integers from 1 to *n*, but recursion can be useful for solving such problems as the Tower of Hanoi.

Iteration using a spreadsheet can be messy for larger projects because you have to cut and paste a lot of cells over considerable real estate. This is error-prone and it consumes a lot of memory as well. All these numbers may no be of actual use, as they may be intermediate values leading towards the last row or column result. Maximum use of range names is a must when doing sizable iterations.

Now, the stopping rule may not be some simple integer value but elapsed time or a diminishing error value. The discrete event simulation in the last chapter went on for a fixed number of events, but it might be just as appropriate to want to run the simulation for a certain length of time instead. In this case we don't know in advance how many rows we'll need to do all the work.

Using Spreadsheet Macros for Productivity

This leads us to macros. Spreadsheets generally provide for a simple programming language. The language has statements to direct execution flow, assign variables, call functions, and compare values. The variables used are generally range names. There is even a single-step and a tracing feature for debugging macros. For convenience, the macro can be assigned to a labeled button. There can be any reasonable number of macros in a spreadsheet.

By way of introduction, let's redo the factorial calculation using a macro. Table 11-9 gives the named ranges we'll need: a cell to hold the iteration variable and the result, two more cells to hold their initial values, and a cell to hold the argument (the number whose factorial we want).

Looking at the spreadsheet macro (see Figure 11-19), the real estate used to hold numbers is negligible and the macro language is seen to be straightforward.

The convenience of assigning a macro to a button is very compelling, so Figure 11-20 provides an example of how to assign one to the factorial macro in Figure 11-19.

TABLE 11-9 NAMED RANGES NEEDED TO SUPPORT THE FACTORIAL MACRO

Named range	Description
START	starting value of the iteration variable I
I	the iteration index variable I
N	the number whose factorial we want, I's upper limit
INIT	the starting value of the factorial (0!)
RESULT	the cell holding the cumulative product, our answer

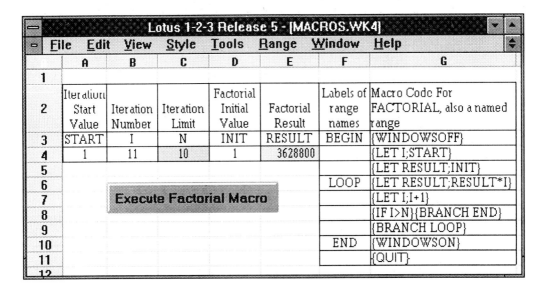

Figure 11-19 An iteration example for the factorial function, aided by a simple macro in column G. The user puts the number whose factorial is sought in cell C4 and presses the macro button. The result is placed in cell E4. The macro begins by shutting off spreadsheet window updates until the macro is done. This is a performance consideration. After initializing the calculation, the macro loops, incrementing the iteration number and updating the result value. When the iteration number exceeds the iteration limit, the macro quits and Lotus 1-2-3 updates the window to show the final result.

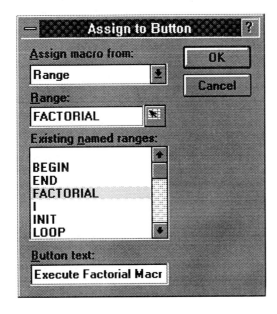

Figure 11-20 The named range was previously defined and called FACTORIAL. It spans all the cells of the macro. The button text is assigned in this dialog box to **Execute Factorial Macro.** Pressing this button runs the macro. The button itself is created via menu sequence **Tools->Draw->Button.** To assign the macro to this button bring the mouse over it, press the right-hand button, and choose **Assign to Macro** from the pop-up menu.

Sec. 11.7   Iterative Methods Using Spreadsheets

11.8 PRODUCING DOCUMENTATION FROM A SPREADSHEET

This may seem like an off-track topic for a book on network capacity planning. It turns out, though, that many studies wind up being put into presentation form by the same people doing the study. The author has certainly done his share of copy-and-paste work! So onwards.

The spreadsheet itself may contain various types of information

- rows and columns of labeled numbers and formulas
- graphs and charts
- drawings
- imported pictures
- complete sheets of composite information
- macros and buttons

Often only some of the spreadsheet's information needs to be transferred to the report. Usually only the results are worth reporting.

These are some of the data formats that are generally available

- ASCII text
- PostScript and encapsulated PostScript (when printing to a file)
- device independent bitmap (DIB)
- bitmap
- Windows Metafile
- screen shot (also a bitmap)
- AmiPro table
- graphics file (TIF, GIF, TGA, JPG, et al)

Figures 11-21 and 11-22 show how formatting choices are presented to the user.

Methods of creating documentation with spreadsheets include

- directly printing a paper report from the spreadsheet print command
- directly embedding the spreadsheet (or parts of it) in another file (cut-and-paste link)
- using dynamic data exchange (DDE) between active applications
- using object linking and embedding (OLE)

Transferring information between spreadsheets and other report-writing programs leads to some data format challenges.

Color issues come up when one computer system can display only 16 colors at time while another can display 256 colors. The 16-color system has to convert the 256-color information to its 16-color palette. Some 24-bit display systems (16.7 million colors) can also create richly colored information that the 256 and 16-color systems cannot adequately display. The lesson here is produce a report that can be viewed by the lowest common denominator (usually the 16-color system). Of course any attempt at printing a color document to a monochrome printer will result in some type of color-to-gray-scale conversion.

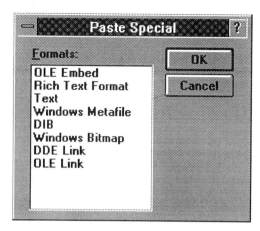

Figure 11-21 After doing a copy of a block of cells in the Lotus 1-2-3 spreadsheet, the AmiPro user is given these format choices when doing an **Edit->Special Paste.**

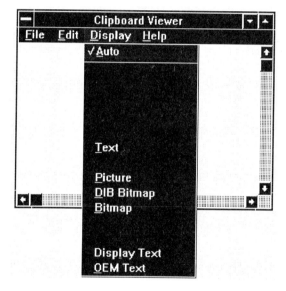

Figure 11-22 Lotus 1-2-3 places the copied block of cells onto the Windows clipboard in all the above formats. Note that the clipboard is not itself able to physically display all these formats and dims the corresponding menu choices.

Fonts available on the machine that produced the data may not be available on the target system, resulting in font substitution. The substitution process may not give pleasing results. Font point sizes may not map over. Adobe PostScript type 1 fonts do not always map well to TrueType fonts.

Scaling between what's seen on the screen at about 90 DPI (dots per inch) and what's seen on the printer at 300 DPI may result in disappointment or joy. Many word processing packages allow you to scale a graphic to fit a frame that fits the page well. A graphic that is shrunk to fit the page seen on the screen often looks pathetic on that screen, but prints beautifully because the WYSIWYG word processor did its best to show you what the page looks like on a 90 DPI screen, but this is only an approximation of what the 300 DPI printer will actually produce.

Printing graphics from inside PC word processors sometimes leaves the user with some choices on just how the images will be rendered on the printer. If the image is scaled up or down then either resampling via interpolation (which looks best and is slower to print) or resizing by pixel replication/discarding is possible. If the printer supports PostScript it's possible to take advantage of its halftone screening features. For conversion from color to monochrome, various dithering techniques may be available, such as nearest color, ordered dither, and error diffusion (Floyd-Steinberg, Burkes, or Stucki). For color reduction scenarios, you generally have a choice of standard windows, optimized, weighted, or non-weighted palettes, and a color depth of 24, 16, 8, 4, or 2 bits corresponding to 16,777,216, 32,768, 256, 16, or 2 colors.

11.9 AVAILABLE COMMERCIAL SPREADSHEETS

Here is a short list of spreadsheet programs the network manager might consider using for network capacity planning purposes

- Lotus 1-2-3
- Excel
- Quattro Pro
- SuperCalc
- Wingz
- ClarisWorks
- Various shareware programs

Many of these programs are available for MS-DOS, MS Windows, UNIX and X-windows, and Mac OS platforms.

12

Mathematics Scratch Pads

12.0 INTRODUCTION

The math scratchpad is a generalized form of spreadsheet that allows you to place numbers, formulas, plots, text, and even imported bitmapped graphics in free form anywhere on the paper. The tools provides the necessary compute engine to recalculate and scan the document from left to right and from top to bottom. There is no row-column constraint as with standard spreadsheets. What-if analysis is as simple as changing some part of the scratchpad. The compute engine recalculates automatically or manually. Data from text files can usually be read into the scratchpad for processing and the results can be written back out as needed. The math scratchpads are one of the best computational tools available.

This chapter reviews the features and usage of the math scratchpad tool as it pertains to practical applications such as network capacity planning. We don't presume to be cover all math scratchpad features exhaustively.

Our focus is on Mathsoft's Mathcad product because the author uses it extensively. The reader is urged to compare features and try evaluation/demo copies of commercial, shareware, postcardware, or freeware products before making a purchase decision. See the last section of this chapter for math scratchpad Web sites.

12.1 WHAT IS MATHCAD?

Mathcad is the tool that's been used extensively in the preparation and illustration of the network capacity planning calculations for this book. Mathcad 5.0 runs on MS Windows, is marketed by Mathsoft, comes with a superb manual, costs a mere $99, and is supported from a Web page at URL http://www.mathsoft.com on the Internet where numerous Mathcad programming examples and pointers to other Internet sites are posted. Version 6.0 has been announced. The following is a list of useful features found in Mathcad

- **Built-in support for units of measure.** Since most numbers used in networking arithmetic have units such as bits per second or bytes per frame, any formulas used to manipulate these numbers should come out with the right units of measurement. Recall that in high school chemistry and physics we were taught how to use dimensional analysis to ensure that our formulas and calculations at least had the right units of measure. To ensure we don't make similar errors, Mathcad can keep track of units—even new units defined by the user.

- **Rich set of math functions.** Mathcad provides internal functions for trigonometry, Bessel, transcendental, statistics, curve fitting, and regression.

- **Plotting capability.** No computational tool is complete without the ability to graph data and Mathcad has quite a variety of two- and three-dimensional customizable plots. Any change in a calculation will result in a re-plot of the data.

- **Arrays and complex numbers.** Mathcad supports vectors and matrices and includes a set of functions for operating on them. It can evaluate finite sums and products in the usual compact mathematical notation.

- **Electronic books.** Mathcad documents can be authored as hypertext-linked electronic documents and a reasonably diverse set of electronic books can by purchased through Mathsoft, including one on queuing theory. These books are math scratchpads and work just like any other Mathcad document, including the ability to copy and paste.

- **Multiple open documents.** Mathcad supports the opening of multiple scratchpads within the main application window, allowing for copy and paste among them.

- **OLE and DDE support.** Mathcad for MS Windows can import and export data using both Object Linking and Embedding and Dynamic Data Exchange. This allows good integration with other tools used by the network administrator.

12.2 A SAMPLE MATHCAD DOCUMENT (FIGURE 12-1)

Page 1

Sample Mathcad Document
Showing the Basic Features of a
Math Scratchpad Tool

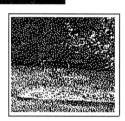

Simple Arithmetic: $\quad 12.5 + 4.6 - 5.3 + 11.1 = 22.9 \qquad \dfrac{(4.5 - 1.2) \cdot 4}{(4.1 + 7) \cdot 4.5} = 0.264$

General Formulas: $\quad \text{Delay}(\lambda, \mu) := \dfrac{1}{\mu - \lambda} \qquad \text{Delay}(0.95, 1.0) = 20$

Formulas may contain variables that can be defined later on when it's time to evaluate the function definition.

$\text{ErrorRate}(x) := 2 \cdot x^2 - 3 \cdot x + 10 \qquad \text{ErrorRate}(3) = 19$

$F(x) := \dfrac{\exp(x) \cdot \cos(x) \cdot \sin(2 \cdot x)}{\sqrt{\sin(x)^2 \cdot \cos(2 \cdot x)^3}} \qquad F(3.14) = 46.208$

Sums and Products: $\quad \text{Total}(x, n) := n^2 \cdot \displaystyle\sum_{i=0}^{n} \dfrac{x^n}{i!} \qquad \text{Total}(5.3, 30) = 1.309 \cdot 10^{25}$

$\text{GeoMean}(x, n) := \displaystyle\prod_{i=1}^{n} \dfrac{i + n^{-i}}{i + x} \qquad \text{GeoMean}(1, 10) = 0.101$

Arrays:

$X := \begin{bmatrix} 1 \\ 3 \\ 4 \\ 5 \\ 8 \\ 9 \end{bmatrix} \qquad Y := \begin{bmatrix} 1 \\ 2 \\ 3 \\ 5 \\ 7 \\ 8 \end{bmatrix} \qquad i := 0..\text{last}(X)$

Graph of the Array Data

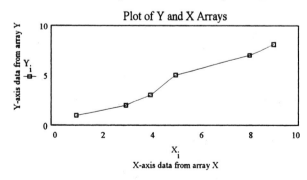

Figure 12-1

12.3 USING MATHCAD TO HANDLE MESSY FORMULAS EASILY

While pursuing a network analysis the network administrator may run into some messy and unpleasant formulas that are difficult to deal with due to the labor involved. There is also a good chance of making a mistake. Math scratchpads come to the rescue by letting the user to enter formulas pretty well the way they're found in the textbooks.

Take the formulas for the multiserver single queue (M/M/C in Kendall notation). They're unwieldy to manipulate by hand. The more complex a formula the more likely that manual manipulation will produce one or more errors. With Mathcad the formulas are entered directly, as shown in Figure 12-2.

$\lambda := 95$ — Arrival rate (per second)

$\mu := 20$ — Server processing rate

$C := 5$ — Number of servers

$M : 100$

$N := 1 .. M$ — Maximum number of events that will be considered in the system

$$P_0 := \frac{1}{\left(\sum_{N=0}^{C} \frac{\lambda^N}{N! \cdot \mu^N} \right) + \left[\sum_{N=C+1}^{M} \frac{\lambda^N}{C^{N-C} \cdot (C! \cdot \mu^N)} \right]}$$

$$P_N := \text{if}\left[N \leq C, \frac{\lambda^N}{N! \cdot \mu^N} \cdot P_0, \frac{\lambda^N}{C^{N-C} \cdot (C! \cdot \mu^N)} \cdot P_0 \right]$$

$$\text{AvgQueLen} := \frac{P_0 \cdot \left(\frac{\lambda}{\mu}\right)^C \cdot \left(\frac{\lambda}{C \cdot \mu}\right)}{C! \cdot \left(1 - \frac{\lambda}{C \cdot \mu}\right)^2}$$

$$\text{AvgTotalWait} := \frac{\text{AvgQueLen}}{\lambda} + \frac{1}{\mu}$$

$$\text{AvgInSystem} := \text{AvgQueLen} + \frac{\lambda}{\mu}$$

Figure 12-2 Long complex formulas that include sums, exponents, and intermediate values can be entered directly from the textbook. Here we show the M/M/5 queue statistics formulas. Math scratchpads remove the traditional deterrent of having to write a program to implement such formulas.

12.4 GRAPHING AND DISPLAYING RESULTS IN MATHCAD

Results of network capacity plans must often be interpreted and reported in visual form. Mathcad offers a variety of visualization methods

- Direct display of a vector or an array
- X-Y graph with the flexibility to vary:
  - line type
  - plotting symbol
  - line and symbol color
  - grids
  - linear of logarithmic axis
  - multiple data sets per graph
  - graph title and axis labels
- Polar plot
- 3-D plot

Let's begin with an example which displays a vector **P** and an iterated variable N (see Figure 12-3).

$$P = \begin{bmatrix} 0.15 \\ 0.225 \\ 0.169 \\ 0.127 \\ 0.095 \\ 0.071 \\ 0.053 \\ 0.04 \\ 0.03 \\ 0.023 \\ 0.017 \end{bmatrix} \quad N = \begin{bmatrix} 0 \\ 1 \\ 2 \\ 3 \\ 4 \\ 5 \\ 6 \\ 7 \\ 8 \\ 9 \\ 10 \end{bmatrix}$$

Figure 12-3 The array **P** holds 11 values and Mathcad displays a column with the vector's index next to the value stored there. The variable N is an index variable ranging from 0 to 10. This method for displaying results is suited to small amounts of accurate information but imparts little information visually.

To improve the data presentation, we use Mathcad's XY plotting feature and customize it some (see Figure 12-4).

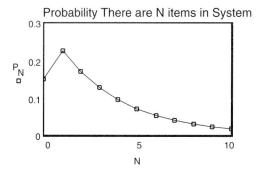

Figure 12-4 This is the same data from the array **P** above, with the addition of an automatic grid, a custom title, and squares to mark each data point. The physical dimensions of the graph can be stretched to any desired size and additional axis labels could have been added.

Should data from a matrix need to be displayed, there are two approaches. The first one is to plot multiple lines on an XY plot. This works well if there are just a few lines, but if there are many lines it will be better to create a 3-D plot such as Figure 12-5.

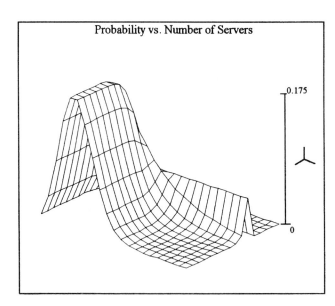

Figure 12-5 This is a plot of the probability density function of the queue occupancy for a single queue multiserver system. The number of servers increases as we move away from the vertical axis and towards the left. This display makes it clear at which point increasing the number of servers no longer improves the system performance, about eight. The viewing angles can be adjusted.

12.5 PRODUCING DOCUMENTATION WITH MATHCAD

After doing a network capacity study, the next step is to prepare the results for a presentation. You may have to convey information in the form of

- graphs
- tables
- a page-long calculation
- maybe an electronic book (hypertext)
- text

Since Mathcad can print a worksheet, a nicely formatted study may pass muster by itself. Indeed, both the commercial and "Internet-free" electronic books are well laid out and a pleasure to read. If the results are better off embedded into a word processing document, data will have to exported from the worksheet.

The following data formats are available on the MS Windows clipboard from Mathcad (see Figure 12-6)

- Windows Bitmap (they scale poorly with nonintegral stretch factors)
- Windows Metafile (WMF) (they scale very nicely at any stretch factor)
- OLE Link
- OLE Embed

Any use of OLE Link and OLE Embed presumes that Mathcad is available on the system where the report will be read.

The Windows Bitmap format includes (surprisingly) only that portion actually visible on the Mathcad screen at the time the data is copied to the clipboard. The Windows Metafile format includes all the copied areas from the worksheet. Even text areas are sent

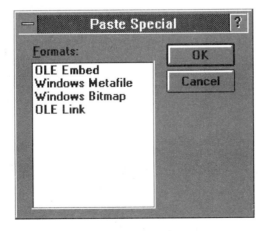

Figure 12-6 This is the **Paste Special** menu in Lotus AmiPro with Mathcad material in the clipboard. The Windows Metafile format is the most useful because the formulas, symbols, and especially graphs used in Mathcad come across very well into AmiPro. Bitmap presentations should be sized as large as possible before bringing them though the clipboard, in order to preserve the appearance as best as possible.

to the clipboard in these formats. When working with bitmaps in word processing documents, remember to deal with these issues

- Size—CRT screens are about 85–95 DPI, printers are typically 300 DPI.
- Storage—approximately length · width · color_depth · compression.
- Performance—it takes time to display, render, and scroll bitmaps.
- Color—anything over 16 colors may not display well on a 16-color display.
- Black-and-white conversion of color bitmaps requires dithering and color reduction.
- Grayscale (16 or 256 shades) vs. 2-color black-and-white.
- GIF and TIF may be compressed somewhat, JPG format can be compressed more.

Note that part of the worksheet may be printed to a file in encapsulated PostScript (EPS) form using the generic monochrome MS Windows PostScript driver or a physical PostScript printer driver. Word processors typically allow EPS files to be imported into frames that can be scaled as necessary. EPS contains all the vector instructions necessary to draw the image at whatever resolution is required, so the resulting image is always smoothly rendered.

12.6 COMMERCIALLY AVAILABLE MATH SCRATCHPADS

Math software is traditionally evaluated annually in IEEE's magazine *Spectrum*. Many of the products listed in Table 12-1 are available on UNIX, MS Windows, and Macintosh platforms. MathPad is available for free on the Internet and runs on the Macintosh. Many of the Web sites indicated point to additional sites with similar orientation. Happy Web crawling!

TABLE 12-1 COMMERCIALLY AVAILABLE MATH SCRATCHPADS

Tool Name	Supplier	For More Information
Maple Theorist	Waterloo Maple Software	`http://www.maplesoft.on.ca/`
MATLAB	MathWorks	`http://www.mathworks.com/`
Mathematica	Wolfram Research	`http://www.wri.com/`
Macsyma	Macsyma	`http://www.macsyma.com/ec.`
MathPad	Mark.Widholm@UNH.edu	`http://pubpages.unh.edu/~whd/MathPad/`
Mathcad	Mathsoft	`http://www.mathsoft.com/`

13

Using the Systems & Networks PlanNet Simulation Tool

13.0 INTRODUCTION

Network performance consultants with Hewlett-Packard's Profession Services Organization use PlanNet to validate network designs for HP customers. The author has used PlanNet routinely for such purposes over the last two years.

This chapter reviews PlanNet's working components and network library modules, including a section on developing customer library modules using BONeS Designer. Next we discuss how to create a network topology and how to develop the necessary traffic generators, both of which are core elements of the simulator. Automatic performance graph generation is discussed and then we review the elements of a professional modeling and simulation report.

Recognizing the verity of "garbage in, garbage out," we look at ways a network manager can validate the simulation results. Frankly, it's very important to be pessimistic about the simulation results, not because we don't trust the simulator (it really is pretty accurate) but because of human error.

PlanNet can be used to conduct what-if scenarios, and after reviewing a sample simulation, we show how to use PlanNet to choose an efficient client-server protocol, study the impact of expanding applications to remote locations, and validate a network design for Email and telnet users.

The chapter ends with a quick review of commercially available simulation tools.

A Note about the Appearance of Screen Shots Used in this Chapter

The reader should note that this chapter contains screen shots of the PlanNet tool in operation. The screens shots were taken on an MS Windows system running WRQ Reflection/X to emulate an X-terminal. The PlanNet software is a UNIX applications that runs on an HP9000 model 715/50 and because it's an X-client, all the PlanNet displays were projected to the PC where screen shots were taken. For this reason the window decorations have the MS Windows look rather than the normal OSF/MOTIF look.

13.1 COMPONENTS OF THE PLANNET SIMULATOR

PlanNet's main components are the model builder, network module library, scripting tools, simulation engine, and report generator.

The **model builder** is a key component of any simulator. It is the graphical user interface for specifying the network topology. Users select from a variety of traffic generation devices, LAN media, WAN media, and interconnecting devices and wire them together to create `the network.` To support what-if analysis the user can save several versions of the topology in a library. All the objects on the network map carry parameters that can be customized by double-clicking them and tailoring the values in the resulting dialog box for that module. The model builder checks for any construction errors when a model is saved A symbol editor is provided to allow the user to create customized icons for the network diagram. The model builder is able to save a topology report in PostScript form.

The **library of network modules** that can be purchased with PlanNet are accurate representations based on the fundamental operation and physics of the network electronics. There is far more to them than simple queues, service centers, and delay centers. Systems & Networks develops these hierarchical modules using their BONeS Designer tool, a separate product. A properly written hierarchical module can be used in PlanNet and be interconnected with any of the other modules.

PlanNet's **traffic scripting tools** are valuable because they help construct realistic network traffic generators. Users can take direct advantage of the scripting language to create fairly arbitrary data flows between a client and a server. Network traces can be converted into traffic scripts using the network toolbox, a GUI that lets you import an ASCII trace and export a traffic script. For a predefined set of network operating systems, protocols, and applications, PlanNet's Scribe tool can be used to synthesize traffic scripts.

The **simulation engine** is the heart of PlanNet. It is a discrete event simulator that coordinates the flow of packets through the various network components, stepping from event to event and keeping track of the clock. Since most simulations sweep one or more physical parameters (such as the bandwidth of a serial circuit), it is advantageous to conduct multiple concurrent simulations using multiple computers that NFS-mount the file system of the licensed system.

A simple GUI **monitors** all simulations in progress. The simulation engine produces warning messages during the simulation to alert the user about possible problems such as unexpected buffer overflows, a missing script file, or a parameter error.

During the simulation, each hierarchical module records its own performance statistics using internal probes. The standard PlanNet libraries track steady-state statistics and not time series information. PlanNet's automatic **report generator** creates customizable graphs of this information. The reports can be saved in ASCII form and they can be printed as PostScript or saved as a PostScript file.

All parts of the PlanNet tool are X-window clients, so you can operate the tool directly at the UNIX workstation console, from another UNIX workstation, from an X-terminal, or from a PC or Macintosh running X-window server software. X-window server products include Walker Richer Quinn's Reflection/X and Hummingbird for the PC and Mac/X for the Macintosh.

13.2 PLANNET'S LIBRARY OF STANDARD NETWORK COMPONENTS

PlanNet comes with a set of optional library components for network devices such as WANs, LANs, interconnect devices, and traffic generators.

Library modules for wide area networking include the serial line, T-1, T-3, WAN Cloud (a collection of point-to-point lines), and a frame relay network.

LAN technologies include libraries for Ethernet, 10-BASE-T, 100-BASE-T, token ring, and FDDI.

Interconnect device libraries include the 10-BASE-T hub, learning bridge, single-protocol router, and multiprotocol router; an Ethernet switch is under development. An ATM switch example is provided with the BONeS Designer tool.

For traffic generation library modules we have four variations. The statistical bursty traffic generator (SBTG) and the voice station. The SBTG sends packets to a destination based on simple statistical properties such as average packet size, and the voice station sends isochronous data. The one-way end-to-end packet delay is measured.

The packet trace script plays back a packet trace directly and the packet trace model generates traffic with the statistics found in a packet trace. Then we have the application traffic generator (ATG), which provides very flexible traffic patterns and, importantly, can provide round-trip response times.

Each module deals with buffering, fragmentation, media speed, and network protocol type. Each module has to measure predetermined performance values appropriate to the module, so the Ethernet module counts collisions (and a lot of other information) while the router module tracks memory utilization.

Network modules are bought separately as needed, but what if no module is available for the devices you need to simulate? Your choices are

- Substitute an appropriate available module and improve the approximation by tailoring the module parameters. A router or bridge module can approximate an Ethernet switch if latencies are set to zero, buffer memory is made equal, and traffic levels are high enough that the cut-through feature isn't being used. An FDDI ring can approximate a 100VG-AnyLAN.
- Purchase the BONeS Designer tool from Systems & Networks, take their five-day training class, get comfortable with this tool, and develop your own custom network module.
- Hire a network performance consultant from Hewlett-Packard, Systems & Networks, or another company to develop the module, test it, debug it, document it, and support it for as long as you use it.

13.3 CREATING CUSTOM NETWORK COMPONENTS WITH BONES DESIGNER

Suppose that you, the great PlanNet guru, has to evaluate the performance aspects of an FDDI switch, a full-duplex Ethernet adapter, a countrywide ATM backbone, or even a company-side business process (because Designer is quite general and it is not limited to development of network components but to entire systems). The standard PlanNet libraries don't contain these devices. What do you do? You can break out a copy of BONeS Designer and develop your own hierarchical module (see Figure 13-1)!

To create a new hierarchical module you begin with an in-depth study of how the device works. Then you determine what performance data has to be collected and how to parameterize the model. After development comes the validation phase.

To develop a new model it is absolutely necessary that you have a complete working understanding of the underlying technology. How do bits, cells, frames, and packets move around inside this device? Where are the buffers, how big should they be, are they shared among multiple queues, and what is the queuing discipline? How should buffer overflows be handled? How do all the timers work? Equally important, what simplifications are allowed? Is it acceptable to ignore certain aspects of the device protocol if it has

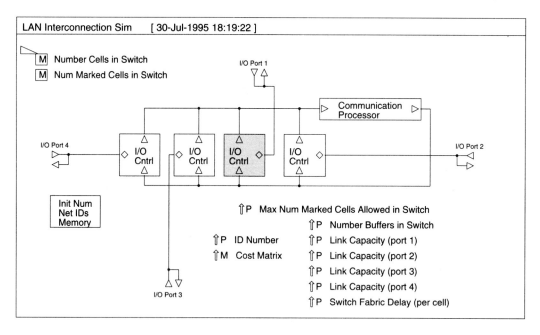

Figure 13-1 This is the hierarchical diagram for a sample module for the BONeS Designer tool. Packets move between blocks which generally contain lower-level blocks to model the physical aspects of the system, which in our case tends to be network electronics.

no bearing on steady-state performance? You also must determine how flexible the module needs to be—what should be parameterized and what are sensible limits for these parameters?

Before developing the module, you also need to decide what performance metrics it should collect. This will be device and technology dependent to a great degree. The usual metrics are throughput in frames per second and bits per second, utilization in percent, average and peak amount of a resource used, discards and overflows, and average time spent in the system. You may also want to record probability density histograms. It is customary to allow the user to turn off a specific data collection. This reduces the amount of unwanted data the user has to wade through and turning off data collection can speed up the simulation too. To allow the new hierarchical module to be used in PlanNet, specific implementation guidelines need to be followed.

With a model design in hand, you use Designer's model builder GUI to construct the hierarchical module. After some effort, a working debugged, tested, and documented module will be ready. The greatest challenge is the validation phase, and there is no better recourse than to compare the simulation results with test results over a reasonable range of parameters. Barring this, a peer review and a structured walk-through can be very helpful in ferreting out subtle errors.

13.4 CREATING THE NETWORK TOPOLOGY AND RUNNING THE PLANNET SIMULATOR

Building the network topology diagram in PlanNet need not be time consuming and the process benefits from a structured approach. Generally, you should work on a small part of the network (such as a geographic location), fill in the detail, and do the remaining locations in the same manner. Lastly you add in the WAN details, try a short shakedown run, then perform a long simulation to get stable results.

To build the diagram for each location, begin by laying down traffic source icons. These are usually clients, so fill in the parameters for each icon, including the name of the application traffic generator script, the destination of the traffic, and the client name. Next, lay down the icons for the traffic sinks, usually the servers, and fill in their parameters too. Now add in the LAN segments (usually hubs), label them, and connect the clients and servers to them. Be sure to turn on all the statistics collectors for these icons because they're needed for debugging and validation purposes. They can be turned off later on if the data is not wanted. Save the map, fixing up any construction errors that PlanNet reports. Repeat this exercise for each geographic location, and take advantage of cut-and-paste to duplicate icons with similar parameters.

With all the geographic locations drawn (perhaps with some North-South-East-West orientation), add in the bridges, routers, and WAN links, again labeling them and filling in all the relevant information about line speed, memory capacity, and vendor-specific router parameters. Connect the routers to the LAN and WAN links and terminate unused connections. Again turn on all the statistics collection features for debug purposes. Save the topology after repairing any construction errors that PlanNet may report.

Before running the simulator, go back and make sure that all the necessary traffic generation scripts are available and check their syntax using the network toolbox. Also make sure that the number of clients and servers have been parameterized and that these parameters have been consistently set up. For example, you may want to vary the number of clients in even steps from a high value to a low value, a range that brackets the target number of clients. Since each step is a complete simulation, don't run too many of them unless you have a snake farm (a healthy number of HP 9000 series 700 workstations on a LAN) to support multiple concurrent simulations.

The first few runs of the simulator should cover only about ten seconds (`TSTOP=10.0`) of simulated time. These runs are shakedowns intended to ferret out any obvious bugs in the scripts, topology, and parameters. After that, run the simulation long enough to get statistically significant results on the performance graphs. You'll find that simulations with more clients don't need to be run as long as simulations with fewer clients. PlanNet's TSTOP parameter can be a function of the number of clients to take advantage of this and reduce the simulation time. For example, it is reasonable to specify `TSTOP=600.0/SQRT(Number_of_clients)`.

After validating the low traffic point of the simulation, run the simulation longer to get the best statistical results, print the graphs, interpret the results, and make appropriate recommendations. Then you bill the customer!

13.5 STANDARD AND USER-WRITTEN TRAFFIC GENERATOR MODULES

PlanNet provides three basic types of traffic generator modules, namely the statistical bursty traffic generator, the packet trace–based generator, and the application traffic generator.

The Statistical Bursty Traffic Generator (SBTG)

The SBTG is useful for generating background noise levels on a LAN or WAN. Round-trip response time measurements are not available with this generator, but statistically generated traffic can be customized to follow the exponential, fixed, uniform, and normal distributions. Both interframe timing and frame sizes can be independently set.

Two Packet Trace–Based Traffic Generators

The first variation of the packet trace–based traffic generator plays back the packet recording with the same interpacket timing, packet sizes, sources, and destinations. The generator represents each traffic source and destination in the recording. For traces that don't play out as long as TSTOP, the simulator loops the playback as long as necessary. The traffic script approach does not provide for any variability because all the timings are fixed. No round-trip packet timing information is available.

The second variation, the packet model, derives statistics from the packet recording and generates packets based on these statistics. This restores the variability in the traffic. No round-trip packet timing information is available.

Application Traffic Generator (ATG) Scripts

The ATG is the best traffic generator because it is the most flexible and provides round-trip response time. This generator models a CPU, disk, and LAN adapter—a very simple thing really, and not well suited for complex servers with multiple CPUs, disks, and LAN adapters. Still, the objective is network modeling as opposed to system modeling. System modeling can be done by creating a BONeS Designer hierarchical module for a complex server and using it in PlanNet.

A single ATG can run multiple scripts concurrently to simulate multiple independent client-server conversations. An ATG script consists of one or more steps, and each step allows for nine parts (see Table 13-1 and Figure 13-2).

Each step or group of steps may be bracketed to start and stop a timer, defining a transaction. If a real-world transaction consists of a few dozen packet exchanges, then bracketing them will give an accurate measurement of the response time for the complete transaction. When all steps in the ATG script have been executed, the script will stop unless a Restart directive is encountered to loop over the script. If the script has not completed when TSTOP occurs, no timing information is available for uncompleted transactions.

Priority has meaning only for media that can support it, which depends on the implementation of the LAN/WAN hierarchical module to which the ATG is connected. FDDI, IEEE 802.5 token ring, 100-VG-AnyLAN, and ATM technologies support it, but there is no point in simulating priorities if the product you use to implement your network does not provide access to the feature.

ATG scripts may be hand-written to simulate anticipated transactions. The PlanNet toolbox boasts Scribe, an interactive tool for generating custom ATGs for specific applications. Network packet traces can be converted to ATG scripts using either the toolbox or the trc2atg *awk* script.

TABLE 13-1 THE NINE SEQUENTIAL PARTS OF AN APPLICATION TRAFFIC GENERATOR SCRIPT

Part number	Part name	Description
1	ThinkingTime	client think time
2	TimeoutPeriod	maximum time the client will wait for a remote reply
3	LocalCPU	number of instructions executed by the client system
4	LocalDisk	number of bytes the client reads from its local disk
5	RequestLength	number of bytes the client sends to the remote system
6	RemoteCPU	number of instructions executed by the remote system
7	RemoteDisk	number of bytes the remote system reads from its disk
8	ResponseLength	number of bytes the remote system returns to the client
9	Priority	relative network priority of the transaction traffic

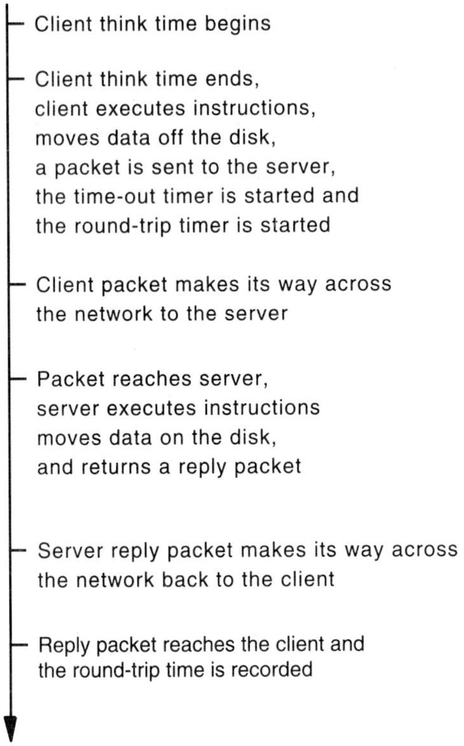

─ Client think time begins

─ Client think time ends,
  client executes instructions,
  moves data off the disk,
  a packet is sent to the server,
  the time-out timer is started and
  the round-trip timer is started

─ Client packet makes its way across
  the network to the server

─ Packet reaches server,
  server executes instructions
  moves data on the disk,
  and returns a reply packet

─ Server reply packet makes its way across
  the network back to the client

─ Reply packet reaches the client and
  the round-trip time is recorded

Figure 13-2 This is the order in which the parts of an ATG script step are executed. PlanNet's application traffic generator script implements a series of packet exchanges between a client generator and one or more server systems. Arbitrary packet exchanges can be modeled this way, and round-trip response times can be accurately measured. Client and server packets are moved through the network, encountering appropriate delays in their travels.

This is an ATG script consisting of two steps:

```
#
# clientservere.atg
#
Step {
ThinkingTime=exponential(mean = 0.043199)
};
StartStats;
Step {
TimeoutPeriod=1.0,
ThinkingTime=0.0,
LocalCPU=0,
LocalDisk=0,
RequestLength=exponential(lower_limit=20,
                          mean = 500,
                          upper_limit=1480),
RemoteCPU=0,
RemoteDisk=0,
ResponseLength=40
};
StopStats;
Restart;
```

The first step models the client think time. The second step does the work. This step is timed, per the StartStats-StopStats keywords. The ThinkingTime is zero in the second step because we put it into the first step to avoid including think time in the transaction duration. Accordingly, the time-out value is set to 0.1 seconds, the client performs no local CPU or disk activity, and sends out a packet whose size is governed by a negative exponential distribution with a mean of 500 bytes. The distribution is bracketed between 20 and 1,480 bytes to avoid sending unrealistically small packets and to prevent fragmentation by the network layer. The remote system performs no CPU or disk activity and merely replies with a fixed-length 40-byte packet. The Restart keyword loops the script.

Note that the ATG will add a 20-byte IP header, so if you are modeling the TCP transport, you have to include the 20-byte TCP header in `RequestLength` and `ResponseLength`. The ATG module will observe the appropriate medium framing rules to insert the appropriate OSI layer II and I encapsulation.

In practice, there may be many sequential steps with various parameters changing to model real traffic. Steps of interest may be instrumented with StartStats-StopStats pairs while other steps need not be instrumented. There is no requirement that the script loop. A long script may not need to do so, but often the workloads we simulate are repetitive and looping is appropriate.

13.6 PLANNET REPORT GENERATION

Each of the PlanNet network modules comes with a predefined set of statistics graphs that can be displayed, printed, saved as a PostScript image, or saved as an ASCII table of values. Each graph can be customized by modifying the axis ranges, labels and colors, by cutting and pasting data from other graphs, and by making other cosmetic changes. Since a simulation may have several iterated variables, a choice of x-axis and y-axis parameters can be made. For example, you might vary both the total number of active users and the line speed of a serial line, so you have some flexibility in displaying this information.

The report generator is an X-client, so a simple screen shot can be taken after the color display has been tailored to suit your needs. A screen shot can be taken of any X-client using standard X-window commands such as

```
xwd -frame > screenshot.xwd
```

The XWD file format may not be supported by your word processing package. The XWD screen dump format *is* readable by HP's *whiteboard* program, a component of the SharedX product. The file may be further processed using the standard X-window command *xpr* as shown here:

```
xwd -frame | xpr -device ps -gray 4 | lp -dlaserjet -opostscript
```

This UNIX command sequence takes a shot of the graphics window, including the frame, and converts it to PostScript form, converting the image colors to a 4 × 4 gray-scale representation, and finally sends it to a spooled LaserJet spool that supports PostScript.

The PlanNet data analyzer window has a print command that allows you to print to a PostScript file. The PostScript file can be converted to Encapsulated PostScript using the *extract-eps* command supplied with PlanNet. EPS images can be inserted into reports and must be printed to a Postscript printer. Finally, since the data can be exported to an ASCII file, there is unlimited potential to use the simulation data outside of PlanNet. Tools such as Lotus 1-2-3 and Mathcad can import ASCII data for display and postprocessing purposes.

Those of you using MS Windows or Mac OS with X-window display emulators to run PlanNet can take advantage of the native screen copy features to record windows. MS Windows uses the **ALT-PrtSc** key pairs and MacOS uses **Command-Shift-3** keys.

Table 13-2 provides a list of tools and programs that allow you to manipulate various image formats.

TABLE 13-2 DEALING WITH POSTSCRIPT IMAGES IN PLANNET SIMULATION REPORTS

File format	Common file name extension	Tool that understand the format
PostScript	PS, ps	GhostView & GhostScript can display PS, convert it to bitmap form, put it on the clipboard as a bitmap, create an EPS file, and insert a preview image into the EPS file.
		PlanNet's `extract-eps` *awk* script converts PS to EPS.
Encapsulated PostScript	EPS, eps, EPSF, epsf	GhostView & GhostScript can display EPS, convert it to bitmap form, and put on the clipboard as a bitmap.
		Adobe Photoshop can display EPS files and convert them to bitmap form.
		HiJaak Pro purports to read EPS files but completely misrenders PlanNet's analyzer files.
		XV can read a bitmap file and convert it to EPS.
		AmiPro, ClarisWorks, and MS Word (and probably others) let you insert EPS pictures into a document but won't render them on screen, but will print them to a PostScript printer.

13.7 CONTENT OF A PROFESSIONAL MODELING AND SIMULATION REPORT

A network capacity design document should contain (in addition to the usual table of contents, list of figures, and modest index) the following information

- Input data used in the simulation
    - type of traffic used
    - transaction volumes
    - packet trace
    - other numerical data used
    - client and server locations
    - topology diagram
    - alternative topologies considered
    - assumptions made in the study

- Output data taken produced from the simulation
  - transaction response time at each client location
  - utilization on LANs
  - throughput of all WAN lines
  - client and server CPU utilization
  - client and server disk utilization
  - other media dependent plots
- Interpretation of the simulation results
  - explanation of the trends in the graphs
  - interpretation of the graph statistical confidence intervals
  - identification of any bottlenecks
  - comparison among the what-if scenarios simulated
- Recommendations based on the results
  - preferred limits on client concentrations
  - best server locations
  - optimum topologies
  - relevant cost impact

13.8 VALIDATING SIMULATION RESULTS

It's a simple to matter to slip up by forgetting a minus sign or misplacing a decimal point in a parameter, mistyping a digit, or using the wrong traffic generator. The simulator will proceed happily and produce results anyway. But as the saying goes, "garbage in, garbage out." The simulation should be checked, and here is a checklist to help systematize the process.

SIMULATION CHECKLIST

1. Warnings and errors in simulation must be understood and deemed harmless.
2. Simulator bugs/features don't apply here: be sure to read the release notes.
3. Check results are independent of the SEED, the random number seed value.
4. Protocol overhead on WAN and router has been added.
5. TCP/IP protocol overhead (HEADERS) are considered.
6. MAC protocol overhead (HEADERS and TRAILERS) is considered.
7. Server instruction overhead has been considered.
8. All node parameters are correct (laborious but necessary).
9. Topology modeled reflects reality.
10. Worst-case traffic and transaction volumes have been identified correctly.
11. Original traffic was representative (steady, bursty).
12. Traffic generator scripts were consistent with quick manual check of parameters.
13. Simulation ran long enough to guarantee steady state on all queues.
14. Reasonable confidence intervals of $\pm 5\%$ or less.
15. Consistent with mean-value analysis at low traffic volumes (sum up delays).
16. Run simulation with one traffic generator and check results are reasonable.

17. Router parameters (latency, forwarding) are correct for specified vendor.
18. Lost traffic (IP datagrams in router, 16 collisions) as expected.
19. Bottlenecks are where they're expected.
20. Performance knees are consistent with bottlenecks.
21. Has a peer review been conducted? Eight eyes are better than four!

"Fudging It"

Occasions present themselves that require we make assumptions or approximations in order to proceed with our analysis. For example, we may have no good estimate for the number of CPU instructions a server executes when handling a transaction, so to ensure that we model the network and not the server, we may assign 10,000 instructions per transaction. Or if an Ethernet switch PlanNet module is not available, a router with zero latency can approximate it (because at low utilization the results will be off by only about a millisecond, and at high utilization the switch will suffer from internal queuing anyway, just like a router). In a pinch, an FDDI module can be substituted for a 100-BASE-T module as long as utilization levels are not too high.

When no good transaction volumes rates are in hand, it may be best to play the transactions back to back to simulate a worst-case scenario, adopting the philosophy that you should simulate the worst case as the average case.

13.9 WHAT-IF SCENARIOS, OR MODELING ALTERNATE TOPOLOGIES

Simulation offers a repeatable, verifiable documented result, based on the best information available, which can incorporate new information as it comes to light. The best use of simulation is to support the successive evaluation of what-if scenarios. Here is a small list of problems that can be solved using simulation methods.

1. Determine the best FDDI priority settings to minimize response time.
2. Determine WAN link speed among multiple sites with given response time needs.
3. Select between 4 Mbps and 16 Mbps token rings.
4. Decide between distributed servers versus all servers on one FDDI ring.
5. Select among several alternative network application (NFS, FTP, X-windows).
6. Determine response time behavior as user counts increase.
7. Study the impact of moving an application to remote business sites.
8. Determine the impact of adding additional servers at various locations.
9. Determine whether many slow servers or a few fast servers is best.
10. Evaluate the burden of network printing on a segment.
11. Locate a bottleneck of the existing WAN/LAN network.
12. Evaluate frame relay versus a point-to-point solution.
13. Choose an alternative backbone topology (FDDI, 100VG-AnyLAN, 100-BASE-T).
14. Incorporate SNMP performance data into the current network model.
15. Find the number of X-stations running an application that a segment can support.

16. Estimate when more users will increase server utilization beyond the acceptable.
17. Evaluate the impact of adding new applications to network servers.
18. Choose between a fast router and an Ethernet switch.
19. Validate that a new enterprise-wide application can by carried by the network.
20. Prove that segmentation can reduce client response time.

13.10 A SAMPLE PLANNET SIMULATION EXPLAINED

Let's follow a simple PlanNet simulation. We're going to study exactly what happens as we add more and more traffic-generating clients to a 10-BASE-T hub. The clients exchange packets with servers attached to the same hub. The steps are basically

1. Develop the traffic scripts.
2. Build the topology diagram.
3. Fill in all the parameters for each device on the topology.
4. Define values for the iterated parameters.
5. Run the simulation.
6. Study and interpret the resulting plots.

1. Develop the Traffic Scripts

To generate traffic, each client executes an application traffic generator (ATG) script capable of producing 1% utilization when only itself and a server are on the LAN. The ATG script for the Ethernet client as follows

```
#
# ethernet.atg
#
Step {
ThinkingTime=exponential(mean = 0.043199)
    };
StartStats;
Step {
TimeoutPeriod=1.0,
ThinkingTime=0.0,
LocalCPU=0,
LocalDisk=0,
RequestLength=exponential(lower_limit=20,
                         mean = 500,
                         upper_limit=1480),
RemoteCPU=10,
RemoteDisk=0,
ResponseLength=40
    };
StopStats;
Restart;
```

2. Build the Topology Diagram

The topology is easily built using PlanNet's **add object** menu and connecting the modules together (see Figure 13-3).

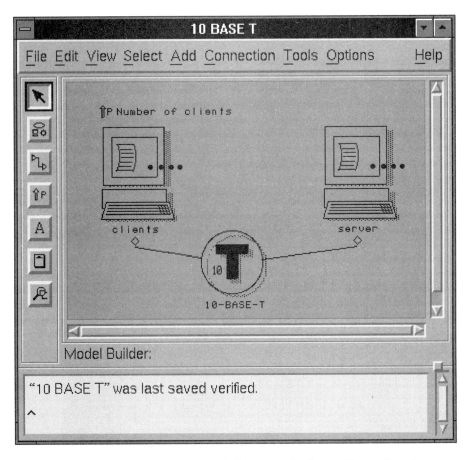

Figure 13-3 This is the PlanNet model builder screen showing the Ethernet client, the servers, and the 10-BASE-T hub. Notice the parameter called *Number of clients* takes on values between 1 and 200. Each of the network devices has an associated dialog box with customized parameters which are presented in Figures 13-4 to 13-6.

3. Define each Network Module's Parameters

Each module on the topology map has a properties and parameters module. For the client, server, and hub in our simulation, we have to fill in the dialog boxes shown in Figures 13-4 to 13-6.

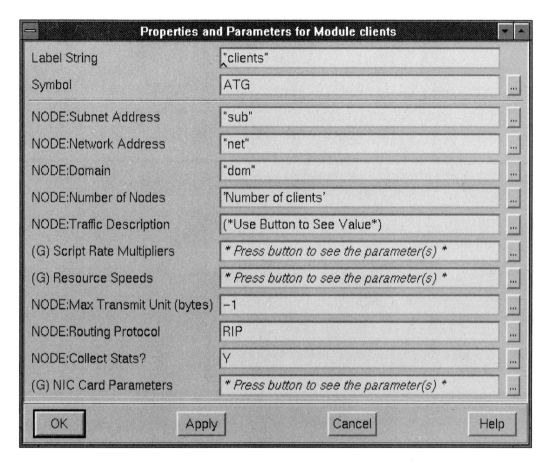

Figure 13-4 This is the property box for the client ATG network module. The fully qualified network name of the device is defined here as *clients.sub.net.dom*. The Number of Nodes represented by this icon is tied to a parameter called *Number of clients* and the Traffic Description field (not seen here) refers traffic to the *Server* node using script *clientservere.atg*. An MTU of −1 means to use the attached LAN medium's MTU, a routing protocol of RIP defines Internet Protocol as the network protocol, and we indicate we want the client module to collect performance statistics during the simulation. We have not filled in custom *NIC Card Parameters* in our simulation, and have taken the defaults.

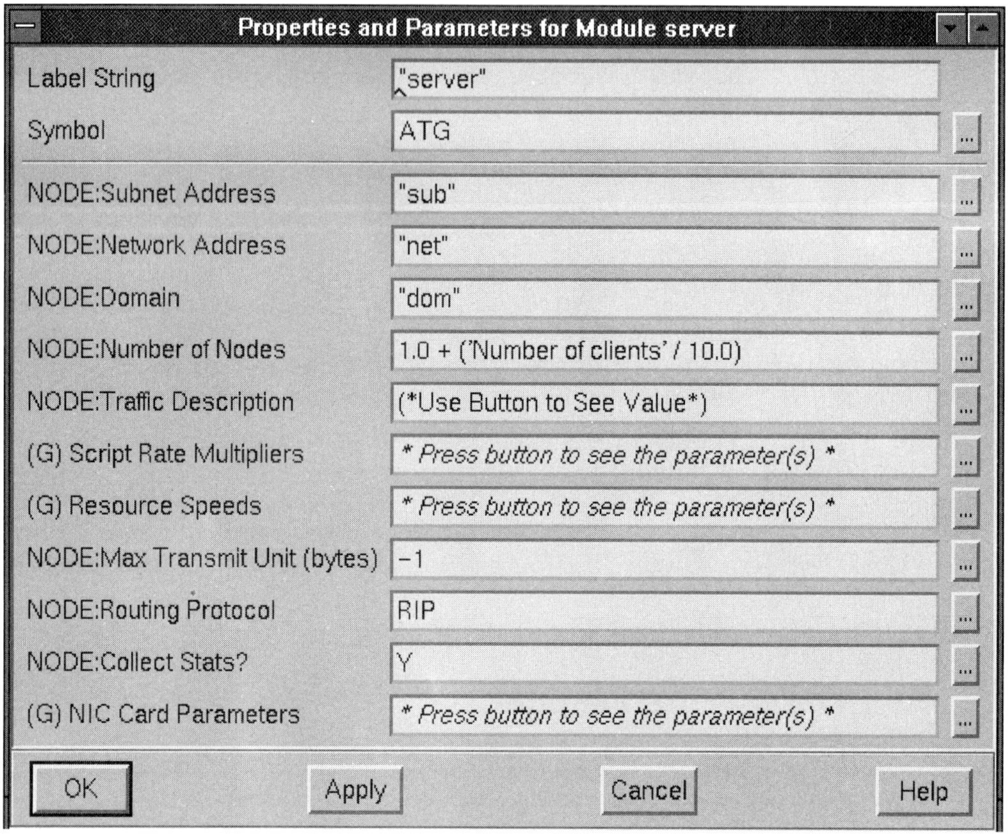

Properties and Parameters for Module server

Label String	"server"
Symbol	ATG
NODE:Subnet Address	"sub"
NODE:Network Address	"net"
NODE:Domain	"dom"
NODE:Number of Nodes	1.0 + ('Number of clients' / 10.0)
NODE:Traffic Description	(*Use Button to See Value*)
(G) Script Rate Multipliers	* Press button to see the parameter(s) *
(G) Resource Speeds	* Press button to see the parameter(s) *
NODE:Max Transmit Unit (bytes)	-1
NODE:Routing Protocol	RIP
NODE:Collect Stats?	Y
(G) NIC Card Parameters	* Press button to see the parameter(s) *

[OK] [Apply] [Cancel] [Help]

Figure 13-5 The server is also an ATG network module, *server.sub.net.dom,* so this window looks like that of the client. The *Number of Nodes* parameter is a function of the number of clients because we don't want the simulation results to depend on the server potentially bottlenecking at either the CPU or the LAN adapter. The *Traffic Description* field is left blank, because this server does not initiate any of its own traffic. It merely replies to client ATG requests.

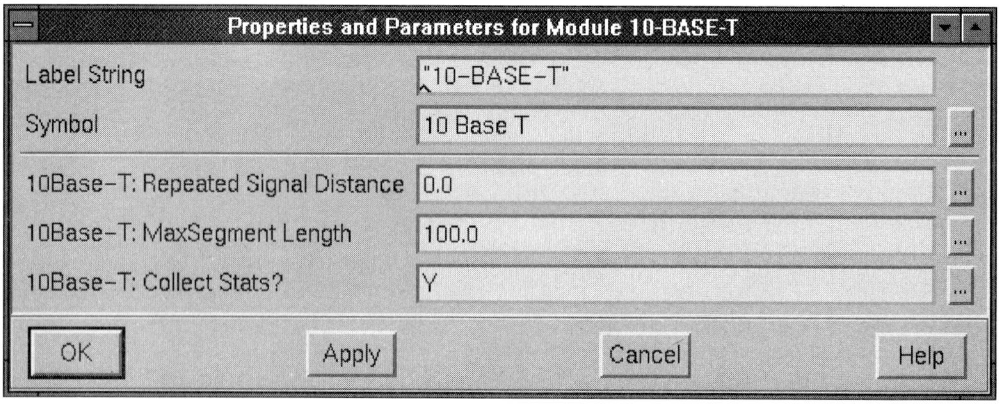

Properties and Parameters for Module 10-BASE-T

Label String	"10-BASE-T"
Symbol	10 Base T
10Base-T: Repeated Signal Distance	0.0
10Base-T: MaxSegment Length	100.0
10Base-T: Collect Stats?	Y

[OK] [Apply] [Cancel] [Help]

Figure 13-6 The properties for the 10-BASE-T hub allows us to vary some distances, but unless you are looking for some very hardware-dependent configuration results, just give the hub a unique name and put in a *"Y"* to collect simulation statistics.

4. Define the Iterated Parameters

The iterated parameter in our sample simulation is the *Number of clients* and we've chosen to make it an integer parameter starting at 200 clients and dropping down to 1 client in steps of 25 (see Figure 13-7).

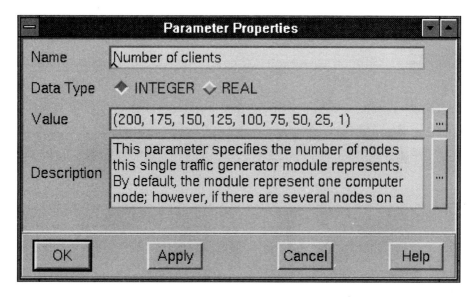

Figure 13-7 The iterated parameter *Number of clients* requires that a completely independent simulation be run for each value. On a single UNIX workstation the simulations run sequentially using the parameter values in the order shown, form left to right. If multiple UNIX workstations are NFS-mounted to the licensed workstation then PlanNet will keep them all busy running independent simulations for successive values of the parameter until all simulations have completed.

5. Run the Simulation

After saving the simulation model (having tended to any construction errors PlanNet may report) you run the simulation. The simulation's progress can be monitored. On a good day, there are no simulation run-time errors or warnings. As the simulation corresponding to each value of the iterated parameters complete, the performance results are available for display (see Figure 13-8).

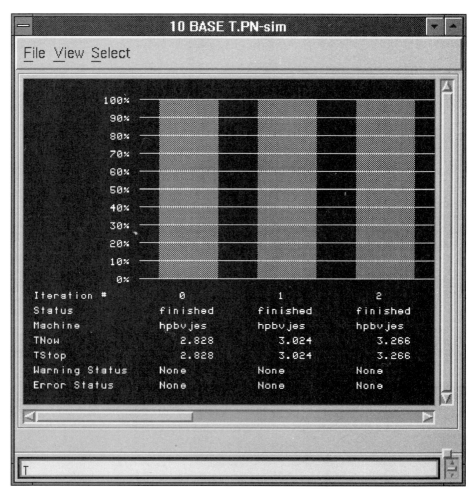

Figure 13-8 This is the PlanNet monitor window showing the progress of each simulation. One simulation is done for each value of the iterated parameters, in this case *Number of clients*. The thermometer-style progress indicators can be seen from across the room. Note that system *hpbvjes* is executing these simulations and it has finished iterations 0, 1, and 2 (the rest are off the screen). The TNOW values represent the simulation time, and they are less than TSTOP during the simulation, and come close to TSTOP at the end of the simulation. There aren't any errors or warnings to report.

6. Study and Interpret the Resulting Performance Graphs

The interesting plots are for client response time, Ethernet utilization, and server CPU utilization. Here we show just the response time curve (see Figure 13-9).

The performance data used to plot the graph in Figure 13-9 comes from the plot table, and it can be saved to a file for use outside of PlanNet. The exact plot table format is given here

```
Plot Name: ATG:clients-Delay For Each Script
Author: johnb

Plot Title: ATG:clients-Delay For Each Script
Y-Axis Title: Delay / Script
X-Axis Title: Number of clients
```

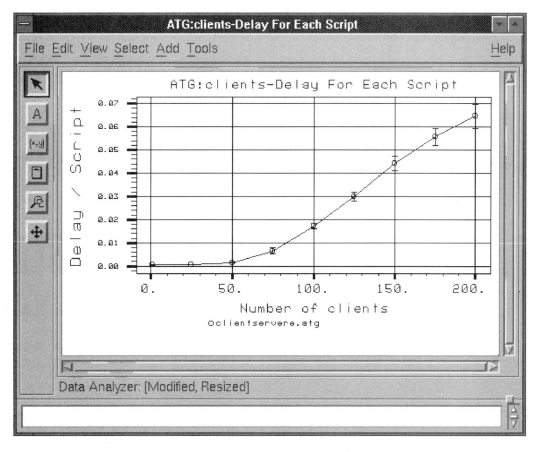

Figure 13-9 This is PlanNet's automatic plot generator, called the Data Analyzer. Here we see the response time curve for the transactions in ATG script *clientservere.atg,* labeled automatically by PlanNet. We can interpret the curve to mean that response time for 50 users remains acceptable but begins to rise to unacceptable levels beyond this. Note that this type of curve appears over and over again in the performance arena, and it's been discussed in several other sections of this book.

```
Date: Thursday, 7/13/95 04:05:11 pm PST
Creation Date: Thursday, 7/13/95 04:05:11 pm PST
Last Save Date: Not yet saved

Library Name: None
Library Path: None

Description: No description available.

  X Title: Number of clients
  Y Title: Delay / Script

 Y0 == clientservere.atg

        X          Y0          Delta0

        1        4.56E-04      1.94E-05
       25        6.75E-04      1.84E-05
       50        1.59E-03      2.82E-04
       75        6.61E-03      1.47E-03
      100        1.72E-02      1.21E-03
      125        2.99E-02      1.79E-03
      150        4.41E-02      3.10E-03
      175        5.57E-02      3.61E-03
      200        6.46E-02      5.26E-03
```

The *X* column represents the *Number of clients* parameter, *Y0* represents the delay in seconds measured for the ATG script *clientservere.atg*, and *Delta0* is the confidence interval. The confidence interval is calculated by PlanNet such that the actual response time (delay) falls within the range $Y0 \pm Delta0$ with 95% probability. For simulations that are in the steady state, increasing the value of TSTOP will generally reduce *Delta0*.

13.11 CHOOSING A CLIENT-SERVER PROTOCOL—FTP, NFS, OR X WINDOWS

Let's review a methodology for determining the best solution for moving CAD drawings around on a network. The requirement is that CAD files reside on a central server and remote users require access to them. The following solutions will be considered

- The user or application script uses the file transfer protocol, FTP, to copy the file from the server disk to the workstation disk and views the drawing locally with a CAD application.
- The user or application script uses an NFS mounted disk from the remote server file system and transparently views the drawing locally with a CAD application.
- The user executes an X-client CAD viewer on the server and uses the local workstation as an X-terminal. The CAD file and CAD viewer remain on the server.

We begin by choosing products to implement each of these solutions in a test bed. We develop a benchmark and teach users how to work each of the three solutions for viewing

CAD drawings. After the training session, a user goes through a typical transaction while a LAN analyzer captures the LAN traffic resulting. If time permits, three transaction traces are taken for each solution. When the benchmark is done, we'll have nine separate packet trace files.

Next we create ATG scripts. The easiest method is to use PlanNet's toolbox or `csv2trc` and `trc2atg` *awk* scripts to reduce each of the nine packet traces to simple one-step ATG scripts. If your packet tracing tool is not supported by PlanNet, then you will have to brush up on your *awk* scripting and first convert the ASCII packet traces to *.CSV* or *.TRC* form. A simple worst-case analysis can be conducted by looping each one-step ATG script to simulate an active session.

A more realistic ATG can be crafted if you can estimate the time it takes to copy the file (FTP or NFS) given the file size, how long the user views the file, and how long the user thinks before repeating. The ATG will contain the following steps

- A user think step. Estimate this by dividing eight hours by the number of drawings viewed in a day and convert it to seconds. Assume this is the mean for an exponential distribution with a reasonable lower and upper limit.
- The file transfer steps. Include enough ATG steps to simulate a file transfer (synthesize it by using *trc2atg* on a section of the packet trace that corresponds to the file transfer part of the transaction, and copy enough of these steps into the script to simulate the file transfer). Use fixed packet sizes in these steps because FTP copies data this way.
- CAD drawing viewing step. The user views the drawing for some number of seconds locally, generating no network traffic. This is another thinking step corresponding to the average viewing time for the CAD drawing. This is probably an exponential distribution too, with a reasonable lower and upper limit.
- The restart step loops the script.

Where should the *StartStats* and *StopStats* statements be placed? If you want to measure the network component of the response time, then bracket just the file transfer component. If you want to measure the transaction duration then bracket both the file transfer and the user viewing time. Here's a short example of an ATG script to implement the above.

```
# ftp.atg
# User think step
#
Step {
    ThinkingTime=exponential(lower_limit=10,
    mean = 30,
    upper_limit = 180)
};
#
# A short file transfer for this example
# but there may be hundreds of these steps
# for a real CAD drawing.
#
StartStats;
```

```
Step {
    TimeoutPeriod=0.02,
    ThinkingTime=0,
    LocalCPU=1000,
    LocalDisk=1460,
    RequestLength=1460,
    RemoteCPU=100,
    RemoteDisk=1460,
    ResponseLength=45,
    Priority=0
};
Step {
    TimeoutPeriod=0.02,
    ThinkingTime=0,
    LocalCPU=1000,
    LocalDisk=1460,
    RequestLength=1460,
    RemoteCPU=100,
    RemoteDisk=1460,
    ResponseLength=45,
    Priority=0
};
StopStats;
#
# User viewing time
#
Step {
    ThinkingTime=60
};
#
# loop the script
#
Restart;
```

The X-window solution does not move the file across the network, but opens it at the server. Network traffic is due to the X-client on the server communicating with the remote X-terminal during the viewing time interval. The ATG script to model this can be crafted as follows

- The user think step. The average think time can be estimated by calculating eight hours divided by the number of drawings viewed, converted to seconds. Make this the mean of an exponential distribution with a minimum and a maximum value.
- File open step. The user opens the file, generating a few packet exchanges across the network. Create an auxiliary ATG script using *trc2atg* on the packet trace corresponding to the file opening part of the transaction and copy enough steps into the script to account for the packets observed. This step generates very little traffic compared to the file viewing step, and you are justified in ignoring it entirely on this basis.
- File viewing step. The user views the CAD file for some given average time. Any panning and zooming done will create X-window traffic on the network. Create an ATG

script from the transaction packet capture file corresponding to the file viewing phase (using *csv2trc* and *trc2atg*). Copy enough of these ATG steps into the final ATG script to simulate the viewing time.
- put in a *Restart* to loop the script.

Bracket the steps between the file open and the end of the viewing interval with the *StartStats* and *StopStats* keywords to measure the transaction response time.

Draw the network topology, complete with the servers, clients, hubs, WAN, and LAN links. Configure each ATG client icon to execute the three scripts concurrently, beginning with the FTP method, and sweep the *Number of clients* parameter from 1 to 15 to simulate from 3 to 45 active users. Run the simulation with TSTOP = 10.0 seconds at first and validate the results for the first point (*Number of clients* = 1). Then run the simulation for larger TSTOP until the confidence intervals are less then 5% for all points. Repeat this method by saving the model under different names for the NFS and X-window methods and by changing the names of the ATG scripts in the client icon parameter box, and running the simulations again.

Note that PlanNet allows you to execute different simulation models concurrently, so if your UNIX system has the horsepower, go ahead and run each simulation when you're ready. Set TSTOP long enough so that you simulate a large number of transactions. If it takes 10 seconds to copy the file and another 60 to view it, then the simulation should be run at least for 700 seconds.

For long simulations, it is essential that the ATG script *TimeOut* value be set realistically so that when a packet is discarded, the ATG will time out and continue generating packets for the rest of the simulation. If the *TimeOut* value is set to infinity, then traffic generators may slowly wink out as packets are lost during the simulation (perhaps due to a router shedding packets during congestion). PlanNet's *trc2atg* awk script sets the TimeOut value to infinity, so change it when you use its output when crafting your own ATG scripts.

After all three simulations are done, and the confidence intervals are acceptable, the results may be compared to choose a solution for viewing CAD drawings. The response time data sets may be compared using cut-and-paste to produce one composite graph. Note that the response times derived from our methodology are for a single packet exchange between the client and the server. To choose among the FTP, NFS, and X-window methods, compare the maximum users each supports (based on response time) and the cost of each solution.

13.12 EXPANDING A CENTRALIZED APPLICATION TO REMOTE LOCATIONS

PlanNet simulations can be used to verify that an application presently running on a local area network will deliver acceptable response time and throughput when new clients are situated remotely across a WAN. Indeed, it is possible to develop a set of guidelines for configuring the remote WAN/LAN site for optimum performance. Simulation can also tell us how many additional remote clients the current server farm can support.

The study begins by collecting traffic traces for the high-volume transactions, which might be the opening, editing, and closing of word processing documents, one of a dozen different financial application transactions, or print jobs. The number of users and the daily transaction volumes must be estimated at each business location—information business analysts can often make available to you. Now you can create ATG scripts for each transaction.

It is not unusual to find that nobody can tell you what the traffic volumes might be or even what people are using the network for. Here is an opportunity to instrument the existing network's Ethernet or token ring segments with HP EASE Traffic Probes or LanProbes and take advantage of the HP Traffic Expert or NetMetrix tool to measure the traffic matrix you need (see Figure 13-10).

Next you draw the entire network topology, complete with the WAN links, routers, hubs, clients, and servers, and with great care you fill in the parameter boxes to reflect the number of users each ATG icon represents, the names of their servers, and the names of the ATG scripts that direct traffic to them.

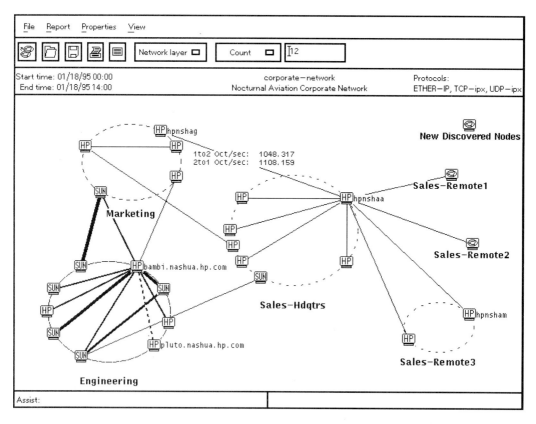

Figure 13-10 This is the NetMetrix Internetwork Monitor display, showing the traffic matrix for an enterprise network. The data to create this display is taken from HP's extensions to the RMON MIB implemented in the HP-UX Power Agent. The current version of the tool allows what-if analysis by letting the user move nodes from one subnet to another and recalculate the new traffic flow.

In order to determine performance bottlenecks, you usually vary the number of active users by introducing a variable, such as *Growth_factor,* and multiply the number of client nodes at each ATG icon by this variable. This iterated parameter may take on the values 3.0, 2.0, 1.0, and 0.5 so that a fairly smooth set of performance curves can be generated.

After clearing up any obvious problems with the simulation model, set TSTOP = 10 seconds and verify that crude performance plots can be pulled up, then run the simulation with TSTOP = 600 seconds overnight. The next morning, look at the response time curves for the remote sites. If they are flat, then no bottlenecks exist. If they start out flat but start to rise at the end, then a bottleneck must exist between the client and the server, so a look at the utilization curves of the LAN or WAN segments along that path is called for. A quick check should also be made of the server CPU utilization curves to ensure that we have not inadvertently driven a server into saturation by forgetting to reduce the server instruction count of a transaction. (Recall that we usually can't depend on the accuracy of the CPU instruction count determined by the `trc2atg` script in PlanNet's toolbox and the model of the server ATG is somewhat simplified.)

Once we run the simulation long enough to reduce the performance graph confidence intervals to around 5%, the data can be used to size the WAN links between central and remote sites, based on the maximum number of user and their transaction rates.

13.13 VALIDATING A NETWORK DESIGN FOR EMAIL AND TELNET USERS

Another application for PlanNet might be to study the impact of Email and telnet traffic on user response time for a given network design. Email is a bulk transfer protocol that runs periodically or nonperiodically while telnet traffic due to interactive applications being run across the network occurs pseudo-randomly during the day. The interactive traffic is effected by the Email traffic much more than the Email is effected by the telnet traffic.

We will measure the degradation of telnet traffic in the presence of continuous Email traffic by simulating several concurrent Email transfers, say from two to five, and by sweeping the number of telnet users from 10 to 50 in steps of 10. This requires $4 \cdot 5 = 20$ simulations.

A short packet trace taken from the middle of an Email transfer can be used to create a simple one-step ATG script using the `trc2atg` script in PlanNet's toolbox. Likewise, a single telnet conversation can be recorded (or synthesized) and played back in a loop. But telnet traffic tends to consist of short 64-byte Ethernet packets (fixed-length single-character packets, echoes, and TCP ACKs) between client and server, with an occasional longer response (possibly with a Poisson-distributed packet length) from the server (in response to the user hitting ENTER and getting a response from the application). Two ATG scripts for telnet might be more interesting, because one can simulate the character-by-character typing and the other can simulate the application responses. The response time for both are of interest. The character-by-character script will have a short think time in its ATG step while the application response ATG script will have a longer think time. The hardest part of a simulation is developing an acceptable ATG script! The ATG scripts `telnet.atg` (for the telnet clients) and `mail.atg` (for the mail hubs) are shown below.

```
#--------------------------------------------------
# telnet.atg
#
# Time between keystrokes (figure 10 cps average)
Step {
    ThinkingTime=exponential(lower_limit=0.01,
    mean = 0.1,
    upper_limit=1.0)
};
# one keystroke and the echo character
# (1 character, 20 bytes TCP header)
# PlanNet add IP & Ethernet headers
StartStats;
Step {
    RequestLength=21,
    RemoteCPU=1000,
    ResponseLength=21
};
StopStats;
#TCP ACK for the echo
Step {
    ResponseLength=20
};
Restart;
#--------------------------------------------------
# mail.atg
#
# Time between packets
Step {
    ThinkingTime=exponential(lower_limit=9.6e-6,
    mean = 0.01,
    upper_limit=0.1)
};
# send a mail data packet and return a TCP ACK
# (1460 bytes of data, 20 bytes TCP,
# PlanNet adds 20 byte IP and Ethernet headers
StartStats;
Step {
    RequestLength=1480,
    RemoteCPU=1000,
    ResponseLength=20
};
StopStats;
Restart;
```

With the hard work behind us, we draw the network topology (see Figure 13-11), set up all the node parameters, and run the simulator.

The response time graphs for the telnet character-by-character ATG are presented here in the form of Lotus 1-2-3 graphs, which have been created from the PlanNet data analyzer Plot Table.

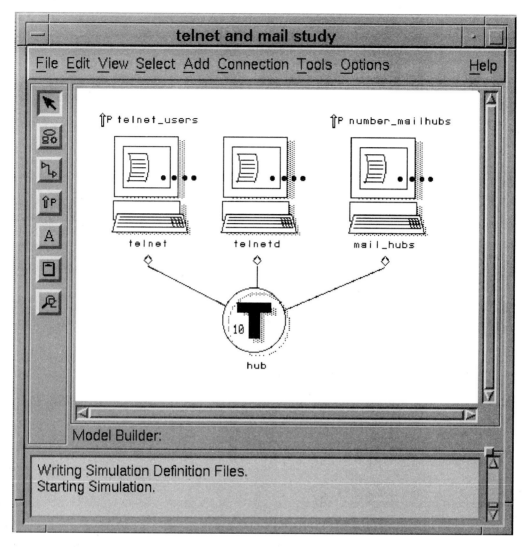

Figure 13-11 Creating the PlanNet topology diagram for the telnet and Email simulation takes only a few minutes. The telnet clients, their server, and the Email hubs share the same 10-BASE-T hub.

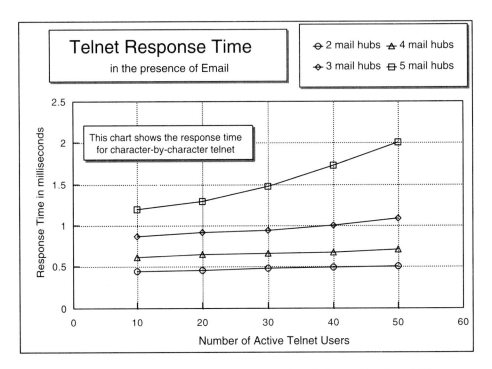

Figure 13-12 Data exported from PlanNet's plot table is easily imported into Lotus 1-2-3 to allow us to customize the data presentation to our liking. Here we see that character-by-character telnet response time for 50 users does not degrade significantly until more than two concurrent Email transfers occur. Telnet traffic response time is not effected by the number of users to any great degree until the number of mail hubs reaches four.

13.14 COMMERCIALLY AVAILABLE SIMULATION TOOLS

The author has some familiarity with the network simulation products listed in Table 13-3, having read about, tried out the demo version, or professionally used them.

TABLE 13-3 COMMERCIALLY AVAILABLE GUI-BASED NETWORK SIMULATION PRODUCTS

Product	Company	Web Site	Notes
COMNET III	Caci	http://www.caciasl.com	UNIX and PC versions of network simulation software.
BONeS Designer	Systems & Networks	http://www.sysnet.com	UNIX/X-windows discrete event simulator suitable for building and simulating arbitrary systems, including networks.
Netmod	University of Michigan	http://www.citi.umich.edu/netmod.html	MS Windows PC software provides GUI for building hierarchical models, provides traffic descriptions and network components, and calculates approximate analytical solutions to network traffic flows.
BONeS PlanNet	Systems & Networks	http://www.sysnet.com	UNIX/X-windows discrete event simulator with library of network modules.
SimScript	Caci	http://www.caciasl.com	PC and UNIX based general purpose simulation language.
VisSim	Visual Solutions	http://www.ultranet.com/biz/vissim/index.html	MS Windows PC software, combined with Pascal-written DLLs in Dr. Dobb's Journal for June 1995 provides discrete event queue-based block-oriented simulation features. A downloadable demo is available.
XNetMod	University of Michigan	http://www.citi.umich.edu/netmod.html	UNIX/X-Windows port of NetMod with hooks into REAL and NEST C-language simulation languages.

13.15 SEARCHING FOR SIMULATION INFORMATION ON THE WORLD WIDE WEB

In his travels, the author has located some useful sites on the WWW. The listing in Table 13-4 is taken from his Web browser bookmarks.

TABLE 13-4 URLS FOR WORLD WIDE WEB SITES SERVING SIMULATION INFORMATION

Web Site URL	URL Description
http://piranha.eng.buffalo.edu/simulation/	COMPUTER SIMULATION: MODELING & ANALYSIS (CSMA)
http://simlab.cs.cornell.edu:80/	Cornell Modeling and Simulation Project Home Page
http://www2.ecst.csuchico.edu/~hfsmith/McLeod/	McLeod Institute of Simulation Science
http://netlab.itd.nrl.navy.mil:80/NS.html	Network Simulation & Analysis
http://eurosim.tuwien.ac.at/hotlink.html	SIMULATION HOTLINKS
http://128.227.100.198/~fishwick/	Simulation Model Design and Execution: P. Fishwick
gopher://hill.lut.ac.uk/11/Software	Simulation Software
http://www.fernuni-hagen.de/www2bonsai/WINF/library.htm	Simulation—Library search
http://www-pablo.cs.uiuc.edu/CS433/notes.html	University of Illinois CS 433 Lecture Notes

14

Comparing Average, Worst-Case, Queuing, and Simulation Methods

14.0 INTRODUCTION

Various network capacity planning methods and many tools are discussed in this book. This chapter is intended to position them relative to each other. The average, worst-case, queuing, and simulation methods are positioned (we'll call them "the four methods" in this chapter). Also compared are the spreadsheet, math scratchpad, and simulation tools. We look at metrics for comparison such as suitability, accuracy, ease of use, work time cost of use, quality of documentation produced by the tool, and training and experience needed. A helpful technique for validating a simulation using a queuing analysis is given.

14.1 SUITABILITY FOR LARGE NETWORK MODELS

As Table 14-1 indicates, the four methods are not equally well suited for analyzing large networks.

TABLE 14-1 COMPARATIVE SUITABILITY OF THE FOUR PLANNING METHODS

Method	Suitability
Average	A fast method that allows us to use simple tools like spreadsheets and calculators for handling any size network.
Worst-Case	Overdesigns and thus increases the cost of the network, but easy to apply to a large network and suited to simple tools like spreadsheets.
Queuing	Can be a very hard analysis for large networks unless the topology falls under one of a small number of well-studied cases found in the statistics textbooks. It is best to simplify the problem by reducing the topology to a chain of independent simple queues and use a math scratchpad or spreadsheet.
Simulation	Well-suited for large topologies with complex traffic. It takes longer to get results because the tool is more complex, and you must handle more information and produce more results. It can take several weeks to generate validated results and a comprehensive report.

14.2 ACCURACY COMPARISON OF THE FOUR METHODS

As indicated in Figure 14-1, the four design methods boast different degrees of accuracy.

It's worth noting that at low traffic levels, all of the methods for determining network response time and utilization will generally agree. As traffic levels increase, the simulation method retains its accuracy while the other methods have greater variation.

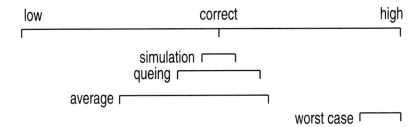

Figure 14-1 The worst-case analysis methodology overestimates and the simulation method gives the most accurate results. The queuing method and average method generally straddle the correct answer. To validate a complex network simulation a network administrator often does a quick average-value check at low traffic levels. Anything within 20–30% is close enough.

14.3 EASE OF USE AND REUSABILITY

The four design methods and their ease of use and reusability vary depending on the tools used when working with them (see Table 14-2).

Reuse with any of these methods improves when the network manager takes a modular approach and retains good notes that document the progress of the work effort. It pays to organize data in smaller files and libraries.

TABLE 14-2 COMPARATIVE USABILITY OF THE FOUR PLANNING METHODS

Method	Ease of Use	Reusability
Average	Very easy method with simple tools such as pen and paper, spreadsheets, and math scratchpads.	When the problem is laid out in a structured modular manner it is easy to modify and expand it for reuse.
Worst-Case	Very easy method with simple tools such as pen and paper, spreadsheets, and math scratchpads.	When the problem is laid out in a structured modular manner it is easy to modify and expand it for reuse.
Queuing	Only if the problem can be stated in terms of the popular queuing solutions is this an easy method.	If the same traffic statistics are required then an existing analysis can be tailored for a new problem. A different statistical distribution may not allow reuse of the mathematics.
Simulation	The simulation tools are generally easy to use after a suitable training period. Creating the traffic generators is not as straightforward but some simulators will synthesize traffic generators based on user-specified workloads and parameters.	Traffic generators are easy to reuse and most network topologies are readily modified, especially with the built-in cut-and-paste tools of the simulator's model-builder GUI.

GUI-based simulation methods are very easy to use but due to price they are justified only for complex problems with hundreds to thousands of nodes that cannot be handled sanely with the other methods.

14.4 WORK TIME REQUIREMENTS

Table 14-3 provides a rough guide to tools that may be used and the amount of time taken when using the tools, given a typical performance analysis. The intent is to compare the tool sets and not to give work effort estimates for problem solving.

TABLE 14-3 COMPARATIVE WORK TIME REQUIREMENTS OF THE FOUR PLANNING METHODS/TOOLS

Method	Productivity tool used	Time required (hours)
Average	Spreadsheet & PC/Mac	2
	Mathcad & PC/Mac	1
	Calculator	4
Worst-Case	Spreadsheet & PC/Mac	4
	Mathcad & PC/Mac	2
	Calculator	8
Queuing	Spreadsheet & PC/Mac	8
	Mathcad & PC/Mac	3
	Calculator	16
Simulation	Simulator S/W & Workstation	1
	Mathcad & PC/Mac	32
	Spreadsheet & PC/Mac	40

The math scratchpad and the spreadsheet tools are not that well suited for doing simulations of any great complexity, but of course any reuse of previous work can cut down the time spent doing a new simulation. Using a programmable calculator instead of a standard one can reduce the work effort estimated in the table.

14.5 TRAINING AND EXPERIENCE NEEDED TO USE THE METHODS

The amount of training needed to successfully use the four design methods varies considerably, as indicated in Table 14-4.

As you move down the list, the methods require more experience in math, statistics, and tools. Placing a well-intentioned but untrained and inexperienced individual behind the keyboard of a full-featured network simulation tool is a recipe for potential disappointment.

TABLE 14-4 COMPARATIVE TRAINING AND EXPERIENCE REQUIREMENTS OF THE FOUR PLANNING METHODS

	Training and experience requirement	
Method	In capacity planning	In using the tool
Average	1 month	1 day
Worst-Case	1 month	1 day
Queuing	6 months	2 days
Simulation	1+ year	5 days

14.6 QUALITY OF DOCUMENTATION PRODUCED BY THE TOOLS/METHODS

Given that the network managers often have to document and present the results of their performance analysis, it's important to consider how the design tools compare in creating usable output (Table 14-5).

TABLE 14-5 COMPARATIVE QUALITY OF DOCUMENTATION PRODUCED BY THE PLANNING TOOLS/METHODS

Tool	Suited methods	Type of documentation	Comments on quality
Spreadsheet	Average Worst-case Queue	Graphs Tables Limited text	Lotus 1-2-3 graphs can be customized to produce high-quality presentations. The tables and text can stand alone. For best results import all these data types into a word processing document.
Scratchpad	Average Worst-case Queue Simulation	Graphs Tables Text regions	The graphs are not quite so nice and the tables are really array representations. A Mathcad document can stand alone and look good, but best results are obtained by copying the information into a word processing document.
Simulator	Simulation	Network map Graphs Tables	PlanNet's maps look nice and the graphs can be somewhat customized but both are exported as black-and-white PostScript. An X-window screen shot will capture the color graphs. You can export the plot's tabular data into Lotus 1-2-3 and create custom graphs. A word processor is essential to integrate the results.

14.7 USING ONE METHOD TO VALIDATE ANOTHER

To validate a simulation you can use the average method to check the first point on the graph where network utilization is low. A rule of thumb can used: if the two are within ± 20% or so they are in agreement. If not, it's necessary to dig in deeper to figure out what's not right. The premise is that you can check the simulator's first point and trust it to do the right things as traffic levels go up, as queues form, and as packets collide or disappear from buffers.

The simulator's second point usually includes some queuing activity within the network. To satisfy a greater degree of personal paranoia, the network manager can complete a simple M/M/1 (single-server single-queue) queuing analysis, connect inputs to outputs, add up flows that converge, assume statistical independence, assume exponential interarrivals and service time, and add up the end-to-end delays as request packets flow between source and destination and reply packets travel back. This validation step can be done with a spreadsheet or math scratchpad.

Let's analyze the network diagrammed in Figure 14-2 with a simplified queuing analysis.

The spreadsheet is constructed by assuming that traffic from all three clients divides evenly between the two servers (see Figures 14-3 and 14-4). For each client the spreadsheet adds up the individual queuing delays in both directions. The LAN delays are ignored because we assume they are negligible relative to the WAN delays. The service rates and the arrival rates have been cooked for this exercise but in practice it will be necessary to use the line speed and average packet size to figure these values. Since the server may emit packets at a slightly different rate and with different packet sizes, there will not necessarily be any symmetry in the forward and reverse directions.

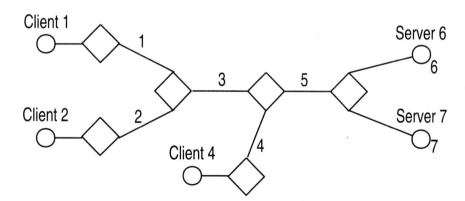

Figure 14-2 This network consists of three client LAN locations (Client1, Client2, and Client4), two server LAN locations (Server6 and Server7), and their interconnecting WAN links and routers. Each queue is numbered, corresponding to either a WAN link or a server. Since each client packet generates a response from a server, the reverse queues will be considered too. We might check a preliminary simulation result by adding up the round-trip delays for each client site.

	A	B	C	D	E	F	G	H	I
1		Forward Queue Direction			Reverse Queue Direction			Validation	
2	Queue	Service Rate	Arrival Rate	Average Delay	Service Rate	Arrival Rate	Average Delay	Client	Trip Delay
3									
4	1	40	10	0.0333333	15	10	0.2	1	0.7
5	2	35	20	0.0666667	25	20	0.2	2	0.733
6	3	40	30	0.1	40	30	0.1	3	0.517
7	4	20	12	0.125	20	12	0.125		
8	5	50	42	0.125	50	42	0.125		
9	6	100	21	0.0126582		21			
10	7	70	21	0.0204082		21	Should be 0 —>	0	
11									

Figure 14-3 A simplified queuing analysis spreadsheet. The columns labeled Forward Queue Direction contain the individual forward queue delay calculations and those labeled Reverse Queue Direction contain the individual reverse queue delay calculations. The column labeled Validation adds up the forward and reverse delays corresponding to each of the three clients. The arrival rate numbers in both directions have been set equal here but they will generally differ. The spreadsheet is set up to provide for this. The WAN link service rates in each direction are generally not the same, reflecting the packet size differences in the forward and reverse directions. A check is done at the bottom right-hand corner to verify that the reverse-direction packets are properly accounted for.

	A	B	C	D	E	F	G	H	I
1		Forward Queue Direction			Reverse Queue Direction			Validation	
2	Queue	Service Rate	Arrival Rate	Average Delay	Service Rate	Arrival Rate	Average Delay	Client	Round Trip Delay
3									
4	1	40	10	1/(B4-C4)	15	10	1/(E4-F4)	1	+D4+D6+D8+@AVG(D9..D10)+G8+G6+G4
5	2	35	20	1/(B5-C5)	25	20	1/(E5-F5)	2	+D5+D6+D8+@AVG(D9..D10)+G8+G6+G5
6	3	40	@SUM(C4..C5)	1/(B6-C6)	40	+F8-F7	1/(E6-F6)	3	+D7+D8+@AVG(D9..D10)+G8+G7
7	4	20	12	1/(B7-C7)	20	12	1/(E7-F7)		
8	5	50	@SUM(C6..C7)	1/(B8-C8)	50	@SUM(F9..F10)	1/(E8-F8)		
9	6	100	+C8/2	1/(B9-C9)		21			
10	7	70	+C8/2	1/(B10-C10)		21	Should be 0 ·	@SUM(F4..F5)-F6	
11									

Figure 14-4 The same spreadsheet as Figure 14-3 shows the actual formulas used in each cell. These formulas correspond with the network diagram in Figure 14-2. Independent values are shown here as numbers and dependent values are shown by their formula. The formula for Average Delay is taken from the M/M/1 case. For other queue disciplines an appropriate formula may be inserted. Note that the formula for Round Trip Delay takes an average value of the two server response times. This is because the model allows the clients to communicate with all the servers.

15

Difficulties in Predicting Network Performance

15.0 INTRODUCTION

Great complexity lurks in the bowels of a network. It's essential to understand that this complexity cannot be fully understood and considered when doing a network performance study. You'd wind up with "analysis paralysis" if you tried to deal with broadcast and multicast activity, CRC errors, device configuration errors, protocol bugs and features, O/S implementation details, the effect of component upgrades, multiprotocol interaction, router CPU overhead, and special transport features that kick in occasionally.

Perhaps this chapter is sobering because it exposes the difficulties in the real world. You tend to ignore them the longer you follow the well-worn paths of network capacity planning.

15.1 BROADCAST ACTIVITY AND ITS EFFECT ON SYSTEM AND NETWORK PERFORMANCE

There was a time (it was during the eighties) when every networking person feared the dreaded broadcast storm. It would create a LAN meltdown and it was caused by the mysterious Chernobyl packet.

Broadcast storms occur when one or more nodes have misconfigured or buggy IP stacks. Note that this scenario is not the only cause of a broadcast storm. The Chernobyl packet does not look like an IP broadcast to its sender but it does to the other node. The other node generates a response that is not an IP broadcast from its perspective but is to the original system. Essentially these two sets of systems begin dueling, creating high volumes of IP broadcasts, which are of course generally wrapped in a MAC layer broadcast packet.

Now MAC layer broadcasts are processed by every node on the attached LAN, propagating across hubs, repeaters, Ethernet switches, and bridges alike, but stopping at the router subnet boundaries. A LAN adapter receives the packet and sends it up the protocol stack to the network layer. If the network protocol is not present, the packet is discarded, incurring a fairly low instruction penalty. Otherwise the packet is processed further, depending on the nature of the broadcast and the type of network protocol, and there will be a greater instruction penalty. The actual instruction penalty will depend on the processing speed of the node. A low-end 80286-based system will take a lot longer to process an IP broadcast than a 66 Mhz PowerPC.

Network capacity plans often ignore broadcast activity for a variety of reasons

- Sources of broadcast packets are not generally known.
- CPU processing time may be high (e.g., a RIP packet).
- CPU processing time may be low (e.g., an ARP packet).
- CPU processing time may be negligible (e.g., a Novell SAP received by an IP-only node).
- Processing time varies with architecture (CPU, O/S, implementation).
- Impact on system performance is not well defined.
- Frequency of broadcast packets is unknown.
- Broadcast levels are normally very low, more like "noise."

Given that broadcast packet volumes don't contribute significantly to filling the network pipes, they may certainly be dismissed from a capacity perspective. To account for end-system CPU hits incurred by a broadcast, simulation tools can provide a pretty good handle on this. Given that each broadcast incurs x-many instruction hits, a traffic generator for subnet `bellevue.hp.com` can be constructed to send traffic to `*.bellevue.hp.c om,` a wild card that matches all destinations on the `bellevue.hp.com` subnet.

15.2 MEDIA ERROR RECOVERY, INTERRUPTIONS TO SERVICE, CRC ERRORS, AND RESTARTS

Capacity planning focuses on performance parameters. Simulation tools can track packet losses in routers (due to buffer overflows) and on Ethernet due to excess retries. That's about as far as our methods can go towards modeling "fringe" network behavior.

The networking medium may encounter a brief interruption in service, such as token ring beaconing, FDDI ring wrap, router reboots, CRC errors, and other error recovery processing required by the standard for that medium. These interruptions certainly effect performance but they don't generally occur during normal operation. When interruptions do happen, there is generally some time-limited transient behavior during which the medium recovers and after which normal performance conditions apply (see Figure 15-1). Network capacity plans generally cover the steady-state network operation, meaning that the performance of the fully functioning network plus the performance of a degraded mode of operation (during some outage) is determined.

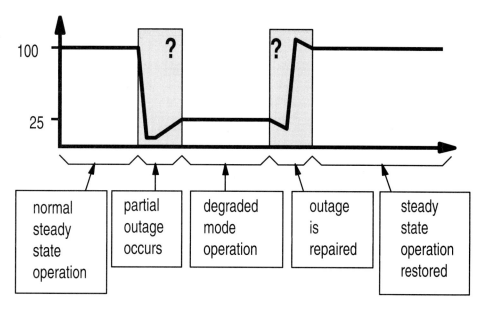

Figure 15-1 Networks that suffer a partial outage enter a transient performance state that is typically not modeled and which settles into a degraded more of operation, which we can model. Failure of a 256 Kbps primary WAN link and the automatic dial-up of a 56 Kbps backup might be an example of this. Once the outage is repaired, the network undergoes another performance transient—again not modeled, and then passes finally to the steady state, which is normal for the network and again falls into a state we do model.

15.3 PROTOCOL BUGS AND FEATURES

Network capacity plans and the associated tools and methods generally don't deal with the following

- random connection resets or drops
- detailed protocol implementation
- limits on the number of concurrent connections
- limits on the size of the buffer pools
- reordered packets
- UDP vs. TCP differences
- hidden internal timers and timing loops

The most sophisticated simulation tools such as REAL and NEST are intended for protocol simulation but the typical network administrator will generally not have the inclination, time, willingness, or expertise to use (and debug) these public domain tools. Many commercially available simulators like PlanNet are relatively protocol independent even though they can model each network protocol in a multiprotocol environment independently.

15.4 OPERATING SYSTEM IMPLEMENTATION EFFECTS ON THE NETWORK

Network and system electronics are all run by their embedded operating systems. Their implementation internals and architecture are generally proprietary even though they outwardly implement industry standards. The following are among the implementation details that will affect performance

- location in hardware or software of OSI layers 1 through 7
- smart LAN adapters that can hold layers 1 to 6
- kernel code vs. daemon code vs. user mode code
- single- vs. multithreaded code
- virtual memory, mapping, and swapping
- /etc/inetd in UNIX vs. TSR/Winsock in MS-DOS/Windows
- disk cache size (for applications doing disk I/O)
- disk cache hit rate

These kinds of details are often not known and putting them into a model ropes the network administrator into doing system-level modeling. This level of detail is usually approximated in a broad-brush approach by adjusting the simulation parameters for CPU time. PlanNet provides quite a bit of flexibility in its server module, allowing you to choose the statistical distribution and its parameters (mean and variance), and lower and upper limits.

15.5 IMPACT OF SYSTEM AND NETWORK COMPONENT UPGRADES

The following list of system and network changes impacts network performance in ways that are harder to determine than a simple increase in line speed

- increased memory capacity (or faster RAM chips)
- faster CPU (higher clock speed or architectural upgrade)
- faster SCSI bus controller
- wider SCSI bus data path
- O/S upgrade (the one that hopefully fixes all your other problems)
- tunable NOS parameters
- new bindery
- bigger CPU cache (from 256 Kbytes to 1 M)
- defragmenting the hard drive

None of these changes makes a clear impact performance and there may be surprises in store after the upgrade, such as a performance reduction or no improvement at all. Any expected improvement in performance can be estimated from published benchmarks or in-house testing. The PlanNet simulator is equipped with a utility called Scribe which takes user-provided parameters about the client and server and generates an application traffic generator (ATG) script for use in the simulation. Some educated guessing is still needed to answer all the questions Scribe poses.

What is the performance impact of swapping a dumb 10-BASE-T hub with one supporting SNMP, RMON, or HP EASE, or of swapping the same type of hub for one made by another vendor? Since 10-BASE-T is a standard, you'd expect no change in performance of the hub's basic I/O functions. But does the extra firmware operating inside the hub really have no other impact?

On the bright side, we can handle certain types of upgrades with a good simulator. Let's remove a one-port Ethernet card from a router and replace it with a four-port Ethernet card. Performance differences here are more straightforward because the router vendor will specify IP forwarding rates between Ethernets on the same card and also between Ethernets on different cards. What about swapping out the router for another vendor's? In this case PlanNet's menu of vendor-specific router parameters (derived from Scott Bradner's tests published annually in *Network Computing* magazine) comes to the rescue. The user can also fine-tune these parameters.

15.6 CONFIGURATION ERRORS IN NETWORK ELECTRONICS

The performance predictions made by a network capacity plan may not agree with real-world measurements because certain network elements are misconfigured. Here is a list of configuration issues that are encountered in network electronics

Routers:
- Error in the routing table (packets take an indirect path).
- ICMP redirects occur.
- Routing loops.
- Time To Live (TTL) is set too short.
- Timers are too short.
- Buffers are too small, too few, with the wrong bin sizes.
- Protocol routing priorities are set wrong.
- Load balancing is poor.
- Packet filtering overhead is larger than expected.

Bridges:
- Overhead due to "security" features that are turned on.
- Spanning tree configuration problems.

Hubs:
- SQE is enabled between hubs although the vendors says not to.
- Redundant links fail-over.
- The 10-BASE-T heartbeat is enabled for some nodes but not for others.

Switches:
- Full duplex is turned on but the server's card is standard Ethernet.
- The port can handle only one MAC address.
- The MAC port table overflows.

Per the theme of this chapter, improper and unexpected operation is generally not handled by network performance analysis methods. This is somewhat of a curse because when there are performance problems on a network, how is one to know if it is a capacity problem, a configuration problem, or an architecture problem? For example, how do we approach the problem, "Response time is terrible but there are no utilization problems"? The answer is that you don't at first blindly do a capacity plan to solve a performance problem. You first conduct a Kepner-Tregoe problem analysis. This is a methodology that takes you from problem statement to final resolution.

15.7 MIXING PROTOCOLS SUCH AS IP, IPX, DECNET, AND APPLETALK

In a multiprotocol network each protocol is independent but can interact with the others because all share the same resources (see Figure 15-2).

Note that tunneling and bridging of nonroutable protocols is a separate matter. SNA can be tunneled by wrapping each SDLC frame in a TCP/IP wrapper and injecting it into the IP network. IPX and AppleTalk may also be tunneled using IP when these otherwise routable protocols are not supported or configured on the network.

Many networks bridge NetBEUI and Local Area Transport (LAT) because these protocols have no routing layer. Remaining protocols are routed. This combination is called *brouting*.

The network layer must provide the functions expected at the OSI model, which are addressing, network-to-MAC-layer mapping, routing and route discovery, fragmentation, and reassembly. The routing protocols will each have their unique address fields, network-to-MAC-layer mapping, and routing and route discovery mechanisms.

IP has 32-bit network addresses, uses Address Resolution Protocol (ARP) to map IP addresses to Ethernet addresses, and allows for static or RIP/OSPF/EGP/ICMP route discovery protocols. DECNET Phase 4 uses a 16-bit network address, rewrites the MAC address of the LAN adapter to correspond, and uses HELLO for route discovery. IPX uses

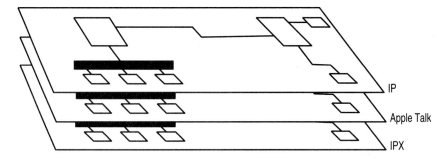

Figure 15-2 Multiprotocol networks may be viewed as multiple logical network layers superimposed on the same physical topology. Each protocol is independent of the others and each is configured using the rules laid down for that protocol. Protocols interact only because they share the same router CPUs and the same network links, i.e., they share resources.

a 32-bit network address plus the 48-bit Ethernet address for addressing; the routers dictate each LAN's IPX address.

Network simulation tools like PlanNet can treat each protocol separately from the others, allowing routers to discover routes and prioritize protocols. The tool does not simulate the actual traffic due to route discovery, network address–to–MAC address mapping, or other nonperformance-related protocol activity. The assumption is that the simulator can figure out static routes at initialization time and that network addresses are treated as strings of characters with a dotted notation to denote subnets (which look just like DNS node names).

15.8 ROUTER OVERHEAD: RIP, OSPF, SNMP, ICMP, ACCOUNTING, AND COMPRESSION

Routers do so much more than simply store and forward packets. There is both CPU and network link overhead in dealing with routing protocols such as RIP, OSPF, and ICMP. SNMP packet overhead can be quite high if the network management station is requesting the ARP cache or address tables. Accounting uses the CPU as does serial line compression.

ICMP overhead includes replying to `ping` echo requests, sending ICMP redirects to end systems that don't know the best route to a destination, and transmitting ICMP source quench requests to avoid buffer overflows when there is congestion. It's difficult to predict the amount of ICMP traffic a router must deal with and this matter is generally ignored in network performance studies.

OSPF is a complex algorithm that recalculates the routing table based on link-state updates within its OSPF area and exchanges information with routers it has established an adjacency with. Packet overhead is relatively low (by design) but the CPU overhead can be high during the calculation period. The duration and overhead of the OSPF calculations varies dynamically with the network and depends on the location of the router in relation to its neighbors. This overhead is therefore generally ignored by capacity planners.

Serial line throughput can improve substantially by turning on compression. If only one CPU drives the router then this limits the number of lines that can be compressed. Some routers have a separate CPU per serial card, which allows the central CPU to perform other tasks. Since the amount of CPU time to perform compression increases with the aggregate data rate across all serial lines connected to the card, the vendor will usually specify a worst-case cumulative data rate. Exceeding this will saturate the card's CPU, limit the throughput, and increase latency. Recall that for every compression there is a decompression at the other end that loads the remote router CPU.

Barefoot routing can be done with minimum latency. CPU switching may be necessary but fast switching yields the lowest latency. But in this security-conscious decade, router IP and TCP port filtering is a powerful and widely used feature. Routers with filtering turned on must process each packet in software, evaluate the packet against each filters installed, and pass it on after all filters have been tested. The more filters, the greater the latency. The PlanNet simulator allows the user to configure additional latency values into the router module. The values will have to come from the router vendor, from the Bradner report, from testing, or from thin air.

SNMP is essential for managing routers but the software that implements the protocol is usually assigned the lowest priority of all programs so it won't degrade the router's performance. There is the packet overhead associated with SNMP, but the way to handle it is to treat the network management station as a client, the router as a server, and model it using a traffic generator.

15.9 SPECIAL TRANSPORT-LAYER FEATURES: VAN JACOBSON TCP AND NETWARE BURST MODE

General purpose simulation tools generally don't include special enhancements to standard protocols. Many modern networks now include TCP/IP as the preferred protocol. Client and server systems from a variety of vendors include TCP/IP implementations with a range of robustness, features and limits—some not documented.

Van Jacobson TCP refers to a TCP implementation with additional features that enhance TCP's operation on an Internet. These features include

- fast start (prevents TCP from dumping a full window into the network on startup)
- exponential backoff (increases time-out limit exponentially on retries)
- honors maximum and minimum TCP timers
- keeps a dynamic round-trip time and variance and sets the time-out accordingly

Needless to say, when such features kick in, the behavior of the data flows is not trivial. Only special purpose simulators such as C-code, NEST, REAL, GPSS, and BONeS Designer can even deal with it. These features create transient phenomena that tools like PlanNet aren't built to track. In fact, the current implementation on PlanNet's application traffic generators has a time-out parameter. If the response packet does not arrive within the time-out period, that transaction terminates and a new think time is generated. There is no flexibility to vary the timer in "real time."

Dealing with Netware's burst mode feature is complicated by the fact that a lot of applications may not be able to take advantage of it. DOS commands such as DIR, DEL, and REN don't move enough data to take advantage of burst mode. Other commands and programs that move more than 768 bytes of data in one I/O operation will work faster. Burst mode allows multiple packets to be outstanding before a transport-layer ACK is expected. This is like sending a big packet and having the network layer fragment the data to accommodate the LAN medium.

From a network performance perspective, burst mode and the application have to considered together. If DIR, DEL, and REN commands send small packets, model accordingly, and if the application can send large amounts of data without an application-type ACK, model accordingly. PlanNet allows you to set a large packet size and the network-layer fragmentation and reassembly is done automatically.

16

How to Find Books and Papers for Reference and Further Study

16.0 INTRODUCTION

The quest for current information on the theory and practice of network capacity planning resulted in a small sample of recently published books and a huge volume of Internet-available electronic material. This chapter lists some good Web search engines and even provides a suggested list of keywords to search on. A list of good books is also given. Now you may spend money at your favorite technical bookstore and spend time crawling the Web!

16.1 USING THE WORLD WIDE WEB TO FIND NETWORK PERFORMANCE INFORMATION

Many publishers, booksellers, companies and universities have home pages on the Web. Prentice Hall is at **www.prenhall.com** and Computer Literacy Books is at **www.clbooks.com** on the Web. Many universities have home pages with a pointer to their technical publications area (often this in the form `ftp://ftp.department.university.edu/pub/techreports`. Most corporations have Web home pages of the form `http://www.corporation.com`. Home pages usually review the latest company products and may even offer a search engine and give pointers to other sites of interest.

For general research on the Web, you'll want to collect the locations of all the search engines you know about into your Web browser hot list. Do not waste your time crawling around aimlessly at promising sites without a good reason. Use your search engines heavily and save the search results in a file for later reference. A brief list of appropriate search keywords is given below and Table 16-1 supplies a starting list of Web search engines. Search with several key words at a time to narrow the search. Remember that many search engines will break down your keyword and search on substrings and words derived from the root words.

KEYWORDS FOR WEB SEARCHES

queue	numeric
WAN	data
LAN	math
Ethernet	software
ATM	tools
network	analyze/analysis
FDDI	predict
video	simulate
packet	performance
token	capacity
switch	model

Documents on the Web come in various formats, including compressed (ZIP, Z, gz), Adobe PostScript (ps, eps), HyperText Markup Language (HTML), plain ASCII text (TXT), CompuServe Graphics Interchange Format (GIF), tape archive (tar), Macintosh Binhex (HQX), Adobe Acrobat Portable Document Format (PDF), and so on. Be prepared with the appropriate helper applications to view these data formats.

The Web sites listed in the first group in Table 16-1 make a good starting point for general WWW searches. You will encounter other sites during the search process even as other sites may pass. A few interesting sites and files for simulation and ATM fans are listed in the second group. Many of these sites contain pointers to other sites of interest, so don't forget to leave a trail of bread crumbs.

TABLE 16-1 WEB SEARCH ENGINES

Web Location (Universal Resource Location, or URL)	Name
General Resources	
http://lmc.einet.net/search.html	Searching the EINet Information Galaxy
http://webcrawler.cs.washington.edu/WebCrawler/WebQuery.html	WebCrawler Searching
http://www.yahoo.com/search.html	Yahoo Search
http://lycos.cs.cmu.edu/	The Lycos Home Page: Hunting WWW Information
http://www.cs.colorado.edu/home/mcbryan/WWWW.html	WWWW—WORLD WIDE WEB WORM
http://www.cs.colorado.edu/homes/mcbryan/public_html/bb/summary.html	The Mother of all BBS
http://www.w3.org/hypertext/DataSources/bySubject/Overview.html	WWW Virtual Library
http://cuiwww.unige.ch/	Welcome to CUI
http://home.mcom.com/home/internet-search.html	Internet Search
http://home.mcom.com/home/internet-directory.html	Internet Directory
http://web.nexor.co.uk/public/aliweb/search/doc/form.html	ALIWEB Search Form
http://pubweb.nexor.co.uk/public/cusi/cusi.html	CUSI
http://www.ais.net/netsearch/	NetSearch(sm)
ATM and Simulation Resources	
ftp://ftp.icase.edu/pub/techreports/93/93-79.ps.Z	ATM performance paper
ftp://ftp.magic.net	ATM information
http://www.atmforum.com	ATM Forum Home Page
file://ftp.cis.upenn.edu/pub/dsl/Archive-LIST/hpcs-ATM-1.ps.Z	ATM paper
http://www.fore.com	ATM vendor
gopher://hill.lut.ac.uk/11/Software	Simulation Software
http://netlab.itd.nrl.navy.mil:80/NS.html	Network Simulation & Analysis
http://128.227.100.198/~fishwick/	Simulation Model Design & Execution
http://isdn.ncsl.nist.gov/	High Speed Networks Group Home Page
http://isdn.ncsl.nist.gov/sources/atmperf/atmperf.html	ATM Performance Measurement: Throughput, Bottlenecks and Technology Barriers
http://www.whitetree.com/ATM_Reference.html	Whitetree ATM Reference Pg.

Bibliography

ALLEN, ARNOLD O. ALLEN, *Probability, Statistics and Queuing Theory with Computer Science Applications.* Boston: Academic Press Inc., Harcourt Brace Jovanovich, 1990, ISBN: 0-12-051051-0.

> Excellent complete mathematically focused textbook about statistics with a strong series of chapters on queuing theory with great examples.

COSTA, JANIS FURTEK, *Planning and Designing High Speed Networks Using 100VG-AnyLAN.* New York: Hewlett-Packard Professional Books, Prentice Hall, 1984, ISBN: 0-13-168685-2.

> Complete treatment of the new 100VG-AnyLAN Technology from a hardware, protocol and network design perspective.

FORTIER, PAUL J., and GEORGE R. DESROCHERS, *Modeling and Analysis of Local Area Networks.* Boca Raton: CRC Press Inc., 1990, ISBN: 0-8493-7405-7.

> Basic LAN operation is covered, then statistics and queuing theory are introduced. Next the performance of LANs is analyzed using queuing theory and simulation techniques.

HELD, GILBERT, *Local Area Network Performance Issues and Answers.* Chichester: John Wiley & Sons, 1994, ISBN: 0-471-94223-5.

> Ethernet, Token Ring and bridge/router performance issues are tackled with plenty of arithmetic and algebraic examples. A PC format floppy contains supporting spreadsheets and BASIC programs.

JAIN, RAJ, *FDDI Handbook, High-Speed Networking Using Fiber and Other Media.* Reading: Addison Wesley, 1994, ISBN: 0-201-56376-2.

> A complete treatment of FDDI is given, including optics, transmission media and cabling, protocols and several performance analysis chapters.

MANASCE, DANIEL A., VIRGILIO A.F. ALMEIDA and LARRY W. DOWDY, *Capacity Planning and Performance Modeling.* Englewood Cliffs: Prentice Hall, 1994, ISBN: 0-13-035494-5.

Good sections on basic methods applied to computer system performance. It includes a PC program floppy for system performance studies.

NEMZOW, MARTIN A.W., *LAN Performance Optimization Blue Ridge Summit.* Windcrest: McGraw-Hill, 1993, ISBN: 0-8306-4277-3.

The text approaches performance improvement as a trouble shooting exercise and has a PC program floppy for performance analysis.

PERROS, H., G. PUJOLLE, Y. TAKAHASHI (EDITORS), *Modelling and Performance Evaluation of ATM Technology.* Amsterdam: Elsevier Scient Publishers B.V., 1993, ISBN: 0-444-81512-0.

Collection of professional papers reporting on theoretical models and simulation results for ATM switches and networks for various traffic types.

PHAAL, PETER, *LAN Traffic Management.* New York: Hewlett-Packard Professional Books, Prentice Hall, 1994, ISBN: 0-13-124207-5.

A very strong performance measurement and monitoring text with a focus on HP EASE

SADIKU, MATTHEW N.O., and MOHAMMAD ILYAS, *Simulation of Local Area Networks.* Boca Raton: CRC Press, 1995, ISBN: 0-8493-2473-4.

Reviews analytical methods and goes over statistics in preparation for C- language simulations of CSMA/CD, Token and StarLANs. A short section reviews simulation languages.

STUCK, B.W. and E. ARTHURS, *A Computer & Communications Network Performance Analysis Primer.* Englewood Cliffs: Prentice Hall, 1985, ISBN: 0-13-163981-1.

Excellent basic treatment of communications and computer systems performance analysis techniques. The book shows its age but wears it proudly.

THOMAS, STEPHEN A., *Queuing Theory.* Cambridge: MathSoft Inc., 1994.

This Mathcad Electronic Book is an excellent tool for studying basic and advanced queuing theory in an interactive math scratchpad.

WATKINS, KEVIN, *Discrete Event Simulation in C.* London: McGraw-Hill Book Company, 1993, ISBN: 0-07-707733-4.

Wonderful treatment of statistics, queuing theory, and discrete event simulation methodology and validation. It includes a PC program floppy for doing simulations.

Index

A

AAL5, 56
Accuracy, 258
   average analysis method, 258
   queuing analysis, 258
   simulation method, 258
   worst-case method, 258
ACK, 251
Adobe Acrobat
   PDF file format, 272
AppleTalk, 55, 268
   LAN vs WAN, 58
   RTMP updates, 115
Application
   central vs distributed locations, 249
   computer-aided drawing, 1
   FTP, 26, 59
   interactive, 43
   Mosaic, 115
   telnet over WAN, 132
   word processing, 1
   X-stations, 238
Array
   Mathcad, 223
Assumptions
   queuing theory, 152
ATG
   FTP example, 247
   mail.atg script for PlanNet, 252
   parameter calibration math, 72
   RequestLength, 235
   ResponseLength, 235
   sample script, 234
   script execution flow, 234
   script parameters, 233
   StartStats, 235
   StopStats, 235
   telnet.atg script for PlanNet, 252
   X-window considerations, 248
ATM
   AAL5, 56
   cell loss, 106
   NFS IOPS, 66
   switch, 56
   switch specifications, 87
   table of interface speeds, 57
   WWW resources, 273
ATM (Asynchronous transfer mode), 146
Average, 108
   accuracy, 258
   document transfer time over frame relay, 129
   table of wait times for M/M/1 queue, 171
   training needed to use the method, 260
   usability of methodology, 259
Awk
   command line example, 38
   command line parameters, 37
   information fields, 36
   netstat output processing, 35
   packet trace processing, 36
   process ping output, 120
   RMON packet traces, 36
   sample output file for PlanNet, 37
   sample packet trace input, 37
   sample script for HP4980 data, 38
   syntax of the language, 37

B

Bandwidth
   compression, 59
   FTP impact, 59

multiple protocols, 59
BER
  bit error rate example, 79
BONeS, 229
  Designer modeler, 230
  special transport features, 270
Bottleneck, 104
  methodology for finding, 105
  WAN, 77
  X.25, 77
Bridge
  latency, 53
  packet loss, 106
  performance specifications, 88
  port table, 54
  principle of operation, 53
Broadcast
  CPU processing overhead, 264
  Mac layer, 264
  Novell SAP, 264
  RIP packet, 264
Buffer
  overflow, 176
  router priority queues, 58
Bugs
  and features, 265
  and simulator implementations, 265
  protocol, 265
Business cycle, 49

C

C language
  modeling libraries, 193
  modeling library sources on the Internet, 194
CDF
  Exponential, 177
  Normal, 177
  Uniform, 177
CDF (Cumulative Density Function), 150
Central limit theorem, 117
Chart
  assistant, 202
  improved presentation, 204
  Lotus 1-2-3, 202
  simple, 203
CIR, 7, 10, 78
Cisco

BusyPer MIB variable, 59
Client
  performance, 62
  performance of location in network, 60
  performance tuning tips, 60
  server performance, 62
Client-server, 3, 44
  FTP, 246
  network topologies, 12
  NFS, 246
  X-windows, 246
Clipboard
  bitmap formats and Mathcad, 226
  data formats, 217
Colgomoroff-Smirnoff, 154
Collision
  description of, 98
  frame loss due to, 99
  late, 99
  percentage calculation, 98
  probability of packet loss, 106
  related LAN measurements, 99
  simulation results for, 98
Color
  in documentation, 216
Compression
  .gz file, 272
  .Z file, 272
  .ZIP file, 272
  GIF file, 272
  graphics file, 103
  HQX file, 272
  line speeds suited, 59
  packet size impact, 60
  PDF, 272
  router overhead, 59, 269
  serial lines, 269
  text data, 60
  ZIP files, 60
Computer Literacy Books
  www.clbooks.com, 271
Configuration
  spanning tree, 267
  SQE, 267
Contamination
  collisions, 46
  dissimilar LAN media, 47
  due to stress testing, 145
  LAN Traffic, 46

list of sources, 47
loaded server, 47
TCP time-outs, 46
Cost of
  customer dissatisfaction, 4
  late product release, 4
  lost sales, 4
  poor performance, 4
CPU
  load factor, 97
  overhead due to serial line compression, 269
  overhead of a MAC layer broadcast, 264
  utilization, 96
csv2trc, 247
Cut-through, 56

D

Decision analysis
  least risk analysis, 91
  potential problems, 90
  table 4-12, 89
  weighed scoring, 90
DECNET, 58
Delay
  computing, 60
Deviation, 108
Disk
  database I/O, 96
  I/O maximum rate, 96
  percentage used, 96
  spawning processes in UNIX, 96
  VM, 96
Distribution
  average of hourly line utilization, 128
  caution about area under the tails, 177
  combining samples from, 117
  Exponential, 111
  Fixed, 113
  hourly line utilization, 128
  Normal, 111
  Normal distribution example, 149
  one-hour of ping responses, 122
  Poisson, 112
  tail of Normal distribution, 118

Distribution *(cont'd)*
  three CDF tails with nearly equal means, 179
  Uniform, 112
DNS
  zone transfer, 115
Documentation
  from math scratchpads, 260
  from simulators, 260
  from spreadsheets, 260
  using spreadsheets, 216

E

EASE, 20
  collision domains, 24
  History Analyzer FTP traffic, 26
  HP History Analyzer screenshot, 24, 25
  HP hubs, 23
  network topology, 23
  Resource Manager packet header decode, 30
  Resource Manager segment statistics, 28
  Resource Manager spider chart, 27
  Resource Manager top connections, 29
  sampling method, 23
  server, 23
  Traffic Expert internet traffic diagram, 31
Email
  simulation with PlanNet, 251
Erlang
  distribution for tandem stages, 173
  formula, 163
  table of values for Erlang's formula, 170
Error
  linear regresssion, 124
  simulation assumptions, 267
Error function
  erf(t), 177
  plot, 178
  tail of the distribution, 179
Estimate
  arrival rate of transactions, 153
  average service rate of a queue, 154
Ethernet
  collision rate, 98
  myths, 75
  NFS IOPS, 66
  performance simulation, 74
  simulation plot of collision rate, 98
  switch, 56
  switch performance specifications, 86
  worst case media access time, 76
Example
  ATG script for FTP, 247
  average and deviation calculation, 108
  awk script for decoding 4980 packets, 38
  business cycles in LAN traffic, 49
  client-server application, 44
  client-server LAN topologies, 12
  closed queue system analysis, 163
  deciding whether to upgrade or replicate, 175
  decision analysis picks a router, 90
  determining the best server location, 71
  fixed buffer queuing analysis, 164, 165, 166
  frame relay propagation calculation, 83
  Jackson queuing analysis, 167, 168, 169
  Lotus 1-2-3 M/M/1 queue simulation results, 207
  Mathcad Monte Carlo simulation, 191
  Mathcad simulation of M/M/1 queue, 186, 187, 188
  measurement contamination, 47
  multi-server queue analysis, 161
  Netmetrix Internetwork Monitor display, 250
  netstat output, 35
  network printing, 43
  Normal distribution, 149
  one hour ping study, 121
  ping round trip time analysis, 33
  ping round-trip time graph, 147
  PlanNet ASCII performance data output, 246
  PlanNet ATG script, 239
  PlanNet ATG scripts for mail and telnet, 252
  PlanNet iterated parameters, 243
  PlanNet module parameters, 241, 242
  PlanNet performance graphs, 245
  PlanNet simulation monitor, 244
  PlanNet topology diagram, 240
  PlanNet topology for mail and telnet traffic, 253
  plot from a Uniform distribution, 114
  print spooler queuing analysis, 174
  probability there are n active users, 150
  productivity loss calculation, 4
  sample from an Exponential distribution, 114
  samples from a Normal distribution, 115
  SNMP traffic overhead calculation, 41
  spreadsheet queuing analysis of a network, 261
  spreadsheet simulator for M/M/1 queue, 183, 184
  spreadsheet to compute active users, 143
  telnet application, 43
  telnet response times with email present, 254
  traffic load for a mix of user types, 48
  WAN delay computation, 61
  WAN performance vs BER calculation, 79

WAN performance vs window size, 79
worst-case analysis using Lotus 1-2-3, 209
worst-case design validation, 149
Exponential
 CDF, 177
 inter-arrival time, 153
 PDF, 177
 service time, 153
Exponential distribution, 111

F

Factorial, 213
FDDI
 backbone for servers, 148
 CDDI, 11
 file server backbone, 11
 MTU, 148
 NFS IOPS, 66
 performance simulation curve, 75
 Vs. 100VG-AnyLAN, 11
FDDI (Fiber Distributed Data Interface), 148
Fibonacci number, 213
FIFO (First In First Out), 154
File
 formats found on WWW, 272
 size of graphics image, 103
File server
 generic model, 63
 NFS tuning, 64
File transfer
 time to perform, 102
Finger pointing
 bottleneck, 104
 correcting the direction of, 93, 105
Fixed distribution, 113
Forecasting
 regression, 124
 six month line utilization, 126
 trend analysis, 124
Format
 bitmap, 200
 DIB, 200
 metafile, 200

rich text, 200
text, 200
WWW files, 272
Forwarding, 53
Frame relay
 architecture, 80
 burst rate, 81
 CIR, 10, 78
 discarding packets, 81
 document retrieval calculation, 129
 hub and spoke toplogies, 82
 interactive applications, 10
 latency, 80
 meshing, 80
 network internals, 11
 OSI model, 83
 performance issues, 77
 performance parameters, 78
 performance parameters explained, 81
 port speed, 78
 propagation delay calculation, 83
 simulating with PlanNet, 10
Functions
 evaluation in Lotus 1-2-3, 201
 hyperbolic, 196
 hyperbolic inverse, 196
 integer-based, 197
 statistics, 197
 statistics calculating, 198
 transcendental, 196
 trigonometric, 197

G

Graphics, 216
 factors effecting performane, 104
 file formats in reports, 216
 file size of image, 103

H

Help
 Lotus 1-2-3, 198
Histogram, 110
 3600 ping responses, 122
Hop count, 71

HTML, 272
Hub
 balanced arhitecture, 52
 principle of operation, 52
 topology rules, 52

I

ICMP, 34, 121
IEEE 802.3, 53
IEEE Spectrum, 226
Integral
 table of CDFs, 177
Interactive application, 43
Internet Advisor, 18
Internet sites
 C language simulators, 194
 math scratchpad, 226
 simulation information, 256
 simulators, 255
IOPS, 65, 134
 maximum rate of LAN media, 66
IP
 fragmentation example, 35
 header, 35
 RIP updates, 115
 TTL, 121
IPX, 268
Iteration, 213

J

Jackson analysis
 example, 167, 168, 169
 queuing theory, 162

K

Kendall notation, 222
Kendall nottion
 explained, 154

L

λ
 estimation method, 154
λ (lambda)
 average arrival rate of transactions in a queue, 153

Lambda (λ)
  average arrival rate into a queue, 153
LAN Analyzer, 17, 18
  CSV data output, 17
  Network Advisor ASCII decode, 19
  promiscuous mode operation, 16
Landiag, 159
LAP-B, 82
LAT, 268
Latency
  frame relay, 80
Little's Law, 156, 184, 185
Load factor, 97
Loading
  averaging methods to discover cycles, 50
  business cycle, 49
  composite user mix, 48
  example of a user mix, 48
  heavy user, 48
  light user, 48
  medium user, 48
  peaks and valleys, 49
Loss. *See* Packet loss
Lotus 1-2-3
  cell content for M/M/1 simulation, 206
  charts and graphs, 202
  copy and paste usage, 200
  finding peaks of functions, 211, 212
  function evaluation, 201
  functions, 196, 197, 198
  graphical solution method, 210
  macro, 214
  paste, 217
  precision and accuracy, 200
  recalculation order, 205, 207
  results for M/M/1 queue simulation, 207
  search GUI, 199
  visualization of worst-case analysis, 208
  visualization results of worst-case analysis, 209
  worksheets for organizing work, 199

M

μ
  confusion with statistics mean symbol, 177
  estimation method, 154
μ (mu)
  average service rate of a queue, 153
M/G/1, 157
  table of queuing formulas, 157
M/M/1, 155, 181, 261
  table of queuing formulas, 158
M/M/1/k, 176
M/M/C
  Mathcad analysis, 222
M/M/n, 175
MAC
  broadcast, 264
Macintosh
  Mac/X, 229
  MathPad version for, 226
MacOS
  screen shot, 236
Macro, 214
  button, 215
  example, 215
Math scratchpad
  quality of documentation, 260
Math scratchpads
  Macsyma, 226
  Maple, 226
  Mathcad, 226
  Mathematica, 226
  MathPad, 226
  MATLAB, 226
  Theorist, 226
Mathcad
  2-D and 3-D displays of arrays, 224
  basic features, 220
  dealing with messy formulas, 222
  diplaying results of array operations, 223
  electronic book, 220
  multi-server queue example, 161
  paste formats, 225
  producing documentation with it, 225
  queuing analysis with 32 servers, 176
  sample worksheet, 221
  trend analysis, 125
Measure, 140
  3600 ping responses, 122
  LAN adapter statistics, 99
  ping, 120
  promiscuous packet capture, 145
  SNMP, 140
Methodology
  bottleneck discovery, 105
MIB
  RMON, 20
Misconfiguration
  of network electronics, 267
MKS Toolkit
  awk command, 19
Monte Carlo
  acccuracy vs number of trials, 193
  Mathcad communication system simulation, 191
  simulation method, 190
MTU, 101
  ATM, 56
  Ethernet, 35
  FDDI, 148
Mu (μ)
  average service rate of a queue, 153
Myths
  Ethernet, 75

N

NEST, 194, 265
  special transport features, 270
NetBEUI, 268
NetMetrix, 250
Netstat, 35
  output example, 35
  output processing with awk, 35
Netware
  burst mode, 270
  performance of DIR, DEL, and REN, 270

Network Advisor, 18
New application
  benchmarking, 9
NFS
  -async option, 68
  IOPS, 65
  Laddis benchmark, 134
  nfsd tuning, 67
  performance and nfsd number, 68
  performance metrics, 65
  response time, 134
  rpc information from netstat, 66
  server block size, 42
  server internal model, 67
  table of tunable parameters, 65
  tuning, 64
  UNIX and RISC, 65
  WAN performance, 65
Nfsdrun, 66
Nfsstat
  NFS performance information, 66
  output example, 66
Normal
  Normal CDF, 177
Normal distribution, 111
  extreme close-up of tail, 120
  tail, 118
  tail of CDF, 119
  tail of CDF close-up, 119

O

OC-3, 57
OLE, 216
  in Mathcad, 220
Open System
  worst-case analysis, 138
OSI
  packet header overhead, 36
Outage, 265
Overhead
  compression, 269
  fragmentation, 100
  RIP, 269
  routing protocols, 269
  SNMP, 269
  table of packet header sizes, 101

telnet, 100
transport handshakes, 100

P

Packet
  arrival rate, 41
  ATM cell loss, 106
  capture with LAN Analyzer, 41
  capture with RMON, 41
  collision excess retries, 106
  exponential distribution curve, 73
  loss in ATM switch, 106
  loss in bridges, 106
  loss probability, 76
  loss rate, 106
  NFS server block size, 42
  size distribution, 41
  statistical distribution examples, 42
  transport retransmission, 106
Packet loss
  predicting, 176
Packet size
  ATM, 146
  extremes, 146
  FTP, 146
  telnet, 146
Packet trace
  and PlanNet csv2trc script, 247
  and PlanNet trc2atg script, 247
Paste
  clipboard display formats, 217
  in Mathcad, 225
  special, 217
PDF
  Exponential distibution, 177
  portable document format (Adobe), 272
PDF (Probability Density Function), 150
Performance
  ATM switch specifications, 87
  bit error rate, 79
  bridge specifications, 88
  change with upgrades, 266
  color image display time, 104

compression over serial lines, 269
degraded mode, 265
DIR, DEL, and REN commands, 270
disk cache, 266
display of color image, 103
during a partial network outage, 265
Ethernet design curve, 71
Ethernet simulation design curve, 74
FDDI simulation curve, 75
file transfer time, 102
hop count, 70, 133
measurement with ping, 120
myths about Ethernet, 75
Netware burst mode, 270
O/S impact, 266
response time, 95
RFC 1242 definitions, 86
router specifications, 88
server location, 69
simulation, 71
token ring simulation, 74
transaction rate, 95
transient mode, 265
Van Jacobson TCP, 270
window size, 79
Performance data
  application dependency, 13
  contamination, 13
  why collect it?, 13
ping, 32
  command line parameters, 34
  ICMP loopback, 34
  Implementation variations, 34
  information reported by, 120
  measuring response time, 33
  network performance characteriziation, 120
  one-hour graph in Lotus 123, 121
  output processed with awk, 120
  round trip time vs packet size, 147
  round-trip time, 146
  sample output, 33
  spreadsheet plot of ping results, 34

PlanNet, 10, 44, 71
   and special transport feataures, 270
   building a topology model, 231
   components, 228
   customer library components, 229
   data analyzer, 235
   model builder, 228
   network modules, 228
   protocol independence, 265
   report generation, 235
   report generator, 228
   simulation engine, 228
   simulation monitor, 228
   trace file created by awk, 37
   traffic generators, 229
   traffic scripts, 228
   vendor-specific router configuration, 267
PlanNet library
   Ethernet, 229
   FDDI, 229
   Serial, 229
   T-1, 229
   T-3, 229
   token ring, 229
Poisson distribution, 112
PostScript, 216, 235
   EPS, 236
   extract-eps command, 236
   vs TrueType, 217
PPP, 60, 77
Preamble, 53
Prentice Hall
   www.prenhall.com, 271
Price
   worst case network design, 147
Print spooler
   queuing analysis, 174
Printing, 43
Priority
   PlanNet protocols, 233
Problem solving, 3
Promiscuous
   packet capture methods, 145
Protocol
   AppleTalk, 55
   bugs and features, 265
   DNS, 115
   HDLC, 77
   ICMP, 34, 121
   IP, 35
   mixing, 268
   NFS, 67
   PPP, 77
   RMON, 20
   SLIP, 60
   SNA, 55
   SNMP, 14
   TCP, 35
   X.25, 82
PVC
   frame relay, 80

Q

Queue, 160
   average length calculation, 155
   average wait time in the system, 156
   CDF of system wait time, 156
   closed system, 162
   closed system analysis, 163
   conditions for good results from theory, 158
   fixed buffer analysis, 164, 165, 166
   formula for number of items in the system, 155
   Jackson analysis, 162
   Jackson analysis example, 167, 168, 169
   Lotus 1-2-3 example of an M/M/1 queue, 205
   M/G/1, 157
   M/M/1, 155
   multi-server, 160
   open system, 138
   router priority queue, 58
   service rate, 152
   simple model, 153
   simulator, 181
   spreadsheet queuing analysis of a network, 261
   table of probabilities for multi-server queue, 171
   tandem stages, 172
   transaction arrival rate, 152
   validation of results, 159
Queuing
   assumptions, 152
   training to use the method, 260
   usability of methodology, 259

R

Random number
   sample from a Uniform distribution, 114
   sample from an Exponential distribution, 114
   table of generation methods, 113
REAL, 194, 265
   special transport features, 270
Recovery
   and degraded mode of network operation, 264
   from buffer overflows, 264
   from CRC errors, 264
   from service interruptions, 264
References
   WWW sites, 273
Report
   input data information, 237
   interpretation of simulation results, 237
   modeling contents of, 236
   output data information, 237
   recommendations, 237
Resources
   in tandem, 139
Response time, 2
   99% are less than 5 seconds, 118
   average, 93
   client-server, 63
   histogram, 110
   hop count impact, 133
   network, 63
   network round trip, 133
   NFS laddis benchmark, 134
   Normal curve, 118
   percentiles, 93
   psychology, 93
   tandem resources, 140
   tandem stages queue, 173

telnet over WAN, 132
telnet traffic mixed with email, 254
vs number of users, 94
Response time vs
  number of printers, 6
  number of users, 6
  utilization, 6
Response time Vs.
  server upgrade, 8
  X-terminal population, 8
RIP
  broadcast packet, 264
Risk
  choosing the least risk solution, 91
  overprovisioning, 5
  underprovisioning, 5
RMON, 20
  9 groups, 20
  MIB tree diagram, 22
  packet capture, 23
  packet distribution measurements, 41
  RAM requirements, 22
Router
  compression, 58
  compression overhead, 269
  connecting dissimilar LANs, 55
  fragmentation and reassembly, 55
  latency, 54
  multiple protocols, 55
  performance specifications, 88
  PlanNet vendor-specific models, 267
  principle of operation, 54
  priority queues, 58
  routing protocol overhead, 269
  routing table, 54
  Scott Bradner test, 267
  SNMP support, 59
  WAN hardware and encapsulation, 77
Rules of thumb
  Ethernet performance statistics, 20
  Ethernet utilization, 9

WAN performance metrics, 20
X-terminals on a LAN, 9

S

Sampling frequency
  Heisenberg Uncertainty Principle, 40
  network overhead calculation, 41
  Nyquist sampling theory, 40
  SNMP polling interval, 40
  too much data, 40
SAP
  Novell broadcast, 264
Saturation
  behaviour of network resources, 140
Scott Bradner, 267
Screen
  capture with ALT-PrtSc, 200
Screenshot
  History Analyzer, 24, 25
  History Analyzer FTP traffic, 26
  Probe Manager, 21
  Resource Manager packet header decode, 30
  Resource Manager segment statistics, 28
  Resource Manager spider chart, 27
  Resource Manager top connections, 29
  Traffic Expert internet traffic diagram, 31
Search
  network performance keywords, 272
  WWW, 272
Search engine
  WWW sites, 273
Segment monitor
  HP EASE, 20
  RMON probe, 20
Sendmail, 115
Serial line, 16
Server
  client traffic and EASE, 69
  dual homing, 69

Ethernet switch connection, 70
FDDI connection, 70
generic model for file server, 63
location with best performance, 69
performance impact of network, 62
Service
  queuing theory interpretation, 152
SIMPACK, 194
Simple Times, 15
SIMULA, 194
Simulation
  accuracy, 258
  ATG script calibration arithmetic, 72
  data source and sink packet flow, 72
  design curves, 73
  design curves for LAN media, 71
  training to use the method, 260
  usability of methodology, 259
Simulator
  accuracy check, 184, 185
  BONeS Designer, 229, 255
  C language libraries, 194
  COMNET-III, 255
  custom PlanNet modules and Designer, 230
  Lotus 1-2-3 and an M/M/1 queue, 205
  M/M/1 queue events, 182
  Mathcad plot of time in system, 188
  Mathcad simulation of M/M/1 queue, 186, 187
  Monte Carlo results, 192
  NEST, 194
  Netmod, 255
  of protocols with NEST and REAL, 265
  PlanNet, 229
  PlanNet model builder, 231
  protocol independence of PlanNet, 265
  quality of documentation, 260
  queue, 181

Simulator *(cont'd)*
  REAL, 194
  SIMPACK, 194
  SimScript, 255
  SIMULA, 194
  spreadsheet M/M/1 queue implementation, 183, 184
  states of operation, 181
  validation checklist, 237
  VisSim, 255
  what-if scenarios, 238
  WWW resources, 273
  XNetMod, 255
Sizing
  serial line, 7
SLIP, 60
SNA, 55, 58
Sniffer, 18
SNMP
  basic model, 14
  categories of MIB variables, 17
  command line programs, 15
  COUNTER variable, 14
  exporting collected data, 15
  GAUGE variable, 14
  GET, 14
  MIB tree, 15
  performance data collection, 14
  PUT, 14
  RFC 1213, 15
  serial line performance, 16
  Simple Times, 15
  table of useful MIB variables, 18
  trap, 14
  useful MIB variables, 16
Solution
  decision analysis, 89
SONET, 57
Spanning Tree, 53
Speed
  ATM media, 58
  compression of serial lines, 60
  NFS IOPS, 66
  NFS writes for large files, 68
  serial links, 7
  T-1 line, 7
  WAN circuit, 79

X.25 switch, 84
Spreadsheet
  ClarisWorks, 218
  document transfer time over frame relay, 131
  Excel, 218
  Lotus 1-2-3, 218
  quality of documentation, 260
  Quattro Pro, 218
  queuing analysis of a network, 261
  SuperCalc, 218
  Wingz, 218
SQE, 267
Statistics
  average, 108
  combining samples, 116
  continuous, 109
  deviation, 108
  discrete, 109
  distributions found in networking, 115
  Exponential, 109
  Exponential distribution plot, 111
  Fixed, 109
  Fixed distribution, 113
  Normal, 109
  Normal distribution plot, 111
  PDF/CDF of hourly line utilization, 128
  Poisson, 109
  regression and prediction, 123
  table of distribution formulas, 110
  Uniform, 109
SVC
  X.25, 82
Switch
  ATM, 56
  ATM specifications, 87
  cut-through, 56
  Ethernet, 56
  Ethernet specifications, 86
  FDDI backbone, 57
  frame relay, 80, 83
  X.25 performance, 84
Switches
  cascading, 57
  connecting work groups, 57

T

T-1, 77
Tail
  3600 ping response distribution, 122
Tandem stages, 172
  response time curve for, 173
TCP
  header, 35
  segment size, 35
  Van Jacobson, 58, 270
TCP (Transmission Control Protocol)
  ACK, 251
telnet
  simulation with PlanNet, 251
Throughput
  and network round trip time, 133
  MTU dependency, 78
  WAN calculation, 78
Token ring
  NFS IOPS, 66
  performance simulation, 74
Tool
  spreadsheet to calculate active user count, 143
Tools
  awk, 36
  HP Internet Advisor, 18
  HP Network Advisor, 18
  HP Probe Manager, 21
  HP Probe Manager screenshot, 21
  LAN analyzer, 19
  LAN analyzers, 18
  MKS Toolkit, 19
  netstat UNIX command, 35
  Ping, 32
  PlanNet simulator, 10
  PlanNet traffic script, 37
  rules of thumb, 20
  segment monitor, 20
  Sniffer, 18
  UNIX tracing, 32
Topology
  PlanNet model builder, 231
Traffic
  interactive application, 43

measured with HP EASE, 250
measured with LanProbes, 250
network printing, 43
synthesis and estimation, 42
Traffic Expert, 250
Traffic generator
 PlanNet ATG script, 233
 PlanNet SBTG, 232
 trace-based generator, 232
Training and experience
 for average analysis method, 260
 for queuing method, 260
 for simulation method, 260
 for worst-case method, 260
Transaction
 batch job, 95
 hypertext markup language, 115
 queuing theory interpretation, 152
 rate, 95
 resources used by, 95
 vs number of users, 95
Transient, 265
Transport
 Netware burst mode, 270
 time-outs and queuing theory, 159
 timers expire, 140
 Van Jacobson TCP, 270
Trc2atg, 47, 247, 248
 accuracy of CPU time estimate, 251
Trend
 cyclic, 123
 graphic relationship, 125
 high water mark, 123
 high water mark analysis, 126
 hourly raw line utilization, 127
 linear regression math, 124
 Mathcad analysis, 125
 regression, 123
 six month line utilization forecast, 126
TrueType
 vs PostScript, 217
TSTOP, 232, 233, 251

TTL, 121, 267
TTRT (target token rotation timer), 144

U

Uniform
 Uniform CDF, 177
Uniform distribution, 112
UNIX
 netstat command, 35
 packet tracing, 32
 ping, 34
Usability
 of average methodology, 259
 of queueing methodology, 259
 of simulation methodology, 259
 of worst-case methodology, 259
User
 characteristics, 141
 interactive, 101
 maximum number, 101
 non-interactive, 101
 sorting conversations from a packet capture, 146
Users
 determining number of active users, 141
 effective user count, 143
 heavy, 141
 light, 141
 medium, 141
 probability there are at least n users, 142
 probability density function for, 143
 probability there are n active, 150
Utilization, 2
 CPU, 96
 disk, 96
 memory, 96
 network, 97
 percentage, 96

V

V.35, 82
Validation
 example, 261

λ and μ are Exponential, 154
 network design for Email and telnet traffic, 251
 of a simulation with the average method, 261
 of a simulation with the queuing method, 261
 queuing theory results, 159
 simulation checklist, 237
 using rules of thumb, 261
Van Jacobson
 TCP, 159, 270
Variance, 108
Vendor
 math scratchpad, 226
VSAT
 network round trip time, 134

W

Wait time
 exponential probability curve, 61
WAN
 AppleTalk, 58
 bit error rate, 79
 bottleneck, 77
 HDLC encapsulation, 77
 IP, 58
 PPP, 77
 SNA, 58
 T-1 circuit, 77
 throughput calculation, 78
 window size, 79
What-if
 PlanNet simulation of 3 protocols, 247
Who command
 counting logged in users, 101
Window
 and network round trip time, 134
 impact on throughput, 134
 X.25 rotating window, 85
Work load
 changes at fiscal quarter end, 139
Work time requirements
 of queueing method, 259
 of queuing method, 259

of simulation method, 259
of worst-case method, 259
World Wide Web
  Computer Literacy Bookshop, 271
  information search, 271
  Prentice-Hall, 271
  www.corporation.com, 271
Worst case
  example using Lotus 1-2-3, 209
  multiple concurrent requests, 144
  number of users, 141
  user count calculation using statistics, 142
  vs best case, 144
Worst-Case
  accuracy, 258
cost of network design, 147
FDDI vs Ethernet solution, 148
training needed to use the method, 260
usability of methodology, 259
validation of design using statistics, 149
WWW
  cool sites with network content, 273
  resources, 273
  search engines, 273

X

X.25, 77, 82
  packet switch performance, 85
  principle of operation, 82
  RS-232 interface, 82
  switch performance graph, 84
  topology, 84
X-windows, 248
  Hummmingbird, 229
  Mac/X, 229
  UNIX, 229
  WRQ Reflection/X, 227
  WRQ Relfection/X, 229
  xpr, 235
  xwd, 235

LICENSE AGREEMENT AND LIMITED WARRANTY

READ THE FOLLOWING TERMS AND CONDITIONS CAREFULLY BEFORE OPENING THIS SOFTWARE PACKAGE. THIS LEGAL DOCUMENT IS AN AGREEMENT BETWEEN YOU AND PRENTICE-HALL, INC. (THE "COMPANY"). BY OPENING THIS SEALED SOFTWARE PACKAGE, YOU ARE AGREEING TO BE BOUND BY THESE TERMS AND CONDITIONS. IF YOU DO NOT AGREE WITH THESE TERMS AND CONDITIONS, DO NOT OPEN THE SOFTWARE PACKAGE. PROMPTLY RETURN THE UNOPENED SOFTWARE PACKAGE AND ALL ACCOMPANYING ITEMS TO THE PLACE YOU OBTAINED THEM FOR A FULL REFUND OF ANY SUMS YOU HAVE PAID.

1. **GRANT OF LICENSE:** In consideration of your purchase of this book, and your agreement to abide by the terms and conditions of this Agreement, the Company grants to you a nonexclusive right to use and display the copy of the enclosed software program (hereinafter the "SOFTWARE") on a single computer (i.e., with a single CPU) at a single location so long as you comply with the terms of this Agreement. The Company reserves all rights not expressly granted to you under this Agreement.

2. **OWNERSHIP OF SOFTWARE:** You own only the magnetic or physical media (the enclosed media) on which the SOFTWARE is recorded or fixed, but the Company and the software developers retain all the rights, title, and ownership to the SOFTWARE recorded on the original media copy(ies) and all subsequent copies of the SOFTWARE, regardless of the form or media on which the original or other copies may exist. This license is not a sale of the original SOFTWARE or any copy to you.

3. **COPY RESTRICTIONS:** This SOFTWARE and the accompanying printed materials and user manual (the "Documentation") are the subject of copyright. The individual programs on the media are copyrighted by the authors of each program. Some of the programs on the media include separate licensing agreements. If you intend to use one of these programs, you must read and follow its accompanying license agreement. You may not copy the Documentation or the SOFTWARE, except that you may make a single copy of the SOFTWARE for backup or archival purposes only. You may be held legally responsible for any copying or copyright infringement which is caused or encouraged by your failure to abide by the terms of this restriction.

4. **USE RESTRICTIONS:** You may not network the SOFTWARE or otherwise use it on more than one computer or computer terminal at the same time. You may physically transfer the SOFTWARE from one computer to another provided that the SOFTWARE is used on only one computer at a time. You may not distribute copies of the SOFTWARE or Documentation to others. You may not reverse engineer, disassemble, decompile, modify, adapt, translate, or create derivative works based on the SOFTWARE or the Documentation without the prior written consent of the Company.

5. **TRANSFER RESTRICTIONS:** The enclosed SOFTWARE is licensed only to you and may not be transferred to any one else without the prior written consent of the Company. Any unauthorized transfer of the SOFTWARE shall result in the immediate termination of this Agreement.

6. **TERMINATION:** This license is effective until terminated. This license will terminate automatically without notice from the Company and become null and void if you fail to comply with any provisions or limitations of this license. Upon termination, you shall destroy the Documentation and all copies of the SOFTWARE. All provisions of this Agreement as to warranties, limitation of liability, remedies or damages, and our ownership rights shall survive termination.

7. **MISCELLANEOUS:** This Agreement shall be construed in accordance with the laws of the United States of America and the State of New York and shall benefit the Company, its affiliates, and assignees.

8. **LIMITED WARRANTY AND DISCLAIMER OF WARRANTY:** The Company warrants that the SOFTWARE, when properly used in accordance with the Documentation, will operate in substantial conformity with the description of the SOFTWARE set forth in the Documentation. The Company does not warrant that the SOFTWARE will meet your requirements or that the operation of the SOFTWARE will be uninterrupted or error-free. The Company warrants that the media on which the SOFTWARE is delivered shall be free from defects in materials and workmanship under normal use for a period of thirty (30) days from the date of your purchase. Your only remedy and the Company's only obligation under these limited warranties is, at the Company's option, return of the warranted item for a refund of any amounts paid by you or replacement of the item. Any replacement of SOFTWARE or media under the warranties shall not extend the original warranty period. The limited warranty set forth above shall not apply to any SOFTWARE which the Company determines in good faith has been subject to misuse, neglect, improper installation, repair, alteration, or damage by you. EXCEPT FOR THE EXPRESSED WARRANTIES SET FORTH ABOVE, THE COMPANY DISCLAIMS ALL WARRANTIES, EXPRESS OR IMPLIED, INCLUDING WITHOUT LIMITATION, THE IMPLIED WARRANTIES OF MERCHANTABILITY AND FITNESS FOR A PARTICULAR PURPOSE. EXCEPT FOR THE EXPRESS WARRANTY SET FORTH ABOVE, THE COMPANY DOES NOT WARRANT, GUARANTEE, OR MAKE ANY REPRESENTATION REGARDING THE USE OR THE RESULTS OF THE USE OF THE SOFTWARE IN TERMS OF ITS CORRECTNESS, ACCURACY, RELIABILITY, CURRENTNESS, OR OTHERWISE.

IN NO EVENT, SHALL THE COMPANY OR ITS EMPLOYEES, AGENTS, SUPPLIERS, OR CONTRACTORS BE LIABLE FOR ANY INCIDENTAL, INDIRECT, SPECIAL, OR CONSEQUENTIAL DAMAGES ARISING OUT OF OR IN CONNECTION WITH THE LICENSE GRANTED UNDER THIS AGREEMENT, OR FOR LOSS OF USE, LOSS OF DATA, LOSS OF INCOME OR PROFIT, OR OTHER LOSSES, SUSTAINED AS A RESULT OF INJURY TO ANY PERSON, OR LOSS OF OR DAMAGE TO PROPERTY, OR CLAIMS OF THIRD PARTIES, EVEN IF THE COMPANY OR AN AUTHORIZED REPRESENTATIVE OF THE COMPANY HAS BEEN ADVISED OF THE POSSIBILITY OF SUCH DAMAGES. IN NO EVENT SHALL LIABILITY OF THE COMPANY FOR DAMAGES WITH RESPECT TO THE SOFTWARE EXCEED THE AMOUNTS ACTUALLY PAID BY YOU, IF ANY, FOR THE SOFTWARE.

SOME JURISDICTIONS DO NOT ALLOW THE LIMITATION OF IMPLIED WARRANTIES OR LIABILITY FOR INCIDENTAL, INDIRECT, SPECIAL, OR CONSEQUENTIAL DAMAGES, SO THE ABOVE LIMITATIONS MAY NOT ALWAYS APPLY. THE WARRANTIES IN THIS AGREEMENT GIVE YOU SPECIFIC LEGAL RIGHTS AND YOU MAY ALSO HAVE OTHER RIGHTS WHICH VARY IN ACCORDANCE WITH LOCAL LAW.

ACKNOWLEDGMENT

YOU ACKNOWLEDGE THAT YOU HAVE READ THIS AGREEMENT, UNDERSTAND IT, AND AGREE TO BE BOUND BY ITS TERMS AND CONDITIONS. YOU ALSO AGREE THAT THIS AGREEMENT IS THE COMPLETE AND EXCLUSIVE STATEMENT OF THE AGREEMENT BETWEEN YOU AND THE COMPANY AND SUPERSEDES ALL PROPOSALS OR PRIOR AGREEMENTS, ORAL, OR WRITTEN, AND ANY OTHER COMMUNICATIONS BETWEEN YOU AND THE COMPANY OR ANY REPRESENTATIVE OF THE COMPANY RELATING TO THE SUBJECT MATTER OF THIS AGREEMENT.

Should you have any questions concerning this Agreement or if you wish to contact the Company for any reason, please contact in writing at the address below.

Robin Short
Prentice Hall PTR
One Lake Street
Upper Saddle River, New Jersey 07458